WATSON PARKER

DEADWOOD
THE GOLDEN YEARS

UNIVERSITY OF NEBRASKA PRESS
Lincoln and London

♾

Library of Congress Cataloging in Publication Data

Parker, Watson.
  Deadwood : the golden years.

  Bibliography: p. 265
  Includes index.
  1. Deadwood, S. D.—History,   2. Deadwood, S. D.—
Description.
F659.D2P37   978.3′91   80–24100
ISBN 0–8032–0973–8
ISBN 0–8032–8702–X (pbk.)

First Bison Book printing: 1981
Most recent printing indicated by the first digit below:
                                    7   8   9   10

Contents

List of Maps and Illustrations

MAPS

ILLUSTRATIONS

Preface

THIS IS THE STORY of a mining camp that began more than a hundred years ago in the Black Hills of the Dakota Territory, and of the busy little city that grew up upon its ashes. It is a tale of miners and merchants, of commerce and technology, of society and sinners, and of the town which loved them all. It is a tale of the times when economic hell began to bubble during the Panic of '73, and came to a boil in the Black Hills two hundred miles north of the Union Pacific depots at Sidney and Cheyenne. It is the story of prospectors and miners, investors and Indians, bums and bunco steerers, businessmen and speculators, matrons and madams, the tale of a town with a glint in its eye for present opportunities and a gleam in its memory for the many glories of its lurid past. It is not the story of Deadwood's characters, although many of them stagger in a somewhat unsteady procession across its pages, but instead it is the story of the character of the town itself, for Deadwood was a little city that had a life, and a spirit, and a soul of its own, as much as a town can have them, and its personality is worth recording before the colors fade.

The story of Deadwood is told here in roughly chronological order, with many a temporary flashback and topical excursion. It begins with the early placer gold rush to the Black Hills during the summer of 1875, and it follows the miners underground in their pursuit of the hardrock ores during the 1880s, and then comes back up to the surface and into the dark, Satanic mills which ground those ores exceeding fine. Deadwood's business and professional population, which so heroically adapted itself to the needs and the opportunities of the new and volatile community, is gazed upon with awe and wonder as the pioneer members of Deadwood's "stagecoach aristocracy," who came before the railroads came, built up a Victorian city in the wilderness of the Black Hills. The great chlorination, smelting, and cyanide mining excitements of the 1890s and 1900s play a major part in the story, for it was these speculative and fluctuating manifestations of new technology which gave Deadwood repeated booms, and kept her from withering away completely as did so many other once prosperous western mining camps.

Deadwood's people and their pastimes throw some light upon the uneven nature of the town's citizens and society, as does a brief excursion, here undertaken without fear of lasting ill effects or moral disintegration, through the city's raucous badlands of vice, corruption, and entertainment. The murky and devious byways of Black Hills promotion and publicity conclude, summarize, and to some extent explain the wily endeavors which made Deadwood so prosperous a town and kept her thus through wildly changing times, for in the town's attitude toward advertising, and toward the local history which was that advertising's handmaiden, lies the explanation of Deadwood's deeply rooted orientation toward her gaudy past. It is a tribute to Deadwood's promotional efforts that so small a town so quickly became well known and to this day continues to epitomize in the public mind the bold, bad, wild, and prosperous mineral frontier.

Few writers, I suppose, have finished a history without saying to themselves, "But there is yet more to do," when they came to the end of their labors, and I am no exception. A dozen histories of Deadwood could be written, and I hope one day they will be, to deal in detail with each of the many aspects of the city's sometimes excessive past. If my survey of the kind of a town that Deadwood was during her boom times from her inception in 1875 until her partial collapse in the 1920s leads to such a happy outcome, no one will be more gratified than I, for all that I have tried to do here is to catch the spirit of the town as a whole throughout a period of some fifty years and portray both the stabilities of Deadwood's nature and the many permutations and changes which came upon her as the result of the alternation of her good years with her bad. I have tried to present Deadwood as a whole, a compound of people, business, technology, society, whoopee, and promotion, all intermixed and interacting to produce the small but prosperous city which to this day remains a monument to the vitality and endurance of the mining West.

Doubtless I have included in my history an untruth or two, for that is inevitable when a historian gets his stories secondhand, from other people and from sources which now and then are imprecise. I want to assure my readers, however, that although some of my tales may be untrue, they are not novelities, but are old, well-worn, and

familiar falsehoods which the town has long since taken affectionately to its bosom. In extenuation I should point out that in many
cases the lively lies and misconceptions which Deadwood's citizens
cherished were more important in shaping Deadwood's history than
truer and more sober truths would have been, and I say, therefore,
about my more suspicious tales, what an old-timer said to me after
pouring a real stretcher into my gullible and receptive ear: "If that
ain't true, it ought to be!"

Deadwood is as friendly a town as she ever was, and maybe even
friendlier. I don't know that I have ever before met so many helpful
people all together in a bunch, and all of them assisted me in ways
beyond counting and certainly beyond adequately thanking. Mrs.
Marjorie Pontius of the Deadwood Public Library has, over many
years, been a valued friend and an able guide to the many sources
of Deadwood's history. Mrs. Pauline Rankin and her assistants,
Scott Stewart, Barbara Hintz, Sandy Bochmier, and May Huffman,
of the Adams Memorial Museum at Deadwood were of tremendous help to me in making use of the files and facilities of that
repository of so much Deadwood lore. Dayton Canaday, director of
the South Dakota State Historical Society at Pierre, as well as his
able staff, have for many years provided me with useful materials,
research, and suggestions. Dora Jones of the Leland D. Case Library of Western History at Black Hills State College at Spearfish
has been of great help in tracing down rare and essential materials
from that outstanding collection, and Leland D. Case himself, who
knew me when I was wearing three-cornered trousers, has ever
through the years been a staunch and gallant guide through the intricacies of Black Hills history. The Deadwood Chamber of Commerce, at first under the guidance of Nell Perrigoue and later under
equally able hands, has aided me for thirty years or more in my
searches for Deadwood tales, and has generously shared with me
historical rarities which, as far as I know, no one else possesses.
Deadwood's chief of police, Robert Kelley, generously gave me a
wealth of information about Deadwood's lively present and many
thoughtful insights into her even more sprightly past. Clyde Mitchell, Albro Ayres, and George Hunter were generous with their time
and reminiscences, as was Fred Borsch of Galena. The lively "dragons" associated with Deadwood's "Dragons Are Too Seldom" puppet theater showed me, as much as anything that I encountered,
that the spirit which brought young folks to the Black Hills a

hundred years ago to gamble their energy and skills against the mountains' riches is not dead yet but continues to find a happy home in Deadwood.

The library of the South Dakota School of Mines and Technology at Rapid City, with its splendid collection of Black Hills materials, to which have recently been added the files of the Black Hills writer Mildred Fielder, has been of constant support and assistance; and I wish to thank especially Estelle Helgerson and Philip F. McCauley for their help over the years. Professor Paul Gries, of the School of Mines, whose *Black Hills Mineral Atlas* must ever be the companion of all who work with Black Hills mining, has ably guided me to ghost towns, both in the library and on the ground. The Rapid City Public Library, under the direction of Marjorie Smith, taught me to enjoy research, and more recently, under the direction of Helen Hoyt, it has been helpful in ways beyond number in guiding me through its collections and in rounding up obscure materials. Thirty-five years of delighted acquaintance with the Chicago Corral of Westerners, and with its outstanding monthly *Brand Book*, have supplied me with scholarly details about the Hills and the West which are not available in any other way. The Black Hills Corral of Westerners has been a much-needed guide down many of the trails of Black Hills history which otherwise would have been unnoticed and impassable, and the Society of Black Hills Pioneers at Deadwood has similarly given me many happy and informative contacts with those old-timers to whom Deadwood's history is not a story but a lifetime.

First among those many individuals whose aid and friendship were invaluable in my researches is my father, Troy L. Parker, late of Hill City, who accumulated for me a library of Black Hills literature and history and throughout his life guided and encouraged me to seek out for myself "the way it really was." His many insights and his contemptuous "*That* cat won't fight!" whenever I came up with a peculiarly original historical error have steered me through many problems. My sister and her husband, Dr. and Mrs. Roland E. Schmidt, continue this familial tradition of skepticism and encouragement, both of which have been of constant help. My daughter, Rebecca Ellen Parker, surveyed the demographic changes in Deadwood as demonstrated in the early censuses of the area, making more than one interesting discovery. Mr. and Mrs. Bob Lee of the *Sturgis Tribune* have been generous without stint in sharing their encyclopedic knowledge, and in directing me to others who knew still more of various details of Black Hills history. Mr. and Mrs. Cushman Clark of Deadwood have opened doors beyond counting and have shared with me their extensive knowledge of Deadwood and its past, as did Mr. and Mrs. Stan Lindstrom. All three families were deeply involved in the research and writing which in 1976 produced *Gold—Gals—Guns—Guts*, a compendium of the history of the northern Hills. Robert M. Bryant, Sr., son of Frank Bryant, the discoverer of gold in Deadwood Gulch, and his daughter and son-in-law, Mr. and Mrs. Linfred Schuttler of Spearfish, were of much assistance in clarifying the many confusing details of that discovery.

Professor and Mrs. Carl A. Grimm of the South Dakota School of Mines and Technology have for over thirty years been sturdy guides to the byways of the Black Hills, and I have hiked and driven many thousands of happy miles in their always wise and kindly company. Their son Eric found for me in Minnesota files details of early gold rushers which I certainly would have missed. A. I. Johnson, Keystone's foremost mining engineer, has for years responded graciously to all of my many questions, and if I remain ignorant of many of the details of Black Hills mining, it is my own fault, not his. Similar gratitude is due to Otis E. Young, Jr. of Arizona State University at Tempe, whose writings on Western mining have been an invaluable guide. Mr. and Mrs. Richard Warren Lamb of Rapid City have over the years given me a sense of what the Hills lumber and cattle industries were really all about, and have repeatedly shared with me their resources of local history. Paul Martin of Hot Springs, who accompanied Seth Bullock and the Roosevelt boys to Medora, was able to give me a personal account of that notable and exciting expedition. Carl Underwood of Hill City has told me of many an adventure up to Deadwood, and stocked my memory with a fund of lively anecdotes. Mr. and Mrs. George Frink of Mystic told me much of the lore of the central Hills, and especially of President Coolidge's visit to Governor Sam McKelvie's nearby cabin. Professor C. M. Rowe of the South Dakota School of Mines shared with me his information on the Hills and the proposed state of Absaroka. Hugh Lambert of Albuquerque, New Mexico, has been a companion in exploring, assessing, mapping, and recording Black Hills ghost towns, so many of which contributed to the prosperity of Deadwood in its early days.

Professor Charles Goff of the University of Wisconsin–Oshkosh directed me to the letters of Oshkoshians in the Black Hills which I could not have found without his aid. Robert LeClair found for me accounts of the gold rush in the *Manitowoc Pilot*. My students in a 1978 seminar on western history—Eugene E. Detert, John A. Lammers, Mary Niebergall, and James Ziebell—did yeoman work in surveying Deadwood's history during the 1890s, and I have depended heavily upon their efforts. W. Eugene Hollon, my preceptor at the University of Oklahoma a good many years ago, so enjoyed the old-timers' tales I told him that I have included some of his favorites here to do him honor.

The maps were designed and drawn by Karen Fonstad of Oshkosh; any deviations from reality which may be found in them are due either to the obscurity of my instructions to her, or to the vagaries of the early Black Hills maps upon which we both relied.

I wish also to thank the Deadwood Public Library and the Adams Memorial Museum for permission to reprint photographs in their collections, and the Chronicle Publishing Company for permission to quote from Badger Clark's "The Cat Pioneers."

My wife Olga's continuing research, encouragement, and assistance, and her aid in correcting those petty errors which a historian ignores as he sweeps onward to grander fallacies, have been of so much value that this work could hardly have been begun, let alone completed, without her help.

I would also like to thank an unknown but valued benefactor who in the 1950s sent me a copy of the Burlington Railroad's 1904 pamphlet *Mines and Mining in the Black Hills* and thus started me on the trail of lost mines, ghost towns, and Black Hills and western history. I have lost his name, but I have not forgotten his kindness.

I have lived in the Black Hills on and off for well over fifty years. During this time I have naturally heard a good many tales, stories, anecdotes, and pithy sayings, and of course some of these had to do with Deadwood and have thus found their way onto my pages. I cannot identify all of those informants who over so long a time have so greatly helped me, but I can at least identify and express my gratitude to "the old-timer" whose many remarks are quoted here and there throughout these pages: his name is Legion.

DEADWOOD

The Golden Years

ONE

Hope in the Mountains

"These Hills was old when God was just a little
boy."

An old-timer

THE HORSES waded belly-deep in flowers, and the soldiers fashioned
nosegays to decorate their horses' bridles. It was the summer of
1874 and Gen. George Armstrong Custer was just about to start the
Black Hills gold rush.

Custer had not come to the Black Hills to start a gold rush, and
indeed his official reports of gold in the area tended to be deprecia-
tory rather than enthusiastic. He had been sent into this, the last
unsettled mountain fastness of the Great Plains, to find in the heart
of the Sioux reservation a spot for a military post from which those
hostile and disgruntled Indians might be controlled and kept from
their continuing depredations against both the whites and the other
Plains tribes around them. Instead of locating a site for a post, however, Custer seems to have utterly lost track of this objective, and to
have been carried away with the fertile beauty of the Black Hills
and the possibilities occasioned by his men's discovery of trifling but
promising placer gold deposits along French Creek below the site of
present-day Custer, South Dakota. Custer and his men spread the
word that the mountainous Black Hills were fair and fertile, a
wooded fairyland of hopes and promise rising from the rolling
plains of the Dakota Territory.

The Black Hills, so called from the deep green pines which
clothe them, and which, viewed from a distance, fade into a dark
and shadowy lavender upon the horizon, occupy the southwestern
corner of what is now the state of South Dakota. Rising to heights
of over seven thousand feet, with an average elevation of more than
a mile above sea level, they loom three or four thousand feet above
the surrounding prairies and, especially from the east and north,
give a sombre appearance of secrecy, mystery, promise, and adventure. They are encircled by the branching arms of the Cheyenne

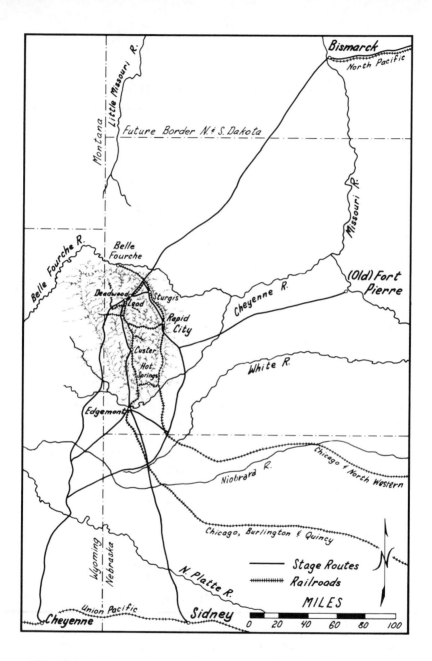

The Black Hills, in the southwestern corner of Dakota Territory, with some of the stage trails and railroads which served them

River, whose Belle Fourche ("Beautiful Fork") goes around them to the north, and whose South Fork encircles them on the south, both nearly meeting again at Pumpkin Buttes to the west of the Hills in Wyoming. These hills, which occupy an area about sixty by one hundred miles, are the remnant of earlier, richer, mightier mountains, and they contain the distillation of the riches which once towered high above them. The mineralized areas of the Hills tend to be more or less coextensive with the tall timber of the area, and the thoughtful miner, schooled in other mineral areas, can easily surmise that the wealth of the timber and minerals alike must be due to some series of geological upheavals which both warped and enriched the soil of these towering mountains. The deep valleys, plentiful streams, rich mountain meadow pastures, and the abundant pines combined with mineral resources to make the Black Hills, in the mid-1870s, a land of opportunity in a time of grief and troubles.

General Custer was by no means the first white man to explore the verdant Black Hills, although he was unquestionably the most notable, a notability which, of course, was considerably enhanced in 1876 when he perished with much of his command in the disastrous Battle of the Little Big Horn, a battle which was to some extent brought about by his earlier opening of the Hills. In 1742, the French brothers François and Louis-Joseph de la Vérendrye may have approached the Hills from the northeast, and seen Bear Butte, an outlying sentinel of their mountainous mass. White men are said to have early entered the Hills for gold—a common belief in all mineralized areas and one that should not be taken too seriously—and in 1834 a group of miners commemorated by the Thoen stone found near Spearfish, South Dakota, supposedly "got all the gold [they] could carry" but perished before they could carry it far. Argonauts bound for California in 1852 are also said to have entered the Hills and prospected, only to fall before the arrows of the Indians, and traces of their brief enterprises are said to have been found in the course of early gold rush exploration and excavations. Lt. Gouverneur Kemble Warren in 1857 nearly encircled the Hills, and left at least three spots which early maps entitled Camp Warren. His magnificent map of the area named the streams of the foothills and the mountains of the interior insofar as these were visible to him as he skirted the perimeter of the Hills.

Capt. William Franklin Raynolds in 1859 followed the path of the Vérendryes and arrived at Bear Butte, which he climbed with

considerable aplomb before passing to the north of the Black Hills
to go around their outlying mountain suburb, the Bear Lodge
Mountains of Wyoming, on his way to the Devil's Tower. Accompanying Raynolds was the geologist Ferdinand V. Hayden, who
prospected in the bed of Bear Butte Creek and, indeed, returned to
the site in 1866, and later, in 1869, announced to the American
Philosophical Society that gold was certainly available in the area.
None of these announcements, however, had the impact that Custer's had when he reported on 3 August 1874 to the adjutant general
of the Department of Dakota that

> gold was obtained in numerous localities in what are termed gulches.
> No discoveries, so far as I am aware, were made of gold deposits in
> quartz, although there is every reason to believe that a more extended
> and thorough search would have discovered it. No large nuggets were
> found; the examination, however, showed that a very even, if not a very
> rich distribution of gold is to be found throughout the entire valleys. In
> other words the "prospecting" showed that while the miner may not in
> one panful of earth find nuggets of large size or deposits of astonishing
> richness, to be followed by days and weeks of unrewarded labor, he
> may reasonably expect in certain localities to realize from every panful
> of earth a handsome return for his labor.
>
> It has not required an expert to find gold in the Black Hills, as men
> without former experience in mining have discovered it at an expense
> of but little time or labor.[1]

This was the kind of news the nation was ready to hear. The Panic
of 1873 was firmly under way, distributing unemployment and poverty with a liberal hand. Drought lay heavy upon the Midwest, and
such crops as did sprout were nibbled off at ground level by an
attack of grasshoppers reminiscent of the plagues of Egypt. The
farmer, the bankrupt, and the jobless alike were free and eager to go
adventuring. The Union Pacific Railroad had long since reached
both Sidney, Nebraska, and Cheyenne, Wyoming, scarcely 175
miles south of the Black Hills and their reputed gold fields; the
Northern Pacific Railroad was approaching Bismarck, in present-
day North Dakota; and steamers on the Missouri River met the
Black Hills trails at Sioux City and Fort Pierre. A mobile and interested population heard of gold "among the roots of the grass" and
had more than one convenient way to get to within grabbing distance of it. It is of such opportunities that gold rushes are constructed, and despite vehement governmental objections, the Black

Hills rush got under way in the late fall of 1874, six months after Custer's tentative discoveries.

The Black Hills had been set aside as a part of the Great Sioux Reservation, by the 1868 Treaty of Fort Laramie. The fact of the Hills' location in the desolate plains area that the Indians and the government agreed upon for a reservation dictated their inclusion in the Sioux reservation. Included they were, and the U.S. Army was charged with the strenuous duty of keeping out the miners, a task beside which the labors of Sisyphus dim into inconsequentiality. Repeated edicts, orders, and directives from military authorities high and low were seriously uttered and diligently but ineffectively enforced, for keeping miners out of the Black Hills was a bit like trying to shovel fleas with a grain scoop: interesting and active work, but not a labor likely to be crowned with complete success or satisfaction. Too many frontiersmen knew where the Black Hills were— three major military expeditions, under Colonels James A. Sawyers, Nelson Cole, and Samuel Walker, had marched past the area on their way to the 1865 Powder River Campaign in Wyoming, and Custer's more recent 1874 expedition had taken a thousand white men and one black woman (Sarah Campbell, Custer's cook, who later settled in Galena), into the very heart of this Sioux reservation.

It is not strange, then, that miners soon started for the gold mines of the Hills or that many of them got there. Several early expeditions were discouraged and turned back by the military in late 1874 and early 1875, but one, known to fame as the Gordon party, did manage to make its way across the Badlands from Sioux City to encamp in the bitter winter of 1874–75 on the site of Custer's gold discoveries in the center of the Hills. Several army expeditions from posts in Dakota pursued these doughty prospectors, but met in each case with severe weather and disappointment, and it was not until April 1875 that Capt. John Mix and his command from Fort Laramie located the Gordon party, safe in an eighty-foot stockade on French Creek. Mix found the miners (who included one white woman, Annie Tallent, whose notable history, *The Black Hills*, published in 1899, has ever since been a source of much Hills lore) safe but hungry, and as eager to accompany him to civilization as he was to carry out his orders to remove them from the Hills.

Out the Gordon party went, to Fort Laramie, and the news of their discoveries, suitably enlarged and embellished, soon reached a public made expectant by earlier newspaper hints of their adventures. No less an authority than the *New York Times* told of their successes, reporting on 1 March 1875 that

> they sank twenty-five prospect-holes and struck gold in every instance. From the grassroots to the bed of the rock they found numerous gold and silver bearing quartz lodes, and the specimens Mr. Witcher [Eph Witcher, a member of the Gordon party who had gone out of the Hills for help] has brought back are pronounced very rich. The party never saw an Indian while in the Hills. Mr. Witcher describes the parts of the Hills they saw as having magnificent valleys, seemingly limitless forests of pine, and abundance of elk, deer and other game.

The publicity continued, for John Gordon, guide and leader for the party, was subsequently arrested and involved in a long series of acrimonious and well-publicized broils with the governmental authorities as he repeatedly attempted to return to the riches which he had found in the Black Hills.

By the summer of 1875, however, the Gordon party was only one of many miners' expeditions that had begun to invade the Hills, skillfully evading army patrols by traveling among the sinuosities of the prairie gullies, and later on avoiding capture in the mountains, valleys, and forests, which provided both gold and protection. Gen. Philip Sheridan, commander of the Military Division of the Missouri, might storm and rage in Chicago, and threaten the arrest and expulsion of any miner found within the confines of the Sioux reservation, but the miners themselves were in the Black Hills and cared little for his anger. A government geological expedition under the direction of Walter P. Jenney and Henry M. Newton also toured the Hills, escorted by several hundred soldiers under the command of Col. Richard I. Dodge. Jenney reported on 9 June 1875 that "the greater part of the Black Hills [are] in Dakota Formations . . . and are of a recent geological age and not auriferous."[2] Such an announcement would have discouraged Jason himself, but Jenney, before long, was forced by new discoveries to change his mind about it. On 17 July he wrote, "I have discovered gold in paying quantities in gravel bars, both on Spring and Rapid Creeks, from twenty to thirty miles northeast of Harney's Peak."[3] Colonel Dodge but expressed his "fair and candid opinion" when he reported, "The Black Hills, in many respects, [are] the finest country I have ever seen."[4]

The army continued in its efforts to expel the miners, sending in Gen. George Crook and an ample additional force of soldiers to scour the Hills for the invading treasure seekers. Crook, however, wisely combined the mailed fist of the military with the velvet glove of supple diplomacy, and he actually was able peacefully to gather up the greater part of the miners in the Hills and take them back with him to civilization by promising them that they might return as soon as the Hills were legally opened to settlement by the extinction of the Indian treaties which protected the reservation. The fifteen hundred or so miners gathered in Custer City for removal cheerfully passed a resolution "tendering thanks to President Grant for the manner in which he had caused his commands to be executed," and departed from the Hills.[5] To ensure that the miners did not return, Capt. Edwin Pollock, with a company of infantry and two of cavalry, a force which soon had to be substantially augmented as the problem of removing miners became more and more acute, was stationed at a military post established at Custer City. The miners, however, continued to sneak into the Hills to hide and prospect in hidden valleys, and by November President Grant, noticing that the troops in the Black Hills merely increased by their desertion the number of miners in the area, withdrew the soldiers and abandoned military efforts to keep the miners out. As Captain Pollock and his men departed from the Hills, they met hundreds of prospectors on their way from Fort Laramie into the gold fields.[6]

The frontier towns encircling the Black Hills—Sioux City, Yankton, and Bismarck on the Missouri River, and Sidney and Cheyenne on the Union Pacific—all saw in the possibility of a gold rush the opportunity for the prosperity denied to them by the agricultural and financial depression of the 1870s. Although the spring of 1875 had been cold, and "people who were obliged to thaw their whisky before they drank it were not likely to become feverish about any topic whatsoever," the summer of 1875 would certainly offer possibilities for promotional activities. Once the soldiers were out of the Hills, it seemed likely that some sort of boom times could be cultivated. Outfitting towns held great public meetings for the purpose of securing and disseminating travel and advertising information—only, of course, because without it "greedy and restless neighbors . . . would divert travel from this point," as the Yankton people put it, "and thus subject the immigrants to untold inconveniences." Public opinion in these outfitting towns held that advertising conveyed a positive blessing upon the pilgrim bound for the Hills, and that the Argonaut ought to be grateful to Yankton and Sioux City, where the people "sit up nights trying to prevent each other from

enticing him into a difficult route and subjecting him to untold inconveniences." This fear that some other city might inconvenience
the miner bound for the Hills seems to have to a considerable extent
dominated the thinking of the businessmen of the surrounding territory.[7]

The publicity generated was probably not swallowed whole by
its intended audience, for the average pilgrim was no ninny, and
when he read a blurb full of rosy adjectives, he probably did not
succumb entirely to its blandishments. When a frontier town, for
example, spoke of the Black Hills in these terms, only a real innocent was likely to believe them:

> The gold is there. It is in almost every gulch, on every hillside, on every
> mountain top, in placers and in quartz. It is there for the poor man and
> for the capitalist. It is to be divided among the laborers, merchants,
> mechanics and manufacturers. There is enough for all who will come,
> and those who wish to flee from the hard times of the East and avail
> themselves of the hidden trasures of this, the last and richest gold field
> on the globe, had better make their arrangements to come early. This is
> a show where the front seats cannot be reserved.[8]

Gulled or not, the pilgrims did come to the Black Hills. Ferocious
weather in the late spring and early summer of 1875 (it rained on
sixty-seven consecutive days and snowed on 2 June) had not de-
terred the rushers, and they gathered themselves into bands in many
a town and city all across the country. Old prospectors and miners
from California, Nevada, Colorado, and Montana left their waning
claims to seek the new bonanzas. The clerk and the cooper, the merchant, the lawyer and the farmer, the white man and the black—all
headed toward the wealth that Custer had revealed and the Gordon
party had confirmed. A New Haven, Connecticut, group included
enough trades and occupations to found and maintain a city: auger
maker, blacksmith, mason, gunmaker, toolmaker, machinist, ex-
plorer, miner, molder, carriage trimmer, and broker. This caravan
of commerce planned to come to Yankton to complete their outfits,
each man buying there two woolen blankets, one rubber blanket,
two pairs heavy leather boots, one pair rubber hip boots, one Win-
chester rifle, one Smith and Wesson revolver, and one navy (Colt?)
revolver. Apparently they planned to be well equipped to wallow in
gore, and rest in comfort afterwards.

Additional equipment recommended by those who had already
"seen the elephant" (current slang for "having taken in the whole

show") in other western mining districts included a round-pointed shovel, pick and gold pan, two tin plates, a dipper, knife and fork, large teaspoon, some towels, and some matches. Messes of six ought to provide themselves, in addition, with a frying pan, a small dutch oven (a flat cooking pot with a rimmed lid on which coals could be piled to brown the top of the bread that baked inside), a tin pail, a handsaw, a hatchet, and a tent. An expenditure of eighteen to twenty dollars would cover one man's food for a three months' trip to the Hills, the total outfit should not come to more than thirty-five to fifty dollars, and most of that was probably invested in the fire-arms and ammunition. The recommended foods included flour, ba-con, beans (called "false friends" because of their tendency to talk behind one's back), coffee in the bean, baking soda for flapjacks and biscuits, sugar, salt, pepper, and dried fruits. Eked out by judicious hunting, such a larder would sustain rather than enthrall its devo-tees, but it was probably as good as they had got at home. Many parties omitted the tent, and carried, instead, individual tarpaulins to cover each man's blankets and protect them from wear and weather. As trainloads of prospective miners headed for the West, it was amusing, one of them recorded, to see new additions climb aboard, each loaded down with his pack, each pack missing many essential items and stuffed with nonessentials. Every station added a few men bound for the Hills, and as the train moved westward, the equipment of the new passengers, schooled on the frontier, tended to become more and more sensible and judicious.[9]

The prospectors came from everywhere, though predominantly from the East and from the Midwest, for as one of the pilgrims wrote in his diary on 22 January 1876: "Black Hills fever is raging. Guess if nothing happens will make a 'go' of it" and go he did, to become an eminent Deadwood townbuilder and newspaperman.[10] The southern and central Black Hills soon swarmed with several thousand miners. French Creek, on which was Custer City, throve temporarily as the putative capital of the mining region, and pros-pectors tramped and wallowed up and down the banks of the stream in search of placer gold and the lodes which had produced it. Hill City, on Spring Creek, was the second town in the Hills (though such an assignment of firsts is recreational rather than historical, an amusement of the local history buff), and from it, up and down the creek, other towns were formed: Sheridan, Baker Park, Rockerville, and Stand-off Bar. Rapid and Castle creeks had Castleton with its rocky placers, Sitting Bull, Canyon City, Pactola, and Placerville, as well as Hay Camp, which eventually grew into Rapid City, the present-day metropolis of the Hills. Battle Creek, which flows within sight of the granite faces on Mount Rushmore, gave rise to Etta Camp, Keystone, Horn City, Harney, Hayward, and Hermosa. Each of the creeks was divided into several mining districts, each prospered temporarily, and some survive as villages down to the present day, but the discovery of the richer placers and lodes of Deadwood, in the northern Hills, eclipsed them all, and quickly robbed them of their transient populations.

As H. N. Maguire, a Pactola and Rochford promoter and newspaperman of no mean ability, put it:

> The writer has witnessed many "mining stampedes," many hegiras from old mining camps to new ones; has seen them by moonlight as well as by daylight—in the midst of winter, when the ground was deeply covered with snow, as well as in the genial summer season, with green-grassed landscapes; has witnessed and participated in them at all times, in all seasons, and under all circumstances—but never before knew so sudden, so total and complete, a depopulation of an old mining camp by a rush for a new one, as was the stampede from Custer City to Deadwood in the early spring of 1876.[11]

The 1880 census showed Custer City left with a population of 201; the area around Deadwood Gulch had a population of over ten thousand. By 1880 the gold rush had long since moved north.

Deadwood Gulch, which was to become so famous in the annals of American mining, lies at an elevation of some forty-six hundred feet above sea level but deep in the valley cut by Whitewood Creek, a modest stream which takes its source on the slopes of Deer Mountain and then runs fourteen winding miles northeastward to the prairies, which it reaches at the site of the present-day town of Whitewood. The Whitewood's tributary creeks—Deadwood, Fantail, Whitetail, Englewood, Yellow, Strawberry, Spruce, City, Sheeptail, Peedee, and others—break through the walls, which tower up to seven hundred feet above the valley floor, to join the main stream of the Whitewood and to contribute to it their waters and their placer gold. The whole area is one of heavy mineralization, and as the mountain ores were worn away by eons of precipitation and erosion, the gold rolled down the slopes, fell at last into the valleys, and was ultimately swept into Deadwood Gulch, where, the incline of the stream being somewhat less precipitous, the gold paused in the curves and interstices of the streambed to await the picks and pans of eager miners.

The whole area is still for the most part covered with a thick growth of pine timber, and the gulches and valleys with thickets of aspen and willow. The valley of the Whitewood itself, at the point where Deadwood Creek entered it from the west, was in 1875 choked with a mass of fallen trees, the result of a tornado, a destructive forest fire, or the labors of diligent but long-departed beaver; and this tangle of dead wood is said to have given the name to the area as a whole. It is useful to note, however, that the gold regions of California also had a mining camp called Deadwood and that an Argonaut from those regions may well have brought the name along with him, or at least suggested the use of the old name for a new mining area so appropriate to it. At any rate, Deadwood (accented on the first syllable) became the name for the entire area, just as it is the name for the whole valley to this day, despite the fact that most of it is watered not by Deadwood Creek but by the somewhat larger Whitewood. It is a narrow valley, two or three hundred yards across for the most part, and even more restricted where the stream has cut narrow gaps in harder rocks on its way northward to the plains. This narrowness of course resulted in the towns of the gulch being long and narrow, and singularly prone to serious flooding, for the same waters which carried the gold to Deadwood are equally eager to carry flood, debris, ruin, and disaster.

The miners who claimed to have first discovered gold in the Deadwood area could probably have hired a hall and held a convention, for their names are many and legion, and their claims all clamant and conflicting. Every now and then during gold rush days of the 1870s some busy prospector found evidence of ancient placer workings: a wagon chain dangling from a lofty pine (the assumption being that, contrary to all nature, the pine grew, lifting the long-since deposited chain upwards with its growth), hewn logs now overgrown with saplings, sluice boxes from antiquity buried beneath six or eight feet of detritus, an old grindstone, and crumbling timbers pocked by the bullets of some long-forgotten Indian attack, still standing guard before a tunnel's mouth. Every mining district accumulates such legends and displays such trophies of the past to demonstrate its claim to riches in the present, and each such claim must be taken with considerably more than the customary grain of salt, for miners, anxious to find a market for their mines, are always happy to establish some sort of tradition of antiquity to enhance their value. John S. McClintock, an experienced and curmudgeonly pioneer and Black Hills historian, made a point of visiting each of the supposed artifacts when it was brought to light, and in his opinion none of them were genuine; all were the inventions of greed and imagination. That may be so, but these legends of early occupation of the Black Hills are dear to the hearts of those who live there now, and certainly a few of these precious relics may be assumed to have at least a tincture of truth about them. As the prospector said, "I was a-diggin' and I stuck my shovel into the bar'l of an ol' musket—ifn' you don't believe me come on up to the camp, and I kin show you the shovel."[12]

On 8 March 1875 the *Cheyenne Daily Leader* reported that old trappers and others had once found gold far to the northeast of Custer's Park on the streams that flowed into the Belle Fourche River. The *Yankton Daily Press and Dakotaian* (so spelled at the time) on 5 August of the same year reported that a diligent miner had prospected sixty miles north of the Custer placers on French Creek and had sunk numerous holes on likely bars and taken out from ten to forty cents to the pan of gravel. A miner named Nuckles is credited by Robert Edmund Strahorn, in his 1877 *Handbook of Wyoming and Guide to the Black Hills*, with having taken gold out of Deadwood Gulch in September 1875, but this may very well be an error and confusion with a man named Dan Muckle (or Muskle or Meckles), who came in with a party in early November. Strahorn is less than precise about names, and George W. Kingsbury, in the *History of Dakota Territory*, who mentions Meckles, is even less reliable in this regard. An Ed Murphy from the Montana goldfields is also credited, on his own account but nobody else's, with having been a "first discoverer" of Deadwood's gold some time in the "late Autumn" of 1875. McClintock, just referred to, credits William Smith, John Kane, and three others with a discovery of gold on Whitewood Creek on 7 August 1875, at the mouth of Spruce Gulch, near the spot where the Deadwood rodeo grounds now stand. McClintock further holds that the Blanchard party, coming north from Custer (Smith had come south, up the Whitewood, from the other direction) found gold on Deadwood Creek on 6 September of the same year. McClintock, however, as is often the case with men of strong and acerbic opinions, was not in his own time, and is not yet, universally regarded as the sole fount of wisdom in the matter.

The man most commonly accepted as the first discoverer of the gold of Deadwood Gulch (and remember, this was hardly more than one hundred years ago, so that the matter could, within the lifetime of living men, be checked by personal interrogation) is Frank Bryant, who with John B. Pearson, Thomas Moon (often erroneously given as "Moore"), Richard Lowe, James Pierman, Samuel Blodgett, Dan Muckle, and George Hauser came into the area in August 1875, coming down Spruce Gulch into the valley of Whitewood Creek. Bryant's son, Robert M. Bryant, Sr., of Spearfish, believes that his father found gold just above the mouth of City Creek on 11 August, then built a cabin and sawed out lumber for sluices to work their claim. Pierman's wife was an Indian and had told him of her friends who had brought gold from the Black Hills to cast into musket balls—it is a common tale, told about most gold regions. The little party in addition had a crude map of the Hills drawn by Tom Labarge, Charley DeGray, and Lephiere Narcouter, old hands of the American Fur Company, which seems to have had several small and short-lived posts around the Hills in the 1830s. At any rate, Bryant did not record his claim until November 1875, at which time he, William Cudney, and W. H. Coder posted the customary notice:

> We, the undersigned, claim three hundred (300) feet below this notice for discovery, and nine hundred (900) feet or three claims above this notice for mining purposes.[13]

The claims ran, as the notice indicates, three hundred feet up and down the creek, and from rimrock to rimrock on either side, a generous custom hallowed by western placer mining tradition, but further enlarged in the Black Hills.

Bryant continued in active mining life in the Hills, locating the Blacktail mine, operating the Gold Finch mill, and prospecting in the southern Hills, and in the Carbonate District on Squaw Creek, where the ruins of his little log cabin can still be seen below the Ironsides Mine.

The second discovery of gold in the area seems to have been made on Deadwood Creek on 6 September 1875, by a party composed of A. S. Blanchard, Tom Patterson, H. A. Albien, James Verpont, and a member of Custer's 1874 Black Hills expedition whose name is unfortunately lost. This group had come into Deadwood Gulch from Custer, and of course did not run into the Bryant party, which had come up the Whitewood from the other direction.

A third discovery, again on Deadwood Creek rather than Whitewood, was made by the Lardner party, composed of William Lardner, Ed McKay, Joe Inglesby, Hilan (Pat) Hulin, James Hicks, William and Alfred Gay, and R. Hagard (or Haggart) and guided by Bryant's companions, John B. Pearson and Dan Muckle (Muskle, Mackle). They seem to have been in much the same area as the Blanchard group, and found gold in early November if not before. Seth Bullock, an early sheriff of the community, indeed believes, in his reminiscences, that the Lardner party was the first to discover gold, and his opinion does carry weight, for he was, if not a member of the party, at least on the spot soon enough to talk to many of the men who were. The natural inclination of miners to claim priority in such a matter from mere personal pride was of course augmented by the traditional right of the first claimant to receive an additional placer claim "for discovery." Stronger characters than these have now and then been led from the path of strict veracity by smaller considerations than those which attached to precedence in a placer mining area.

These discoveries were not made in a mineralogical vacuum, but at the north end of an already vigorous gold rush. When John Pearson wrote to the newspapers that Deadwood "lays over Alder Gulch, Montana, the richest placer mines ever before discovered, because Alder Gulch was spotted, while Deadwood is regular and the [pay] streak is wider, and is the richest and most extensive placer gold field that has ever been struck,"[14] it was of course an exaggeration, and at first glance it seems surprising that a prospector with a good find should so wish to advertise to competitors. Most of the men in the Black Hills, however, had several claims and were as eager to sell some of them as they were to work the rest, for as early as January 1876 most of the available claims had been recorded, and almost every latecomer had to buy his claim from an earlier miner who was already in possession. It was thus to the first arrival's advantage to attract as many buyers as possible to any spot where he had claims to sell.

By December 1875 the Lost Mining District, with William Lardner its recorder, had been set up to record the claims of arriving miners. On 1 January 1876 a party composed of J. J. Williams, W. H. Babcock, Eugene Smith, and a Mr. Jackson arrived and located claims. Williams's claim, Number Two below discovery, in three months yielded twenty-seven thousand dollars worth of placer gold. Williams then sold his claim and bought Number Fourteen above discovery, where he washed out another thirty-five thousand dollars. In mid-January a party including Wade Porter and Oscar Cline arrived, and the rush to Deadwood was in full swing. On 10 April 1876 the mining camp of Creek City, on Whitewood at the mouth of Deadwood Creek, and shortly thereafter Whitewood (not the same, of course, as the present-day village in the foothills by that name) just below it was established. William Gay, in April if not before, laid out Gayville a mile or two above the mouth of Deadwood Creek. Other camps quickly sprang up along the streams. Montana City, Elizabethtown (named for Miss Elizabeth Card, the first girl, sixteen, in the area), Fountain City, Chinatown, North (or lower) Deadwood, South Deadwood, Whoop Up, City Creek, Cleveland, Ingleside, Pluma, and Gold Run went from the north end of Whitewood to the southern. Blacktail, Gayville, Central, Golden Gate, Anchor City, Oro City, Pimlico, and Lead, went up Deadwood Creek, and all of these were merely a beginning, for as the placer fortunes shifted, the towns rose and fell beside the mines. Golden City and New Chicago sprang up on False Bottom Creek (so named because the bedrock was said to be a "false bottom" with the real placer deposits beneath, rather than above it), and were soon merged into a new town called Garden City.

Every valley for miles around was pocked with prospect holes,

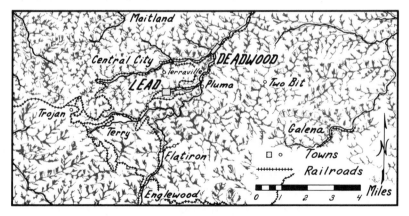

The northern Black Hills mining country, of which Deadwood was the business and commercial center

placarded with claim notices, and dotted with the white tents of incoming hopefuls. These were ideal mines for a poor man, for the gold seemed to extend from the surface downward, at least in some places, and ran from two to fifty cents or more to the pan, and the bedrock, where the bulk of the gold rested, was neither deep, as in other Black Hills placers, nor excessively wet, although there was ample creek water for gold washing operations. By early March 1876 six hundred miners were at work not only in Deadwood but in Whitewood, Gold Run, Blacktail, Whitetail, and Grizzly gulches, and a lucky prospector on Bobtail was said to be taking out $5 an hour. Spring snows delayed more extensive migration into Deadwood Gulch, as the whole area soon came to be called. Cy Iba, an old miner who had worked in California, Nevada, and Montana, said that men could easily make from $5 to $125 a day, although large amounts of snow and cold weather were currently hindering production. It is notable, of course, that the originators of such rumors generally do have some reasonable excuse for their *current* failure to live up to their optimistic predictions. Hope was in the very air, and optimism was epidemic.

The laws and customs of the placer mines had long since been determined and established out of German, Spanish, and Mexican practices that had come to earlier gold rushes in Georgia and California, and had there been adapted to American use. Each mining district (which, in placer, or stream, mining, tended to be a single valley) was empowered by federal statute to make up its own laws, so long as these did not conflict with federal or territorial obligations. Claims were generally taken up on a first-come, first-served basis, but in case a mining district was discovered by a sizable group, it could be laid out into three-hundred-foot claims and the claims distributed by lot, to avoid friction. Some of the prospectors might go away unsatisfied, but it was considered an improvement on going away in a box. Some of the claims on Deadwood Creek seem to have been distributed, early in January 1876, in this offhand manner, when forty claims stretching over two miles were handed out to the fortunate winners in the lottery. The location of a claim had to be marked so that its upper and lower boundaries were clear to all, and a notice, like Frank Bryant's, posted to show its owner, and the claim itself recorded, usually for a fee of from one to two dollars, with an elected claim recorder. Many land titles in the Black Hills date back to just such rough-and-ready, handhewn titles, and

for a hundred years they seem to have for the most part gone un-
challenged.

A miner was obligated to "represent," or work upon, his claim
or claims sufficiently to show that he maintained an active interest
in them—one day of pick and shovel work every one or two weeks
was a frequently used definition of adequate representation—and
this work could also be put in on local public roads if it was incon-
venient for the miner to work upon the placer claim itself. The size
of the Black Hills claims, three hundred feet up and down the valley,
and from rimrock to rimrock on either side, was larger than was
usual in earlier mining rushes, but it was established from the earliest days of the rush and confirmed by constant practice, and claims
of this size were numbered as "No. 10 below Discovery" or "No. 14
above" ("discovery" being implied by "above"). There was some agitation from latecomers to the Deadwood area to reduce the size of
the claims in order that everybody could have a smaller one. An
Irishman named McTigue, another named O'Leary, and miners
McNabb and Smith endeavored to push through this supposed reform, but old-timer Frank Ground, who held a claim in Montana
City at the lower end of the gulch, called a miners' meeting that by
unanimous vote set up a committee, presumably well armed, to es-
cort McTigue and his fellow complainants clear out of the district,
and to keep an eye out for their return.

In legal theory a claim had to be advertised in the local newspaper, but in the absence of these useful publications in the early
days of the rush this requirement fell, by common consent, into a
state of innocuous desuetude, and with the coming of the *Black Hills
Pioneer* in the summer of 1876 to Deadwood it does not seem to have
been taken up again with any vigor. A claim could also be "proved
up" and receive a federal patent, or deed, so that its owner could
hold it in perpetuity, like a homestead or a preemption. The total
cost of a patent, however, was about twelve hundred dollars, and
hardly any of the placer claims were thought to be worth the effort,
for not only did the owner have sufficient title to his claim for mining purposes without going any further, but such a piece of land,
down in the bottom of a valley, with the various rights of adjacent
claimholders impinging upon its use, did not seem to have much
commercial value.

The records of the rush are full of fanciful mining locations,
written out and posted up for amusement and entertainment. Near

Rapid City a local jokester claimed a pine tree, with all its "bends, appurtenances and sinuosities" for mining purposes. Four enterprising Deadwood attorneys in 1883 laid claim to a mudslide on the stairs that led up from Main to Willaims Street, and passersby were cautioned "not to trespass upon or carry away any of this our mudhole under pains and penalties which will naturally occur to them by so doing."[15] The claim notice of course got into the paper as a news item and gave them some free, and perhaps needed, publicity. Gold in the Black Hills appears in several ways. It can be found in quartz, which seems to be the spot where it is originally laid down by nature, and in various other places where the disintegration of the quartz has carried it, like the limestone ledges around Spearfish Canyon or the "cement" conglomerates north of Deadwood, in which ancient placers appeared to have been cemented into solid rock by the percolation and addition of large quantities of iron rust. The eventual though gradual breakdown of all of these deposits ultimately led to the presence of what was known as placer gold down in the valleys, where its weight, nineteen times heavier than water, and correspondingly heavier than most dirt, gravel, or rock with which it might be mixed, brought it to the bottom of things on what was called the bedrock. Here the gold stopped, and if the bedrock layer was fairly smooth or evenly pocketed, the gold could there be gathered up from a thin layer of rich gravel.

At least that was the theory; in actual practice gold could occur from the grass roots down, and from one side of the valley to the other. In the southern Hills it also tended to appear so far down that it was a rare thing for the placer miner to ever get down to it at all, but in Deadwood the bedrock tended to be within a few feet of the surface of the valley floor, and thus its riches were easily accessible. Even so, the valley might be too wet to prospect for gold much below its surface, and the prospector had to first work on the sides of the valley, and guess from the results where the pay streak in the bottom might be. Deadwood Gulch, for example, had two well-defined pay streaks, both of which were well worth digging down to work, and the whole area soon took on the appearance of a prairie-dog town as piles of dirt were interspersed between the shallow shafts that led down to the bedrock. The miner who dug too many such holes, and didn't bring much gold up out of them, might be jokingly referred to as a "gopher" and urged to "gopher" advice to some more experienced miner, but the laugh often rested with the man who dug the most, for in the end he would probably find something at the bottom of one hole or another. Waterwheels, connected by one or two hundred feet of aspen rodding, operated China pumps to clear the water from the wet workings, and diversion ditches and dams were used to temporarily keep the water out of the workings until the bedrock could be swept clean and its gold-bearing gravels recovered.

Aside from his pick and shovel, familiar to any ditchdigger of the period, the gold pan was the essential tool of the placer prospector. This useful instrument was about eighteen inches in diameter and four inches deep, with sloping sides terminating in a flat bottom six or eight inches across. It was purposely made of mild steel in order that it would rust, for the rust that collected upon it gave a certain roughness to the surface of the pan, a roughness that tended to hold fine particles of gold—and many of them were so fine as to be nearly invisible—better than a smoother pan. Modern practice makes pans of copper, rubber, and plastic, with all sorts of patent ripples and sinuosities upon their surfaces, but the old-time prospector seems to have been content with the simple article. It was never used for any other purpose than panning gold, for the accumulations of grease that might result from cooking or washing in it made its surface slippery so that the fine grains of gold slid out of it and escaped. The only cure for such slickness was to throw the gold pan in a low fire and heat it red-hot to remove the offending contamination.

In use, the prospector would put about a peck of promising gravel into his pan, then squat down in the nearest stream—that was what his rubber boots were for—and submerge the pan while gently stirring the gravel to wash the dirt and silt from it. Bringing the pan to the surface, the prospector's practiced hand would throw out the larger pebbles, first carefully rinsing them to remove any clinging particles of gold. Then, alternately dipping and raising the edge of the pan beneath the water while he gently swirled the remaining sand, he allowed the sand to slop over the edge of the pan, working with great care, for the crucial point of the activity was just about at hand. It was at this point that any nuggets might be revealed and removed. Once the sand was out of the pan, leaving behind it black iron, cassiterite (tin ore), and tiny red garnets, all of which were heavy enough to have remained in the pan throughout the washing process, the prospector would give the pan a dextrous swirl that spread its contents out in an arc across its bottom, a sort of a half-moon, and at the far tip of that half-moon, carried farthest by its weight, would be the gold.

A skilled panner could put a dozen flecks of gold the size of the point of a pin into a pan and recover all of them, and much of Deadwood's gold might come in pieces of that size. A gold dollar, for comparison, was smaller and thinner than a modern dime, and nuggets of that size were rare. Once the gold, whatever its size, was brought to one area of the pan, it could be removed with a finger or a moistened toothpick, and stored away in a buckskin or leather bag, often made of a bull's scrotum, for cloth, no matter how fine its weave, was too porous to hold the fine gold dust. Even the most skillful panner lost some of his fine gold and included some heavy sands in his sack, although running a magnet through the grains would remove the iron sands, so that an ounce of gold dust never really ran the customary $20.00 to the ounce, but might be valued at anywhere from $16.50 on up. Miners, however, habitually thought of an ounce of dust as a twenty-dollar gold piece and insisted on making purchases at that valuation. The incredible weight of gold is hard to appreciate. A cubic foot of it would weigh twelve hundred pounds, and a miner could accumulate a considerable value of gold dust and nuggets without having it occupy so much space that its bulk caused him much inconvenience.

Naturally the prospector who did much panning soon developed "the rheumatics" in his back, a weakness in his knees, a cold feeling in the seat of his trousers, and a hand like the foot of an aged ostrich, gnarled and hooked and roughened by the sand, gravel, and cold water in which he labored. He therefore generally turned to more efficient and less contorted ways of getting the gold as soon as he was convinced that his particular batch of gravel showed real possibilities.

The first device to which he might turn was the rocker, a crude machine that was capable of surprising sophistication in the hands of an ingenious builder. Basically it consisted of a perforated box, or riddle, mounted over a sloping trough about the size of a baby's cradle with rockers underneath so that the whole could be rocked back and forth sideways. The miner put his gold-bearing gravel in the top of the box and poured water over it, washing the fine gravel, sand, and silt through the riddle. When the fines had gone down, the box could be lifted off and the remaining coarse pebbles thrown away. As the water and fines fell through the riddle, they fell upon one or more baffles, which provided additional agitation, to ensure that any gold in the mixture was washed free of the other materials. The slurry of sand, water, and, he hoped, gold, then flowed down the trough, over transverse riffles behind which the gold, iron sand, "miner's rubies" [garnets], and cassiterite tended to settle, while the lighter mud, silt, sand, and of course the water flowed on out the end of the machine. Sometimes, if working with very fine gold, mercury could be placed in the riffles to capture the gold by amalgamation, and a piece of carpeting or a sheepskin put at the end of the trough to catch the finest dust. The lanolin in the sheepskin seemed to have a special attraction for gold dust, but none for the sands that passed, and it apparently was just such a golden fleece as this that long ago lured Jason and his fabled Argonauts to the placers along the northern edge of the Black Sea.

The gold could be washed out of the fleece or carpeting later on, and any gold caught in the mercury behind the riffles could be extracted by squeezing the mercury through a buckskin bag, leaving the gold amalgam behind, or by any of several primitive methods of distillation, driving off the mercury by heat (with attendant dangers from inhalation of its fumes) and leaving the gold behind. A rocker was of course small enough to be portable, and if not moved to a new site, a new rocker could be built in a short while from the boards in a wagon body. It had the further advantage of saving water, for the water that ran from the machine could be run into a sump until the silt settled out of it and then used over again. The agitation provided by rocking the rocker made it especially suitable for extracting gold from tenacious, gluey clays, and Rockerville, far to the south, took its name from such a usage, as well as from a scarcity of water that made the use of rockers a necessity.

If a larger quantity of gold-bearing gravel needed to be processed, the miner turned to a sluicing operation. This was a major undertaking, requiring several men for its operation, and a considerable investment of time and labor in making available an adequate amount of water to operate the apparatus. Fifty miner's inches, the amount of water that, under six inches' head, would flow through a hole one inch high by fifty inches wide, were needed to run a string of ordinary sluice boxes—for it took eight tons of water to wash the gold from one ton of gravel, and more yet was generally required to carry away the washed gravel that otherwise would accumulate around the end of the equipment. Water on such a scale could only be obtained by building a dam, usually in cooperation with other parties, and using the water as it became available, for a small party could haul gravel part-time and wash it out the rest of their time. Water that went on down the creek could be reused, although the ability of the water to separate the gold from the gravel diminished markedly as it grew dirtier and dirtier with the silts of upstream operations. Best of all was to use water from some major flume company's ditch from a dam high above the workings, a commercial enterprise of magnitude and importance, which made its money by selling water to the miners down below.

The sluice boxes themselves were made of one by twelve inch lumber, twelve feet long, and set at an incline of four or five inches to the box. A string of five or six was the usual number of boxes, and they were often tapered, so that the lower end of the upper box would fit into the upper end of the one below it. Gravel was dumped into the box at the top of the string of boxes, and water admitted to begin the washing process. The first, upstream, sluice box had a riddle, made out of a loose board drilled full of holes, lying on its floor. This gave a fairly smooth surface over which the man operating that end of the sluice could slide a sluice fork, which looked like a small pitchfork, but with more and flatter tines, removing the large rocks and pebbles. This prevented the rocks from getting into the rest of the string and causing ripples and eddies which might impede its carefully planned operation. The boxes after the first one contained various riffles—sometimes no more than heavy, flat stones, sometimes poles or slats that ran lengthwise of the box, sometimes, as in the rocker, transverse riffles behind which the heavy gold could settle. Each type of gravel required a slightly different mechanism and slope to maximize the retention of the gold: sandy, light gravel being easy to work, and clayey gravel needing much more careful manipulation in order to free the gold from its sticky grasp.

A string of sluices required considerable manpower for its successful operation. A couple of men had to dig out the gravel, and load it into a wagon, or if closer to the sluice, into homemade wheelbarrows (and the wheelbarrows were, like man in Psalm 139, "fearfully and wonderfully made") for transportation to the sluices, and of course a man was needed to operate whatever transportation system was used. At the first box another man was needed constantly to operate the riddle and ensure an even flow of water and gravel at the head of the system, and usually another walked up and down the string of sluice boxes to make sure that everything was going properly. In Strawberry Gulch, by way of an example, the operators of a string of sluices got only $1.50 a day because they did not clean out their riffles frequently enough, and black iron sand and "rubies" built up to the point that the gold washed on over. A clumsy Illinois group had two days' worth of gold accumulated behind their riffles when an unskillful release of a rush of water washed the riffles out of their whole string of sluice boxes and the captured gold along with them. It was this sort of accident, as well as the relative inefficiency of the process in capturing the finest gold, that led to the estimate that a string of sluices caught only 65 percent of the gold that was in the gravel.

Some thoughtful miners who lived downstream from active placer operations simply smoothed out the streambed, put in rocks and poles to act as riffles, and caught the gold that escaped their comrades working upstream from them. Indeed, such a device, called a ground sluice or bedrock flume, could be constructed during the winter, and a large flow of water and gravel suddenly turned into it during the spring freshets, and when the flood had subsided, the riffles and artificial pockets panned for the gold that they retained. It was not considered a very scientific process, but it was cheap, except in labor, and it could be carried forward during the months when frost kept the miners from normal placer workings.

From the earliest days of the rush the cry was "Bring in a sawmill," and the lumber was needed, at least to begin with, to construct the sluices. A sawmill of those days was not, however, a mechanical device, but merely a saw pit over which a log could be rolled, and sawn into boards with a long whipsaw. The sawyer, who directed the operation, marked the log, previously hewn square with a broadaxe, with a chalk line; then, standing on top of the log, he guided the saw along the line while his companion the pitman provided most of the power to operate the saw. The planks were not sawn completely off of the timber, but left joined at one end by a few inches of solid wood until the whole timber had been sawn, so that the timber could continue to provide a platform on which the sawyer could stand to hold and guide his end of the saw. The pitman generally wore the broadest-brimmed hat that he could find, to keep the sawdust out of his eyes, and of course could not look upward to see what he was doing. Most of these so-called pits were actually trestles, six or eight feet high, with a couple of sloping logs leading up to them over which a timber could be slid up onto the trestle for working, but they were still called pits even though they were up in the air. The name pitman of course continued when reciprocating water mills operated the saws, and continues to the present in the sense of any eccentric or reciprocating connection, as in the pitman arm of the steering mechanism of an automobile. The pitman himself, because of the arduous and unskilled nature of his work, was not generally considered to be in the upper ranks of even common labor, but the sawyer was a man of considerable expertise.

The demand for lumber was large in comparison to the amount of it that the available mills could produce, and "men sat on their logs at the sawmill, money in hand, waiting for lumber."[16] Prices for rough twelve inch boards were seventy dollars per thousand lineal (which in this case would be the same as for board) feet, and the lumber to construct a string of sluices came to from fifteen to twenty dollars. Three whipsaw outfits came into the Deadwood area by May 1876—previously the miners had hewn or chopped their own planks for themselves, and a weary work it must have been—and with the arrival of steam-powered mills in the summer of 1876 over thirty thousand board feet of lumber a day was produced, although most of it by that time went not into sluices but into buildings. A cabin could be built of logs, although it was probably cheaper to haul the logs to a mill and have them sawn into boards than it was to accumulate enough logs to build a log cabin, but roofs pretty much had to be of planks, and so did the floors of dancehalls and booming businesses.

An extension of the sluice box was the hydraulic operation, which used streams of high-pressure water to wash away whole gravel banks and send the mass of gravel and water through sluice boxes many feet wide and several feet deep. Such an operation of course used huge amounts of water and produced immense amounts of tailings, but its efficiency in money and manpower—when a bank of gravel large enough to justify the setup and amounts of water sufficient for its operation could be found—was ample compensation. In the few cases where such an operation had any water to spare, this water could be sold to placer miners along the line of the flume that carried the water to the hydraulicking site. Several such companies operated in the Deadwood area, and one grandiose ditch thirty-three miles long was projected by A. Hemme, J. A. Quinan,

A. J. Bowie (the chief engineer of the Father De Smet Mine), and W. L. Kuykendall. It was to carry water from a dam at the head of Spearfish Canyon to Deadwood, using one eighteen-hundred-foot tunnel and several seven-hundred-foot ones to avoid having to make the water run up hill part of the way. Such a flume, if actually constructed, would probably have stuck out over the western edge of the Hills like a fishpole, and the far end of it would have had to have been propped up in the air on trestlework, for no matter how sinuous its path, there simply is not room for a flume that long between any part of Spearfish Canyon and Deadwood. The project was to cost $5 million, and as if the original proposal was insufficient to test the true powers of the projectors, an additional flume to carry lumber and firewood was planned to run along side the three by four foot flume carrying pure and unadulterated water. Water in such quantities was of course not available on the upper reaches of Spearfish Canyon, or anywhere else in the Black Hills, but the general concept at least was sufficiently startling to attract attention.

Flumes and ditches were not all that easy to construct and keep in order. The Fort Dodge Mining Company, working a hill south of Gayville, worked for three years to construct a flume two miles long to simply tap a commercial ditch at the head of Bobtail Gulch. They had a long tunnel to drill through hard rock, and by the time they had completed the tunnel the summer heat had dried up all the water. The next year, when they had completed the tunnel, their ditch ran over porous rock, and the water ran out of the ditch—and into the High Lode mine. The ditch at that point was then lined with planks, and the water turned on again, but where the ditch crossed an old prospect hole, the water again drained out of the ditch, and flooded out the miners in the Terra mine below, "making them think there was a subterranean deluge broke loose." Another effort, the huge Boulder Ditch below Deadwood, never was finished at all and in McClintock's fusty phrase "stands today as a monument to folly." [17]

Almost as impressive as the ditches and flumes was dredging, a system of placer mining in which the miners dug a large pond in the creek bed, and a barge with gold separating equipment was floated on it. A digging device on the dredge gnawed away at the edges of the pond, and brought gravel up from its bottom, where the dredge machinery removed the gold and piled up the tailings behind it, as the entire device gradually gnawed its way forward, bringing its pond along with it. A very large dredge of this type is still at work below Deadwood on Whitewood Creek, taking up not only placer gold but mercury and gold amalgam lost from the huge Hidden Treasure mill on the hillside above it. The most important thing in a placer deposit suitable for dredging was to have the gold either evenly distributed throughout the gravel, or a very smooth bedrock, from which the deepest deposits of alluvial gold could be easily scooped up. The Black Hills bedrock was rough and jagged, and a dredge tended to miss the most valuable gold deposits, and the frustration involved generally led to the eventual abandonment of the process.

The most frequent accident in placer mining was the collapse of gravel upon the miner. Burrowing under the gravel overburden in order to reach as much bedrock as possible often resulted in disaster, for gravel is rounded and is very difficult to shore up, as it has a tendency to percolate around any timbers put in to hold it. Once the gravel starts to move, any shorings shift, and the whole comes down upon the miners underneath. Tom Carr, for example, was buried beneath twenty-five feet of gravel on Scott and Gay's claim at Gayville. His companion Morris Tean was killed at once, and Carr was trapped beneath some timbers with the ground water rising slowly towards his chin as his companions dug a fresh shaft down to rescue him. He survived twenty-four hours of this confinement. The newspapers are full of similar accidents as placer-mining shafts, tunnels, and ditches collapsed upon men working in them, for speed rather than safety governed most of the work.

An interesting feature of the placer rush years was that as winter came on, and with it cold weather and lack of usable water, the miners tended to go into deeper diggings, burrowing into the placers and using the harsh weather for what might be considered indoor work, either in the placers or on the lode mines. Water, too, tended to dry up in the late fall, and what was left of it froze solid thereafter, so that most of the winter activities tended toward preparations for the warmer, wetter springtime. This tendency to idleness during the winter months was considered a defect in the Black Hills mines, for it was generally held throughout the West that a region where mining could not be carried forward at least seven months a year would never be of any real value to its operators. There is something about trying to pan out gold when the water freezes in the pan that tends to discourage placer mining.

The yields of the various placer claims have doubtless been exaggerated by their owners, out of both pride and the hope that an exaggerated tale of riches coming out might meet a buyer coming in. The general, overall yield was also distorted in the telling because it was perfectly possible for a prospector to hit a pocket of gravel rich with gold, and not find another similar one on his whole claim. Robert Kennon (or Kenyon) on Numbers 14 and 15 below Discovery in Deadwood Gulch sometime during July 1876 took out $3,000 worth of gold in fifteen hours—gold was "lying around loose like so much old iron." [18] Number 3 below Discovery, mined by Hildebrant and Company, shipped out $15,000 worth of gold in December 1876, and seems to have extracted $50,000 during the year. James Scott, of the Scott and Gay Claim No. 4 above Discovery took out $30,000 all told. Up to 9 October they had gotten about $10,000, then they "tapped the pay streak" and on the "9th cleaned up $1,178, on the 10th took out $1,434, on the 11th $1,869 and on the 12th $1,114, a total yield of over $5,500 for four days of placer working." In early December 1876 Scott himself carried $10,000 of the gold to Cheyenne, just to make sure it got to the bank. Dublin Lyons, carrying $3,500 worth of gold to Cheyenne, reported that he had seen three kegs of gold on one claim—probably small wooden powder kegs—and that the gold dust was accumulating in such large quantities that the miners didn't know what to do with it.

E. D. McEvena (or McEuena) and A. J. Botsford's claim employed twelve men, and mined from twenty ounces of gold upwards, a total of from $1,000 to $1,500 daily, during the summer of 1876. Richard Hughes's pocket diary recorded that "claims here on Deadwood are paying from $100 to as high as $2,000 per day." [19] The fifteen best placers during 1876 were estimated to have produced amounts of gold as follows:

Allen, Florado (or Flarida) & Co	$65,000
Johnson & Co	70,000
Pierce & Co	80,000
Scott & Gay	30,000
Thompson & Co	30,000
McAleer & Pierce	75,000
Gilmer, Salisbury & Co	40,000
Hildebrant & Co	50,000
Simson & Co	50,000

Neal & Co	26,000
Neal & Co. (another claim)	30,000
Spencer & Morton	25,000
John Kane	30,000
Jack McAleer (another claim)	30,000
George Stokes	30,000 [20]

In each case the "& Co." represents companions or partners, as in the "Governor and Company of Adventurers of England Trading into Hudson's Bay," rather than any actual incorporation. The rounded figures and the frequent appearance of $30,000 as the gold production, indicates that the estimates made were fairly rough ones. It should be remembered, too, that wages in Deadwood ran $4.00–$5.50 per day per man, and that the gold extracted would nowadays be worth not $20 per ounce but many times more. At modern prices, Allen, Florado and Company's gold production could have been over $2 million, which tends to give the sort of impression that it made on the people of its own time.

The greatest placer of them all was the Wheeler Brothers' No. 2 below Discovery, where cleanups ran from $500 to $1,000 every twenty-four hours, the result of the labor of from sixteen to thirty employees. It was owned by W. P. Wheeler, C. Farham, R. Ryan, and Joseph Weber, and apparently another Wheeler. Estimates of its yield up to 8 September 1876 run from $100,000 to $500,000, at which time the operators sold the claim for $3,000 and the buyers took out that much gold the first day they dug for gold. The Wheelers took their gold, and any other gold other miners wanted to ship to Cheyenne, and accumulated a wagonload weighing 1,600–2,500 pounds—about $500,000 worth at $20 an ounce, allowing for iron and tin sands mixed in with the gold dust—and this massive shipment is often cited as if the Wheeler group themselves had mined it all, which accounts for the extremely high estimates often put on the productivity of their claim. One of the Wheeler brothers said that when the costs of mining were deducted, his group only got $40,000 each—it was enough to retire on—and very few others came near it, although one claim, offered in February 1876 for a sack of flour—and refused—was said to have yielded $250,000 thereafter. It is hard to guess which claim this might have been. Another prospector refused an offer of $25,000 for his claim, and a week later sold a one-eighth interest in it for $25 worth of supplies.

Stories of this kind are always a bit dubious, as is the tale of the "seedy individual who arrived in Cheyenne with a delapitated carpet bag" containing $103,000 in gold. It would have weighed about 350 pounds, and such a carpet bag would not have just been delapidated—its bottom would have fallen clear out, even if the seedy individual could have lifted it unaided.

Most of the pilgrims were not as successful as the Wheelers. Scotty Philip came into the Hills in July 1876 with one hundred pounds of flour, and planned to prospect until the flour gave out, and when it did give out, he went east to settle on the prairies, where the town of Philip is named for him now. Most of the other rushers were even less successful and went home poorer than they came.

At times employment was readily available, at other times less than a third of the population—during the rush it consisted almost entirely of employable males—was at work, with wages at from four to six dollars a day, and find your own board and lodging. Apparently many loafers came to the Hills for the fun of it, and it was frequently claimed that anybody who could work and would stay on the job could easily find employment. One diarist recorded that he "lay around camp" and another wrote of a companion, Fritz, "I don't know whether he tries to get work or no but there is one thing sure, he *don't* work." Another laborer got twenty-four dollars for cutting wood and three dollars for gold panning, for his entire month's work. Fritz's commentator went to every claim looking for work, and "sometimes they would talk to us but more times not." The *New York Times* correspondent reported ten thousand men in Deadwood Gulch in mid-summer of 1877, and hardly thirteen hundred of them gainfully occupied at their own work or anybody else's, and the rest were "simply wandering about fomenting a stampede to some other locality, cursing the luck that sent them to the Black Hills, or philosophically waiting for something to turn up."[21]

Stampedes to new diggings were one of the principal entertainments of the unemployed, and often of the employed miner also, for the prospector is so constituted that he would rather search for good luck elsewhere than profit from it nearby. The Bear Lodge Mountains in nearby Wyoming beckoned; so did the Wolf Mountains, wherever they might be and nobody knew for sure, but fifteen hundred miners rushed toward them. The Big Horns doubtless held big nuggets, and off the miners took, to return in a ragged and starving condition a few weeks later. Banjo Dick Brown sang from the stage of the Gem:

> My brother Bill is going away,
>> He wants me to go, but I think I'll stay,
>
> .   .   .   .
>
> He packed his load in half an hour,
>> Two gallons of whisky and a pound of flour,
> He sported his watch and went on tick,
>> For a side of bacon and a can of lard,
> Now look at his fate! My, isn't it hard,
>> He walked all day and most of the night,
> And now he is back, a sorrowful sight,
>> to the Cabin he built in Deadwood.
>
> .   .   .   .
>
> Leave not your friend or your girl behind,
>> For how do you know what you may find
> Or what's been done since you've been gone?
>> Your girl not here, the air is light,
> With your good friend she took her flight,
>> Not caring for the love forlorn
> Who now returns all tattered and torn
>> Bringing no gold from the Big Horn
> To the girl he left in Deadwood. [22]

Nobody knew for sure how many prospectors there were in Deadwood and the surrounding gulches. Estimates for the summer of 1876 ran from a carefully calculated fifty-one hundred (composed, however, of rounded hundreds for each of the various camps) to a grandiose ten thousand, a figure which was reached by the 1880 census, and may be either high or low for the earlier days of the rush. The spring and summer populations were undoubtedly far higher than those during the fall and winter, when anybody who had nothing to do and little money to do it on moved back to the states for work and comfort.

Estimates of the total gold production during the placer rush are necessarily inaccurate, with the earliest estimates tending to be the most optimistic. The following chart may disappoint searchers after marvels, but is probably within 100 percent of being correct (at $20 an ounce):

1876   .   .   .   . $1,200,000
1877   2,000,000

1878	2,250,000
1879	2,500,000
1880	3,305,843
1881	4,000,000 [23]

By the end of 1878, however, placer mining was beginning to fade out, and hardrock lode mining was beginning to contribute a larger and larger share to the total gold production. Some estimates put the early years' production at double these figures, and the truth of the matter is that with gold going out of the Hills to Cheyenne, Sidney, Pierre, Yankton, Sioux City, and Bismarck, and nobody keeping track of it, it is almost impossible to do more than guess at the total amounts which may have actually been produced.

Probably L. Parkhurst had the right idea about making money in Deadwood when he advertised a $3,500 "nugget":

> The largest yet found in the Black Hills. I offer my Spring Creek Brewery for sale; all in complete and running order. The finest spring in the Territory running through the top of the brewery. Located in Lower Deadwood. The biggest thing in the Black Hills. Pressing business at home is the only cause for offering the above business for sale.

Some claim holders eventually did get rich, not from mining but from selling or renting their claims to businessmen who wanted to build on the property. For the average miner a claim would "just about pay grub," and those who got a good wage were rare. Even if the gold had been evenly distributed among those who flocked to the rush—say ten thousand men and a few women according to the census of 1880—it only comes out to $330 each, less than a dollar a day for each pilgrim—and as the figures show, it was by no means evenly distributed. As Moses "California Joe" Milner had remarked to Colonel Dodge when he saw the Hills in the summer of 1875, "There's gold from the grassroots down, but there's *more* gold from the grass roots up." [24]

By 1878 the placer boom to Deadwood had begun to taper off. "The keno men, tramps, and sharpers of all classes who infested Deadwood and other camps" had left for greener pastures. As one of them put it, "There's no genteel work available." The poor men who had come to the Hills to pick up easy fortunes from the gravel either went back home or went to work in the increasingly important hardrock mines that were springing up all around the gulch. Heavy machinery began to take the place of pilgrims on the wagon trails to Deadwood. There was plenty of pay dirt left, and even old claims could be reworked by new methods with new prospects of success, but by the fall of 1878 the prospectors lifted their eyes from the valley floor unto the hills, and by the time the great Deadwood fire of 1879 temporarily destroyed the city, the placer rush was over, for the miners all too well understood what Banjo Dick Brown meant when he sang of the placer rush:

> Oh, I wish that the man who first started this sell
> Was a captive, and Crazy Horse had him in hell!
> There's no use in grieving, or swearing like pitch,
> But the man who would stay here's a son-of-a-bitch![25]

TWO

Ungodly Mills

"By their fires the Sioux Chiefs
Muttered their woes and griefs."

Longfellow

"Deadwood's start was in the mud, but her heart
is in the mountains."

An old-timer

WHEN THE Deadwood placers in the valleys dwindled, the lode
mines in the hardrock came into increasing importance. The mountains, after all, were the original source of the placer gold, and there
was more where it came from, locked into the mountains' rocks and
crannies, if only the miners could get it out at a cost that did not
exceed its value. In practice it seemed to work out—although there
were exceptions—that a mine that couldn't yield over $3,500 a year
for each miner earning $3.50 a day could not stay in business with-
out levying assessments on its stockholders, and such "Dutch dividends" tended to markedly lower the value of the stock on the open
market, and to discourage the investors. It was this constant battle
between costs and production that made the gold mining business
risky, and when augmented by the devious ways and ingenious
swindles of miners of less than sterling probity, the challenge of
getting your money out of your investment was an imposing one.
Mining law was only the first challenge which had to be overcome.

To begin with, the prospector named his claim. A claim without
a name was unthinkable and probably illegal, and the forensic ge-
nius lavished upon the selection of names which would encourage
future buyers or investors would, if employed in popularizing the
Ten Commandments, have made Deadwood a city of saints. The
Safe Investment and the Golden Reward, Golden Crest and the Gilt
Edge Maid, the Golden Sands and the Double Rainbow, the Hidden
Fortune and the Hidden Treasure, the Horseshoe for good luck and
the Deadbroke for bad, the Montezuma and the Whizzers, the Sil-
ver Queen and Queen of the Hills, Two Bit and Two Johns, the
Wasp and the Little Blue, the Vulgar Fraction, and the Seek-No-

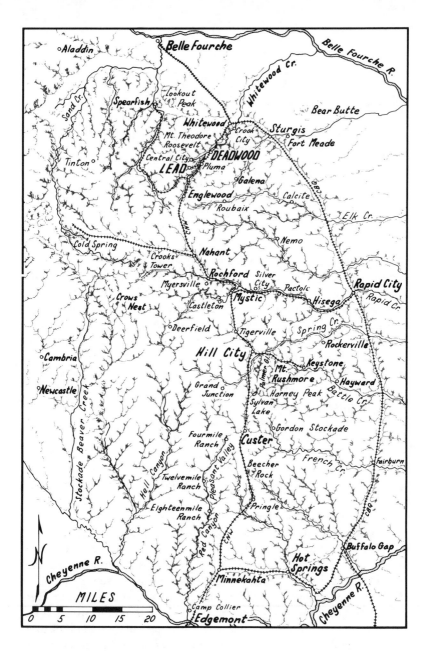

The Black Hills with their mining camps, stage stations, military posts, and a few of their many railroads

Farther all competed for the speculator's dollars. Not all of the names were thus flamboyant, and the more prosaic Hatties and Emmas and Terras played their part, but the name of a mine, as implying something about the creative ingenuity of its promoters, went far toward helping to finance the operation.

Federal law, reduced to its essence, permitted a prospector to stake out a claim fifteen hundred feet long by three hundred feet wide running along the supposed course of a newly discovered mineral vein, the outcropping of which lay within the land so claimed. No claim was allowed until sufficient work—generally presumed to be a shaft ten feet deep or its equivalent in trenching or shallow test pits—had been done to demonstrate the value of the vein. Once the vein had been thus shown to exist, the miner named it, stuck up a claim notice at his workings, put up eight posts at least four inches square at the corners and midpoints of his lines, and then betook himself to the recorder's office to record his claim. The record—which was essentially the same as the claim notice posted on the claim itself—contained the name of the lode, the name of its locator or claimant, the date of location, the number of feet claimed on each side, and the general course of the lode. In cases in which these items were for some reason omitted but the claim could nevertheless be identified, recording was permitted anyway, presumably to provide future employment for the legal profession, the courts, and the surveyors. Ten days or one hundred dollars worth of work a year sufficed to hold the claim almost in perpetuity, and, instead, if the miner preferred to get a patent, or government deed, to his land he could request one as soon as five hundred dollars worth of improvement had been performed, although as soon as he received his patent his land became taxable, which explains why so many eminent mines were advertised as consisting of such-and-so number of *unpatented* claims. Obviously such a haphazard system of laying out claims resulted in a crazy quilt of claims of varying sizes, each fitted in helter-skelter amongst its neighbors and likely to be in conflict with somebody on one side or another. The shotgun as a surveying instrument tended to decide the boundary disputes that arose in the early days, and the system as a whole goes far to explain the presence of over fifty lawyers in early-day Deadwood.

The question of whether mining claims on an Indian reservation were legal at all was kept open by a series of tangled and contorted court decisions. Federal Judge Granville Bennett, in Deadwood,

held that although all claims prior to 28 February 1877 (when the
Hills were returned by the Sioux to the federal government) were
invalid, nonetheless the firstcomer had the better claim. This opinion was upheld in the case *Ahly* v. *Garrison*, which again ruled that
although nobody had any clear titles to Black Hills mining claims,
those who got there first had better titles than those claimants who
came later. The Supreme Court of Dakota Territory, however, on
17 May 1879 ruled that no title at all could be acquired until after
the Hills had been ceded to the government. The legal profession,
at least, found the Black Hills a treasure house of opportunity.

Gold was of course the most important mineral mined in the
Black Hills. Along with it came silver, but although at times equal
in weight to the gold mined, it was of far less value. Tin, in the
triangle between Hill City, Custer and Keystone, boomed in the
1880s, but despite the efforts of an English concern, the Harney
Peak Tin Mining, Milling and Manufacturing Company, which
bought more than a thousand claims and erected a tremendous mill
at Hill City, very little actual production resulted. Tinton, west of
Deadwood on the Wyoming border, also boomed sporadically as a
tin prospect, but never seems to have operated profitably for long,
although it was active as late as World War II. A prospectus for the
Scotland Mining Company near Tinton boasted that their ore ran
from 1.5–2.5 percent cassiterite, the dioxide of tin, and surmised
that this would be worth from $10.00 to $20.00 a ton. Their prospectus pointed out that if the Homestake mine could make money
on ore running $3.50 a ton in gold, the Scotland Company would
probably need its own bank to handle the money brought in by its
tin mining. The problem, as in so many such schemes, was twofold:
the actual, as opposed to the surmised, tin content of the rock, and
the difficulty of getting it out at a profit.

Coal has been found and mined all around the Black Hills, from
Edgemont clear around northward to Rapid City, but the coal mines
of greatest interest to the mines of Deadwood were on Hay Creek
west of Belle Fourche, at present-day Aladdin, Wyoming. When
these mines were finally joined to the rest of the Hills by the Wyoming and Missouri River Railroad from Belle Fourche and the Fremont, Elkhorn and Missouri Valley line on into Deadwood from
Whitewood, coal for smelters was readily available and played an
important part in the development of the mines in the 1890s. Oil,

around Lieutenant Warren's Camp Warren near present-day Newcastle, Wyoming, was available for lubrication, and salt springs in
the same area provided the salt used in the early chlorination process
for extracting gold from its refractory ores. During World War I
tungsten was produced by a couple of mines around Hill City and
by the Homestake and the Wasp No. 2 near Deadwood. Kaolin was
dug and refined for use in water softeners, far to the south, at Ard-
more. Gravel was washed in the Cheyenne River breaks, and fuller's
earth found near Argyle, and even a deposit of "electric metal pol-
ish" was discovered near Carbonate. Several copper mines attempted to get into production, but none seems to have succeeded.
A large selection of miscellaneous minerals—bog iron, iron pyrite,
spodumene (the ore of lithium), antimony, bismuth, cinnabar, ra-
dium and uranium, marl and onyx, lead in conjunction with many
of the silver mines, arsenic, bentonite, clay, and gypsum—all contributed to the stability of the mining industry of the Black Hills,
and by 1890 most of these enterprises were connected to Deadwood
and its supply houses by the rail lines of the Burlington or North
Western railroads. Without these many and assorted minerals, and
the sporadic attempts—some successful—to mine them, it is likely
that Deadwood would have been considerably less active as a center
of mining activity, for although precious metals were the backbone
of the town's commerce, the miscellaneous minerals helped to fill in
the gaps in business, for they tended to boom whenever the precious
metals languished.[1]

Gold, however, was the mainstay and substance of Deadwood's
mineral prosperity. Very few mines were actually located inside the
city limits, and not many mines adjacent thereto, but those mines—
and they were many—that burrowed into the nearby mountains
looked to Deadwood for supplies, financiers (otherwise known as
"suckers"), and entertainment. Your mine might be in one of fifty
different little towns in the Northern Hills, but chances were that
your head office was in Deadwood, and your miners spent their
money there.

Prospecting for gold in quartz deposits called for considerable
expertise, and a liberal portion of good luck. The outcropping of a
quartz vein itself was of course a promising sign, and if gold couldn't
be found in the rock on the surface, the prudent optimist always
surmised that "it would get richer as it went farther down," a popu-

lar miners' delusion which no amount of experience could ever dispel. Quartz once located could be ground to a powder in a druggist's mortar, then panned in a small gold pan, or more often in a trough-like horn to assess the traces of gold which it contained, and a trifling arithmetical comparison of the weight of the gold and the weight of the ore it came from could calculate, usually with considerable optimism, the amout of free-milling gold that could be got from a ton of ore. More refractory ores, in which the gold was held firmly in what amounted to a quasi-chemical bond with impurities in its ore, had to be taken to an assayer whose intricate fire assaying process, dating back to the days of Georgius Agricola's *De Re Metallica* in Bohemia, could determine with remarkable precision the gold and silver content of the ore. Of course this determination relied entirely upon the representative nature of the sample submitted to the assayer's ministrations, and on his own honesty and capability. There were assayers who could find gold in a fragment of a grindstone or the shards of a broken jug, and there were now and then miners who would submit for assay ores which were not representative of an entire ore body. Further, refractory ores might well contain the values claimed by the assayer, but the crude milling processes of the period might not be able to get them out, and more complex processes that came along, although able to extract the values, cost an inordinate amount of the proceeds.

An 1875 Rand McNally and Company's map of the northern Hills showed 125 quartz lode claims running along the northwestern trend of the famous eight-mile-long mineral belt that ran from the Wasp at Flatiron, on Yellow Creek five miles due south of Deadwood, to New Chicago (presently the ruins of Maitland), on False Bottom Creek three miles to the northwest. The claims all ran with the northwesterly trend of the belt, and although most of them are now forgotten or merged into other mining activities, names like the Homestake, Hidden Treasure, Golden Gate, Father De Smet, Golden Terry, and Old Abe would figure for years in Black Hills mining history. Lode mines in the southern Hills, although never of much importance as far as actual gold production is concerned, were also significant in making Deadwood a mining town, for they too looked to Deadwood for financing and supplies. Once the Indian troubles of the 1870s that had slowed down shipments of mining machinery to the Hills were ended, the lode mines began to boom in earnest, a boom considerably augmented by the diminishing returns from the earlier valley placers. Chunks of glassy, milkywhite quartz with gold threads and plates embedded in the rock began to find their way to the outfitting towns to stir up general excitement for the hard rock mines, and every now and then pieces of this "jewlery rock" containing more gold than stone were exhibited, not as selected specimens, but as genuine examples typical of the Black Hills ores.

The quartz lodes in the Black Hills were not like those of other gold mining areas, for the veins had been distorted by millennia of repeated geologic upheaval. One old miner reported, "There is no regularity to anything, and while there may be rich pockets the mining capitalist could go it blind and spend thousands of dollars with a good chance of getting no return."[2] Still, the existence of the pockets, when one did occur, made lode mining wonderfully attractive to those who could afford the time and money to pursue it. By 1878 hundreds of mines and dozens of mills, some of them engineering triumphs of immense size, were hard at work extracting and processing the gold ores of the Black Hills.

Milling processes over the years became increasingly effective, so much so that ores which could not be worked in the 1870s because the gold was too thin in them, or too tightly locked into their integument, were after the 1900s run merrily through the cyanide vats where well over 95 percent of their gold content could be economically extracted. Early processes, however, were not so successful. The free-milling ores, in which the gold was contained mechanically in the rock, were simple to handle although not easy to find. Such rock was ground fine under the stones of an arrastra, a circular stone trough in which the broken ore was laid to be ground beneath stones dragged over it by a patient mule or burro. Often mercury was mixed in with the resulting pulp, to grab the free gold and produce a gold and mercury amalgam, or, if the gold was coarse, the pulp could be merely panned out; the process, in short, simply made placer gravel out of hardrock ore. The mercury, which for nearly a hundred years was an important ingredient of the milling process, was then evaporated in a retort, leaving the gold sponge behind to be melted down into a compact bar, while the mercury itself, recondensed by cooling water, was used again. Mercury is the only commercial product still sold by the biblical talent, in seventy-six-pound iron flasks, and is still of course a standard article of commerce in any mining area.

A more sophisticated form of the arrastra was the Chilean (more usually Chili) mill, which had the arrastra's circular stone trough, but used two immense grindstones to roll over the ore and crush it. It was a more efficient process, using less mule power, and doing a better job, but not many early miners were able to find the time or skill to produce the necessary grindstones. Ball mills, cylinders in which the broken ore, water, and iron balls or rods were tumbled, were tried from the earliest days, but were found, in their then state of development, to be unsatisfactory, although in later years when very fine grinding became standard, ball mills came into their own. Most important in the early days was the California stamp mill, in which five eight-hundred-pound stamps alternately rose and fell into a cast-iron mortar, pounding the ore with water until it could pass out through a fine sieve, to flow over copper tables smeared with mercury, which, as in more primitive processes, converted the gold in the mud and water slurry into a mercury-gold amalgam. A mine superintendent tended to be very fussy about getting just about the same amount of mercury back off his tables as he had handed out to be put onto them—if any was missing, he assumed that somebody was surreptitiously scraping off the amalgam and taking it home with him. Any mill hand buying mercury was looked upon as a thief without further discussion, and the likelihood is that he was one.

Black Hills historians have spent much time in deciding who it was that first brought a mill (for arrastras could be built by anybody) into the Black Hills. The honor is generally accorded to Capt. C. V. Gardner, who early in the fall of 1876 brought in a Blake jaw crusher for rough breaking of ore, and a Bolthoff Ball Pulverizer, and these, operating at the Hidden Treasure, had ground out twenty thousand dollars in gold by the end of the year. It was commonly held, however, that such equipment was better suited to sampling ore than to producing gold, while a stamp mill costing only a little more, say ten thousand dollars set up in the Hills, was an actual piece of production equipment. Such an outfit with ten stamps was brought in by Milton E. Pinney (a name variously spelled) and dropped its first stamps on 30 December 1876, and for ten years hammered out gold at the Alpha and Omega near Central City, in return for a half interest in the mine.

Stamp mills could process ore for $0.65 a ton, and custom mills, taking in anybody's ore, charged about $2.50 a ton, which made free-milling ore yielding $4.00 a ton a worthwhile prospect. The operator of a mill developed an attentive ear, and as long as his stamps dropped evenly at thirty-five strokes a minute, he knew that all was going well, but when the sound became erratic he knew that immediate action was needed, for a breakdown of some kind was imminent, and he braced up the stamps by their cams and took them out of action as the engineer slowed down the steam engine or water power to keep the equipment from kicking itself to pieces as the strain upon it was reduced. That was just one of the hundreds of things he had to think about. James Hargering, a well-known millwright, built about two-thirds of the mills in the Hills in the early days, but very few of them turned out to be paying propositions because the ores treated, assumed to be free-milling, were actually refractory and required a good deal more than simple grinding and amalgamation to extract the gold that the assays showed was there.

By October of 1877, 280 stamps were falling, mainly a couple of miles up Deadwood Gulch from Deadwood, in the area around Gayville, Central City, and Troy, and it was estimated that by the end of the year from 550 to 650 would be in operation, as nine mills were building and five more were on their way into the Hills. In 1878, forty-seven mills were dropping 700 stamps, and by the end of the year although the number of mills had dropped to forty-four, 790 stamps were dropping, handling a daily average of 1,120 tons of ore. In 1879 the *Engineering and Mining Journal* counted only 625 stamps, but these were producing $404,000 worth of gold every month. The Hills had turned from the placers to the lodes, and the steady roar, day and night, of the falling stamps was the sound of money and employment.

Typical of the successful lode mines was the famous Father De Smet, named for the Jesuit missionary who was believed, incorrectly, to have found gold in the Hills while indoctrinating the Indians. The De Smet was discovered about New Year's Day of 1876 by Hilan Hulin, William Lardner, and Harry Gamage, near Central City, and after making its original discoverers rich men, it was sold late in 1877 along with the Golden Gate, Justice, and Belcher claims to Archie Borland, August Hemme, L. R. Graves, and A. J. Bowie, all of California. Bowie, the superintendent—there is dispute whether he was actually a partner—installed two hundred stamps, constructed a luxurious mine office, and built the mine, both above ground and below, to last, and while he was in charge, it is claimed that no miner ever lost his life underground. It was a policy that paid off, for on ore averaging twelve to eighteen dollars a ton he took out sixty thousand dollars a month. The De Smet and its mills were eventually incorporated into the Homestake operations.

With examples like the De Smet and the Homestake (which will be considered later), it is no wonder that Black Hills mines changed hands at fancy prices. The Homestake had sold to George Hearst for $200,000, the North Terra for $100,000 and the South Terra for the same amount. The Florence brought $51,000, the Old Abe $42,500, and hundreds of other lode claim transfers took place in the late seventies at prices up to $25,000. Prices like these, often paid for no more than a prospect hole in the ground which happened to be next door to a more worthy claim, did a good deal to encourage prospectors to climb up out of the placers into the mountains.

The towns around Deadwood boomed and prospered as money to work the lode mines poured into the area. Terraville, Silver City, Blacktail, Anchor City, Troy, Pimlico, Oro City, and Poorman joined the earlier placer towns around Gayville–Central City. Up Deadwood Creek, Pluma and Gold Run boomed. Lead, with its suburbs, Washington and Denver, was the home of the mighty Homestake. It seemed that as soon as a mine and a store were built, a town sprang up around them, and was named for posterity. The mining districts, although by no means entirely fixed, were about as follows:

> White Wood: from the headwaters of Whitewood Creek to the mouth of Split Tail Creek below Deadwood
> Cape Horn: from the southern boundary of White Wood northwesterly to the foothills
> Gold Run: along that little creek
> Boulder: apparently along Boulder Canyon
> Sand Gulch: seems unclear—it may have been along Sand Creek, which runs northward on the Wyoming border
> Bear Gulch: in that area, near Tinton, on the Wyoming border
> Galena: in the silver-lead mining area southeast of Deadwood
> Carbonate: high in the limestone country west of New Chicago
> Bald Mountain: on that peak, where Trojan and Portland and Crown Hill eventually grew up
> Two Bit: between Galena and Deadwood
> Lost Mining District: on Deadwood Creek and its tributaries.[3]

The amalgamation process, as has been pointed out, did not capture all of the gold even from the free-milling ores, and was completely ineffective in removing any from the more stubborn refractory ores. Those mills which did succeed did so by operating on the richest ores available and neglecting the values which were lost. It was a state of affairs which annoyed the mine superintendents and wildly irritated the stockholders until two new processes, the chlorination reduction system and the matte smelter, were introduced. Both were highly imperfect, but they were better than amalgamation, and they flourished until the late 1890s.

The chlorination method, which seems to have been repeatedly invented and forgotten since the days of Agricola, consisted of roasting the troublesome ore at a carefully controlled temperature in order to subtly alter the quasi-chemical combination in which the gold was held. The ore was then ground and mixed with salt and sulphuric acid in a leaden drum, gently heated to generate free chlorine gas, but not so much as to melt the container, and agitated to force the gas to combine with the gold to produce gold chloride. The resulting liquor was after some hours run off over zinc filings, where the zinc changed places with the gold, which was left behind as a black and sooty slime which could be washed off, dried, and melted into gold bars. It was a complex operation, requiring highly trained engineers and foremen, and a skillful watch over the nature of the ore as it went into the mill. The chlorine was not only highly dangerous—the men on the mill floor went about their work with wet sponges over their mouths and noses—but the chemical ingredients of each batch could be used only once, for there was no way to capture and reuse the chlorine. It was a process that also was costly—the roasting, the salt, the acid were expensive, and the impervious containers were hard to get and subject to constant breakdowns and repairs. Still, it was better than letting the gold get away. On Bald Mountain the Portland, Empire State, Clinton, Double Standard (referring not to morals but to the gold versus silver monetary controversy of the 1890s), Big Bonanza, Willy Wassell, and Tornado made use of this process of roasting and bleaching, as it was called, but they did not begin real production until the method was refined and improved about the end of the 1880s.

Chlorination plants became the boom enterprise of the 1880s and '90s, and it was seriously proposed that a sulphuric acid plant, using local pyrites (iron-sulfur compounds), ought to be set up to supply them. The Deadwood Reduction Works, designed by R. D. Clark, was built in Deadwood in 1888 near the mouth of Spruce Gulch, where the fairgrounds are today, and burned in 1889, to be immediately rebuilt. The Golden Reward Chlorination Plant, designed and managed by Professor Franklin R. Carpenter, was also in lower Deadwood, built in 1887 at a cost of two hundred thousand dollars to handle 125 tons of ore a day. It too burned, in 1898, to be replaced with a larger fireproof steel building. A chlorination plant was built in Spearfish to handle the ores from Squaw Creek and Carbonate, Dacy, Cyanide, Preston, Balmoral, American City, Victoria, and other transient towns which hoped to work the limestone gold deposits.

The Black Hills Milling and Smelting Company built a chlorination plant in Rapid City, about where the School of Mines now stands, although it rarely operated satisfactorily. Its chimney was for many years a landmark behind the school, and the mining students year after year attempted to show their skill in blasting by attempting to blow it up. They never succeeded, but to put an end to the nuisance the school only recently had it completely destroyed. Another huge chlorination plant, the Kildonian, was built in 1896 on Deadwood Creek at Pluma, at the mouth of Gold Run, to process one thousand tons of ore a day, and it did yeoman service in custom processing for mines that lacked the equipment to mill their own ores.

The pyritic matte smelting process, developed by Professor Franklin R. Carpenter of the Dakota School of Mines, had a long history but needed to be carefully adapted to Black Hills Cambrian silicious ores. In essence the process was simply smelting with limestone mixed in with the ore as a flux, coke as a fuel, and iron pyrite added to collect the gold and silver as it was melted out of the ore. The process reduced ten tons of ore to one ton of iron matte, which was then sent to Denver or Omaha for further refining. The process cost about ten dollars for a ton of ore, and of course the shipping and further refining were in addition to that cost. The Olaf Seim mine between Deadwood and Central, now shown to tourists as the Broken Boot, produced much of the pyrite, which also included small amounts of gold, so the problem of assessing whose was what when doing custom smelting must have been vexatious. The Deadwood and Delaware Smelter built in 1888, and later absorbed by the Golden Reward, did large amounts of custom work, and produced over $2 million a year in gold and silver matte. The smelters were connected to the mines by a tangled web of narrow-gauge and later standard-gauge railroads, and the tooting of their little engines became as typical of Deadwood Gulch as the steady rumble of the stamp mills. The great bank of glassy slag at the lower (northern) end of Deadwood is a testimony to the quantity of ore processed by a single smelter, the Golden Reward.

By 1887 some of the larger mines had already paid enormous dividends:

The Homestake $3,843,750
Deadwood Terra 900,000
Father De Smet 1,125,000
Iron Hill (Carbonate) 112,500

Other bullion-producing mines included the Highland, Caledonia, Portland, Buxton, Retriever, Uncle Sam (at Roubaix), El Refugio, and Richmond.[4] In 1896 there were thirty-one stamp mills with an aggregate of fourteen hundred stamps in the Hills, most of them in the Lead and Central area. There were four chlorination plants, three cyanide plants, one Moffat Oxydizer (whatever *that* was) and a matte smelter, with a combined capacity of over seven thousand tons of ore a day, and an annual gold output estimated at from $5 to $8 million. The Black Hills mines were booming, but the best was yet to come, for in the late 1890s the cyanide process was introduced to the Hills, and ores previously considered worthless suddenly became profitable to mine and mill.

To suppose that Deadwood's mining industry moved forward in a smooth progression from the primitive to the modern would be an exercise of the imagination unjustified by the observable facts. Actually as one process ran out of ores on which it could operate effectively, a stygian gloom would descend upon the miners, followed by diligent search for yet another mining or milling process which would somehow rescue their individual mines and the future of the community as a whole. Instead of a smooth progression, Deadwood's mineral industry moved forward by a series of violent, erratic, but certainly energetic jumps. Interspersed throughout this acrobatic performance were a series of extraordinary hindrances, and not the least of these was the activity of the Indians of the vicinity.

It is easy, nowadays, to be sympathetic toward the Indian, to want to improve his present existence, to assist him in preserving his ancient tribal customs, and to weep with him over the loss of his lands and his traditions. The frontiersman could allow himself no such luxury; the Indian, a hundred years ago, posed a constant, skillful threat to the well-being and to the existence of any small group of frontiersmen, miners, ranchers, lumbermen, or travelers who might be even temporarily isolated or outnumbered. The threat was always there; and unlike the problems posed by the wilderness itself, the Indian menace appeared to be direct, human, and malign. Whatever a frontiersman did, he had to bear in mind that somewhere out in the forests or the prairies an Indian, who might well be distinctly unfriendly, was waiting, eager to win honors by counting coup upon those whom he regarded as invaders of his ancestral lands.

Prehistoric man does not appear to have lived within the Black Hills; hardly any trace of him has ever been found within the higher granite peaks or along the limestone ridges, and there seems to be good reason to believe that the awesome nature of the Hills, the violence of the storms within them, and the difficulty of traveling in anything but small groups through valleys tangled by fallen trees and beaver dams all combined to keep the Indian and his ancestors out of the higher Hills. Small bands might enter this towering and hostile home of the manitou in search of honors and adventure, but in the main the Indian seems to have preferred to keep to the more fertile, grassy prairies of the foothills, seeking there the jack-pine lodge poles for his tipis and shelter for his wintering. The mountains around the Hills—the Devil's Tower, Inyan Kara, Sundance Mountain, and Bear Butte—all figured in Plains Indian ceremonials (the Indian with good sense conducting his rites at the bases rather than the tops of these imposing prominences), but as a rule the interior of the Black Hills was but rarely visited. It is common for the modern Indian, and various white scholars, to claim that this tribe or that venerated the Black Hills and that the tribe visited them regularly. If today, after scholarship and a more enlightened attitude on the part of the public, inconsistencies in such tales are still not finally resolved, it should be apparent that one hundred years ago misunderstandings must have been vast.

Whatever the tribe that possessed an actual claim to the Black Hills—and the Kiowa, Crows, and Cheyennes all had successive claims of a sort—the area was included in the Great Sioux Reservation established under the Treaty of Fort Laramie negotiated in 1868. This treaty required the Sioux to keep the peace—indeed that was the reason for it—and in exchange a huge area in the Dakotas was to be permanently set aside for their use, and the white man, except for such government officials as might have business there, were to keep out of this reservation. In addition, those Indians who settled permanently upon the reservation were to receive rations for four years from the time of settlement, after which it was hoped they would have learned to become agriculturally self-supporting. It was hoped that these agreements would bring lasting peace to a frontier which for years had been the scene of violence and mayhem as the red and white races clashed with each other.

Unfortunately, as General Crook put it, the Sioux regarded the treaty as "an instrument binding upon us but not binding upon them" and continued their depredations outside the reservation area. In 1870, 15 men were killed on the Missouri River below Fort Peck; in 1871, 39 were slain along that same river; in 1873, 7 were killed near Fort Rice, and in 1874–75, 137 were killed in Indian attacks extending from the Yellowstone River in Montana as far south as the Niobrara in Nebraska. In spite of these attacks, which were probably due mainly to the inability of the Indian leaders to control young braves eager to accumulate in peacetime the honors which their elders had long since achieved in war, the United States government continued to supply rations to the Sioux, and even continued these supplies well beyond the four-year period agreed upon in the treaty of 1868 and by 1876 had disbursed for this purpose some $6 million in excess of the treaty stipulations. With the discovery of gold in the Black Hills, and the inrush of miners to the area, the U.S. Army did its best to keep the miners out, but the Great White Father was no more successful in controlling his young men than the Indian chiefs were in controlling theirs, and by 1876 the peace-keeping provisions of the Laramie treaty were a dead letter, violated by Indian and white alike. When, in February 1876, the secretaries of war and of the interior recognized that this warfare was pretty much an ongoing state of affairs, the Indians were ordered to return from their raids and hunting to their agencies; and when many refused, full-scale military operations against them were begun.

It was, of course, difficult for the Indians to return to unappetizing reservations during the dead of winter, but it certainly was possible, for some did so, and the rest doubtless could have, camping in bad weather and traveling in the good, had they desired to obey the government's commands. Then, the government could have ameliorated their conditions, had it wished to do so.

By the spring of 1876 Indians and whites alike were disillusioned by the behavior of each other, and eager for a war that would settle their differences for good. The Indian, although fed, was not fed liberally, and the rascality of his agents now and then kept him from being fed at all. His traditional raids were onerously restricted, his hunting lands curtailed, and the white man was occupying the Black Hills, in the very center of his newly won reservation. The white man, on the other hand, saw constant depredations in direct contravention of a most solemn treaty and in spite of continued generosity toward those who were thus breaking the agreement; and, unable to keep the miners out of the Black Hills, the federal government offered to buy that section of the Sioux reservation in exchange for a continuation of the now long since expired rationing provisions of the Laramie treaty plus whatever rent or purchase price for the Hills the Indians and government commissioners could mutually agree upon.

In spite of two attempts to negotiate with the various Sioux tribes no agreement could be reached, and by 1876 war was so thoroughly in the air as to be inevitable, and it probably would have gone forward in any case, as the young warriors took every opportunity they could find to attack the incoming Black Hills miners and the miners vigorously fought back. What came to be known as the Sioux War of 1876 was under way.

The story of this war—of General Crook's defeat on the Rosebud, of General Custer's disaster on the Crow reservation at the Little Big Horn, and of Crook's disastrous "mud and horse meat" march from Montana southeastward to Deadwood—has been told repeatedly. The army's fruitless attempts to "surround ten Indians with one soldier" were of course unsuccessful, but the troops succeeded in so disrupting the Indians' hunting and subsistence that gradually they abandoned the warpath and grudgingly returned to their reservations, where in August 1876 an agreement ceding the Black Hills was extracted from a handful of their leaders in return for continued rationing and care, an agreement which in 1889 was amended and confirmed by the marks or signatures of 4,473 members of the various tribes concerned.

Deadwood in 1877. *Centennial Collection—Deadwood Public Library*

Downtown Deadwood today, from cliffs at Mount Moriah Cemetery. *W. Parker photo*

Delmonico's Hotel and Restaurant, J. H. and W. E. Adams' Banner Grocery, and the Bella Union saloon and variety theater. *W. Parker photo collection*

The Deadwood flood of 1883 was one of many that through the years afflicted a city built in the bottom of a Black Hills valley. *Centennial Collection—Deadwood Public Library*

Lucretia "Aunt Lou" Marchbanks, who presided over the kitchen of the Father De Smet Mine and was thus gratefully denominated "the superintendent of the superintendents" of all the Black Hills mines. *Adams Memorial Museum*

A Black Hills cowboy posed beside the photographer's woven willow fence, his pistol worn butt foremost in the hope of a quick draw should the occasion ever require. *Centennial Collection—Deadwood Public Library*

A warlike citizen of advanced years and acromegalic countenance, posed well-armed in his go-to-meeting vest and watch chain. *Centennial Collection—Deadwood Public Library*

Poker Alice Tubbs, gambler and madam of Sturgis, who often paid a visit to Deadwood's gambling hells. *Centennial Collection—Deadwood Public Library*

Miners and ore cars at the working face of an open cut in one of the many mines near Deadwood. The sheet-iron plates provide a smooth surface from which to shovel the broken ore. *Centennial Collection—Deadwood Public Library*

Placer mining at Blacktail in 1908 was not much different from the gold rush of the 1870s: wet, dirty, backbreaking work. *Centennial Collection—Deadwood Public Library*

It was in the Black Hills and along the trails that led to them that the scourge of Indian warfare fell most heavily, as isolated small groups of miners or individuals now and again succumbed to Indian attacks. A party of forty or more "well heeled" and prudent prospectors was virtually immune to the Indian menace, but when a scout or hunter or an imprudent traveler went out alone or with only a few companions, there was always, even after the official conclusion of hostilities, the chance that they would not return, and as a result only the bold or the numerous set out. As Jerry Bryan remarked in Cheyenne: "Some of the would-be braves just now remember that they must wait here to hear from friends. We don't expect to hear from anybody, consequently we are off."[5]

Even a well-armed and sizable party was not safe from assaults—they tended to shoot each other. Richard Hughes, coming into the Hills, was in a party on Rapid Creek which was disturbed by a wandering horse, and one of his companions seemed inclined to fire—within a few feet of Hughes's head—at random into the darkness as long as his ammunition held out. On the trail between Buffalo Gap and Custer (admittedly one on which caution was thoroughly justified, for the party found at least one murdered man along the way) a guard, mistaking a comrade for an attacking Indian, shot him dead in the darkness. All told, some thirty-five to forty incoming pilgrims were killed by the Indians during the troubles of 1876, although estimates as high as one hundred were not uncommon. McClintock and others list many of these deaths: six Iowa men killed on the White River; George Miller, in a party from Montana, killed about where Beulah is now; McGonigle and Riley killed near Crook City; a large herd of stock run off near Bear Butte, and a man named Wigginton wounded and his companion killed; thirteen Indians and one miner slain on Deadwood Creek; Norman Storms shot through the body and killed south of the Cheyenne, and his companion, one Rowser, wounded; Ernest T. Stober killed somewhere between Deadwood and Custer; William Ward and a companion killed four miles north of Belle Fourche (the old town, not the present-day one); an unknown man killed in Centennial Valley; Mark V. Boughton's cattle run off on Lower False Bottom Creek; Charles Mason killed by the same Indians who shot Preacher Smith; Isaac Brown and Charles Holland killed near Spring Creek, east of Spearfish; Charles Nolin, a mail rider, killed on the outskirts of what is now Sturgis; and forty-nine members of Captain Stone's

company of Cincinnatians killed on the way to the Hills, an item
that was probably an exaggeration, and the acceptance of which
probably leads to some of the markedly higher total figures of
deaths; Captain Dodson's (or Dotson's) cattle run off from the Centennial Prairie area; Milton Provence shot from ambush while hauling hay from Crook City to Deadwood, to die instantly; and at least
one Indian killed, and the body dragged into town from the Crook
City area by a chap identified only as Old Spiegel. These were not
times when a careless or lonely man was safe even on the outskirts
of the settled portions of the Hills.

It is interesting to note that although the deaths from Indians
were many, the wounds were few. Very probably, in those days, and
in the absence of proper medical care on the frontier, anybody who
received a bullet wound worth noticing died of it shortly thereafter.
There is also some evidence—the Metz massacre in Red Canyon
being one example—that white bandits now and then murdered
passing travelers, and of course did their best to make sure that there
were no surviving witnesses to testify against them; some of these
murders were doubtless blamed upon the Indians who also lurked
and raided in the area. Nevertheless, with every discount which
reason can properly apply to the statistics, the Indians were a considerable menace to the miners in the mountains. Oddly, there does
not seem to have been any passionate personal animosity toward the
Indians; they were regarded as something of a natural phenomenon,
annoying and dangerous, but a problem to be mastered rather than
hated.

The pioneers in Deadwood did not endure without reprisal. On
26 July 1876 the Lawrence County Commission voted a reward of
$25 each for Indians brought in dead or alive. Considering the risk
involved in producing one in either condition, the offer was probably no more than a symbolic sign of approbation for those engaged
in Indian warfare. Seth Bullock reported that the offer went up to
$50, payable "in clean merchantable gold dust" to anybody bringing
in an Indian's head, which probably meant, although it did not so
specify, that the Indian who had previously owned the head was
absent on other business. In August 1876 Brick Pomeroy shot an
Indian who had stolen some of his horses, and a Mexican cut off the
corpse's head and took it to Deadwood, where he collected $66 in
contributions from the crowds—it sounds as if the county board's
offer was not taken seriously, for he didn't pause to try to collect it—

and spending the money riotously, he was, in his turn, shot and killed in a Crook City bar by the irate Pomeroy, who had originally killed the Indian. In July 1877 the Lawrence county board upped its offer to $250 for the bodies, dead or alive, of Indians captured within the county, and Bullock, at least, claims that this was the reward given to the Mexican who brought in Pomeroy's Indian head, paid by the board of health on the supposition that "killing Indians was conducive to the health of the community." Another source says that the Mexican was paid $300, and indeed the general confusion involving the various rewards offered and supposedly paid—mostly for this one incident—tends to lessen the credibility of the entire transaction, and about all that is completely clear is that the county board did indeed in 1877 make an offer of $250 for Indians taken dead or alive. The offer, however, does not appear to have produced much effect, and the Deadwood citizens turned, with cries of anguish, to the federal government for assistance in combating the Indians who surrounded them.[6]

The federal government, not unreasonably, was unsympathetic to the plight of the "white inhabitants of the Black Hills," who, Charles F. Goerham, acting secretary of the interior remarked, "are there not only without authority of law, but in actual violation of law." Furthermore, there seems to have been, in both the Black Hills and in the outfitting towns around them, an ambivalence regarding such appeals for military aid: it would be nice to have it, but to request it forcefully would indicate how badly it was needed, and thus discourage badly needed business. By the summer of 1876, however, the threat to the lives of the Black Hillers outweighed the threat to the outfitting business, and heartfelt appeals for military assistance began to fill the editorial columns of the newspapers.[7]

Dependence upon the military, unfortunately, was not well placed. The average soldier, firing at the kitchen door from a distance of one hundred yards, missed it about half the time, and a good deal more training and fire discipline than he generally got was necessary to make him improve his marksmanship. It was said among the hardened frontiersmen that the average soldier did cause a good many casualties among the Indians—they injured themselves laughing at the soldier's efforts to hit them with the U.S. Army's single-shot, wood-burning, trapdoor Springfield rifle, a weapon markedly inferior to the repeating Henrys, Spencers, and Winchesters supplied to the Indians by their government agents.[8]

In late May 1876 Gen. W. T. Sherman wrote to Gen. P. H. Sheridan in Chicago that the miners in the Black Hills were there illegally and wrongfully, but that inasmuch as governmental measures to open up the Black Hills country were going forward, the Indians should not be allowed to scalp and kill anybody, and he authorized Sheridan to provide military protection to those miners who were leaving the Hills, and to those freighters who were hauling in supplies for the miners already there. This modest and amiable attitude was of course completely upset by the disastrous defeat of General Custer and much of his Seventh Cavalry Regiment in the Battle of the Little Big Horn on 25 June 1876, and the increased Indian depredations which followed the Sioux withdrawal from the Crow reservation in Montana, back toward their own agencies and into the area around the Hills.

Fortunately, succor was at hand, in the form of Gen. George Crook's troops, who made their way from the Rosebud Battlefield in Montana toward the Battle of Slim Buttes in northwestern South Dakota, and onward, in their famous and disastrous "mud and horsemeat march," into Crook City and Deadwood. Col. Wesley Merritt led a reconnaissance down the Cheyenne River to the mouth of Rapid Creek, and on southward to Fort Niobrara in Nebraska, and Maj. Peter Dumont Vroom and a battalion of the Third Cavalry from Fort Robinson came into the Hills and camped in the vicinity of Bear Butte, to provide still further protection while Crook himself led his troops from Deadwood southward to Custer, where his men so disabled themselves by "nameless dissipations" that he had to withdraw his command entirely from the Hills to keep it in anything like fighting trim.[9]

The arrival of General Crook's command in Deadwood in mid-September 1876 was greeted with wild enthusiasm, with most of the town's population crowding into Main Street "cheering, yelling and prancing around as if the day of jubilee had come" while Crook, bowing and smiling right and left, waved his weather-beaten hat at the delighted multitude.[10] Mayor E. B. Farnum, noting the condition of the troops, indicated the way to the public bathhouse, and mentioned to Crook and his staff the names of the best of Deadwood's ready-made clothing stores, and soon the command looked reasonably human again. Crook and his staff were royally entertained at the Grand Central Hotel, after which the general addressed the crowd for half an hour, describing the rigors of his Indian campaign, his destruction of a small Indian village at Slim Buttes, and his hopes that the government would soon take still further measures to protect the Black Hills from the Indians.

After his address the general and his officers retired to Jack Langrishe's theater, where they shook hands with all comers, a form of social activity which probably showed as much self-control as campaigning against the Indians, and Judge Joseph Miller, after an appropriate oration, presented the general with a petition signed by 625 citizens who praised the population and productivity of the Hills, lamented the murder by the Indians of over 100 citizens during the preceding four or five months, and urged "the establishing of a temporary military post at some available and convenient point in the northern end of the Hills" in order that "the rich natural resources of this country may be by the strong arms of the military forces fostered and protected" and the "murdering bands of Indians who surround" the area be forced to sue for peace. It was a noble effort, but Crook replied that he and his superiors believed that "the operations of the troops which [were] about to be inaugurated" would "afford better protection than the permanent location of a detachment at any one point," and he recommended that the citizens organize themselves into suitable militia bodies for their own "temporary protection in case of any unforeseen emergency."[11]

This prudent advice from General Crook was not actually needed, for there was already a movement toward creating "a Black Hills Brigade," for, as the *Pioneer* commented, "the irregular organizations which have gone out against the Sioux have been more successful than any of the more formidable movements" of the regular troops. Most of the Hills mining camps established their own militia companies—that in Custer, under "Captain Jack" Crawford was known as the Minute Men because they never got so far from town that they could not return in a minute—and cavalry companies were projected for Deadwood, Gayville, Spearfish, and Crook City, and that of Crook City, at least was actually formed and officered—its captain, W. M. Foster of South Bend; its first lieutenant, Lemington McCarty of Central City; and its second lieutenant, William Lardner of Golden Gate—and had an enrollment of thirty-four enlisted troopers. The mere creation of such a body of militia and the inclination of other Hills towns toward military preparedness doubtless did much to slow down Indian attacks on population centers, but the lonesome individual was still a tempting target for any wandering braves who had not satisfied their thirst for distinction in earlier battles with the regulars.

During the early months of 1877 the soldiers were again sent into the central Black Hills to protect the miners during a long and severe winter, and the next winter more news of Indians on the warpath again brought soldiers to the area. Early in 1878 General Sheridan sent investigating officers to the Hills to hunt for a suitable spot to establish a military post to guard the miners from those Indians whose nearby reservations made it easy for them to raid into the eastern Hills. The site selected was on the western side of Bear Butte, where troops were first stationed at a Camp Sturgis, then moved to the southwest of the Butte to a Camp Ruhlen which, when it took on an air of permanence, was renamed Fort Meade, and the nearby town of Sturgis founded to provide the troops with homelike comforts. The newspapers continue to mention various Indian troubles until the summer of 1881, so these various military precautions doubtless were to some degree needed, and once well established they did so much for the prosperity of the northern Hills that it was politically impossible to abandon them; and Fort Meade, now a veterans' hospital, continues in existence to the present day.

By 1880, however, Indian hostilities had calmed down to the extent that Red Cloud ("the noted old coffee cooler") and members of his band could come to Deadwood to testify in a trial, and to gain good will put on various dances in the street one afternoon and later that evening in the Gem Theater, where the music "was not only splendid but loud" and made the whole lower end of the city shake as Joe Gondolfo beat the tomtom for them. The Indians put on squaw dances and scalp dances and war dances generally, and appeared to exhibit only a little regret that these performances could not be followed up with some sort of action appropriate to their themes.[12]

The Indian excitements accompanying the Messiah Craze of 1890 again brought considerable distress to the eastern edge of the Black Hills, and the towns from Hot Springs, Buffalo Gap, Fairburn, and Hermosa all prepared to defend themselves against a renewal of the Indian wars. The prompt action by the military in stationing soldiers along the eastern rim of the Hills, and in sending the troops into the reservations to put down what seemed at the time likely to be a dangerous uprising, protected the Black Hills but resulted in the tragic Battle of Wounded Knee, after which the Ghost

Dance excitement died away, and good relations with the Indians were resumed. Sheriff W. A. Remer found a letter addressed to the Deadwood jail and presumably written by a white participant in the Messiah movement, which told of its writer's journey to the Hills to preach to the Indians, saying in part that

> it is only by peace and loving union with other flowers that the wild violets, which you have all seen, grow larger, brighter, and more beautiful and are called pansies, and now these pansies, which are only educated violets, lead the whole race of flowers in their beauty and education, as you may, by following their example, lead all the races of men.

It was an interesting conceit, and perhaps typical of the better side of the ghost dance movement, the other side of which was the tensions and animosities which led to Wounded Knee.[13]

Indian troubles, of a sort, burst out again in the Battle of Lightning Creek, near Newcastle, Wyoming, when in 1903 Sheriff William H. Miller and Louis Falkenberg were killed, as were four Indians, when Miller's posse attempted to suppress Indian hunting in eastern Wyoming. It is doubtful that anybody thought of it as the start of a new Indian war, for by that time the Indians were no longer sufficiently a threat to be either feared or hated: the Black Hills mills at last had ground them down.[14]

THREE

Dust in the Balance

"A bird in hand is the noblest work of God."
William Smith, early prospector

"You can count the hardrock mines that are actually in Deadwood on the fingers of one foot."
An old-timer

DEADWOOD was a mining town, but it was not a town full of mines. The hardrock lode mines that inflamed and supported Deadwood's businessmen lay in the surrounding country. Many of the miners brought their ores to the Deadwood mills and smelters for processing; all of them brought their business. Nearby the city of Lead (pronounced "Leed" from its leads, or veins of ore) might have twice the population that Deadwood had, but Deadwood did ten times the business. Neither was a suburb of the other—their inhabitants would have blenched at the thought—but economically they were complementary, and the gold that came out of Lead and the gold and assorted minerals that came from the other Black Hills mines provided the wealth that kept Deadwood businessmen in business. Deadwood was the industrial supply center, shopping center, financial hub, and hellhole of raucous entertainment for the whole area, and it gloried in its reputation as "boss city of the Hills."

Deadwood's business district, during its early days as an untamed placer mining camp, looked like "a lot of lemon boxes dumped out in a back yard, some of them propped up on broomsticks." An early eastern reporter took note of three saloons, a hotel, and a blacksmith's shop all "clinging to a ridge with their forepaws, while their main structure strung out behind," and another observer commented that it would have been "more economical to establish oneself in a balloon in the first place." Even such unpromising city lots as these, however, sold at prices ranging from twenty-five to five hundred dollars, and a considerable building boom was under way during the summer of 1876 with many houses going up to replace the tents and brush shanties of the firstcomers in the gulch.

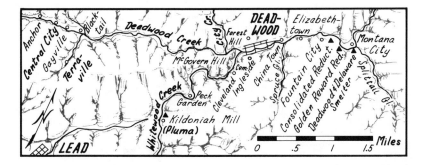

The towns and mining camps around Deadwood

"Dealers in grub" were by no means plentiful, as prospector Jerry Bryan put it, for "everybody seems to deal in Whiskey. You will see the glass standing on the barrel head in a Tent or Brush shanty as well as the log cabin. Everything fluctuates here except Whiskey and labor. Whiskey is at the top notch and labor at the lowest. . . . I would have done as well if I had remained in Cordova [Illinois]." During the busiest weeks of the summer of 1876 ten thousand men were said to be at work up and down Whitewood and Deadwood creeks, the latter being described with more vividness than accuracy as being "about three miles long and fifty feet wide." Other observers put the population at about one thousand; both estimates appear to be inaccurate.[1]

By late summer of 1876 the assessed valuation of Deadwood was estimated at one hundred thousand dollars, although it is hard to see how that could have been a very precise appraisal. By the end of September there were two hundred buildings in town, and the buildings themselves were of a noticeably better quality with crude log cabins giving way to two- and three-story frame business structures. By mid-October the population of Deadwood alone was estimated at three thousand (some of those ten thousand having doubtless gone home for the winter, and a large part of the rest perhaps had never been there to begin with) and there were 173 businesses in town, including Wagner's Hotel, the Grand Central, the IXL for creature comforts, a physician, a drugstore run by Julius Deetkin, two practicing attorneys, Furman and Brown's General Store, and

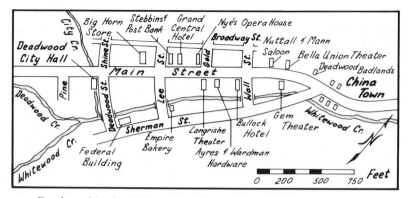

Deadwood in the 1870s, with a few modern additions

a theater. Many of these businesses were still conducted in big wall tents, and in others "lascivious pictures were profusely displayed, and the clinking of glasses was ever to be heard."[2]

As late as June 1877, many of the miners still lived in tents whose dingy whiteness dotted the hills in every direction. A little later a correspondent for the *New York Times* guessed that ten thousand people were within the area around Deadwood, four thousand of them in Deadwood itself, and two thousand "floating" around generally, and noted the presence of "an academy, church, two daily newspapers, four banks and 20 lawyers." Only about two hundred out of this population were engaged in business, five hundred more in active mining, and the rest were "simply wandering about fomenting a stampede to some other locality, cursing the luck that sent them to the Black Hills." Well they might be impatient: the reporter estimated that the yield of gold from the area would, if evenly distributed, come out to about ten cents per man. The city itself was "disorderly, sinful, sickly," its streets "thronged with speculators, tramps and bummers . . . and cappers on every corner watching for the next victim." *Frank Leslie's Illustrated Magazine* called it "one of the liveliest and queerest places west of the Mississippi," and it probably was, a city of a single street, and "a very singular street it is" although, as an army surveyor reported, it was "the commercial center of the most important mining district in the Black Hills."[3]

"The man who is going into the Black Hills to look around him, buy an interest in a mine, or engage in business . . . wants no outfit beyond what he can take in a leather bag," said Edwin A. Curley in his 1877 *Guide*, although he allowed that a Smith and Wesson .44 revolver and a first-rate rifle would not be a useless burden. Everything else a newcomer might need, unless he happened to be in some trade or profession requiring special instruments, could be got cheaper and probably better, because suited to the country, than he could bring it in with him, for Deadwood was set up to take good care of strangers. All of the usual shopping and service facilities of a major western city were available, and every nook and cranny of the city which could house a business was occupied by some sort of entrepreneur. By 1878 even the narrow gaps between stores on Main Street, spaces from a foot to a yard in width, were occupied by vendors of soap, peanuts (there were five peanut roasters in town), candy, and other notions, and the lucky owners of such trifling pieces of real estate collected handsome rents from them.

Deadwood's advertising during the 1870s pretty much gives the tone of its varied businesses. "If you want a nice, cosy shave," said an early ad in the *Pioneer*, "go to Flaherty's, opposte [sic] Nuttall & Mann's Hall." D. M. Gillette, manufacturing jeweler, created the Black Hills gold jewelry, which is still manufactured in the Hills, using different colors of gold to produce a grape, leaf, and vine pattern which "imitated real fruit to perfection." Gaston and Shankland's New and Second Hand Store sold everything, but particularly guns and ammunition, the owners of such things tending to have a high turnover. The Dakota Warehouse, with a capacity of five hundred tons, and "a first class powder magazine," would store goods and later sell them for their owners at reasonable commissions.

By the middle of 1878 Deadwood businessmen had mutually agreed to shut down on Sundays, but it didn't last. Sunday was the only day the outlying prospectors had to come to town, and despite Agricola's urgings that Bohemian miners needed two days off a week, one to shop and one to worship, the Black Hills miners needed to do their trading on the Sabbath, and not so many of them went to church services as to seriously interfere with Deadwood's business or prosperity.

By the 1880s Deadwood's business boom had tapered off: only

twenty-five buildings were under construction, plus half a dozen additions to business buildings. Klambeck and Slater on Whitewood Creek a mile upstream from town were making five thousand bricks a day, and burning them, probably in self-kilns, in lots of seventy-five thousand, against a spring building boom of larger proportions. A car load of aptly named "Hazard [Blasting] Powder" came in the summer of 1880, with Carl Cushman, general agent for the company, in charge of it. Lumbermen all over the Hills fixed prices for common lumber at twenty-five dollars per thousand board feet, in lengths from twelve to twenty feet, and fifty cents a thousand extra for every two feet longer than that. These found a ready market because the balloon frame construction that came in after the Chicago fire and the great Deadwood fire of 1879 needed extra-long studdings. In 1883 a flour mill was running continuously, and producing enough grist not only for the Black Hills community but some extra to ship to Pierre for transshipment to the Indian reservations upriver.

By 1904 a foundry had come to town to serve the mills that needed castings; a cigar factory was in full session; the Deadwood creamery was the largest in the state; *two* brick plants (one, Phillips and Bartlett's could make thirty thousand bricks a day, and the bricks included $2.40 to the ton in gold); two planing and finishing lumber mills, and a couple of steam laundries. Austin Maabs advertised, "Will move and raise houses, anywhere" which, considering the mountainous terrain of Deadwood and the towns around it, shows both the self-confidence and enterprise of the Deadwood businessman, and the optimistic mobility of Deadwood's citizens.

The population too was changing. The 1880 United States Census listed 20 percent of the population as miners; in 1890, only 5.8 percent. In 1892 there were said to be no idle men in Deadwood, with miners getting $3.25 a day and mechanics and skilled laborers $3.50–$6.00 a day, farm hands $30.00–$45.00 a month and board, teamsters $30.00–$50.00 a month, and woodchoppers $0.75–$1.00 a cord (a pile 8 by 4 by 4 feet, containing 128 cubic feet of wood). It is hard to compare wages then with the wages of today. Gold, for example, was then worth about $20 an ounce and now twenty or thirty times that. In other words, gold, and presumably money, would buy twenty or thirty times more in 1880 than it will today, although an actual survey of prices does not show quite so large a disparity. Money, on the other hand, went farther then in covering the customary needs of a wage earner, for when he had fed his family even at the then somewhat elevated Deadwood prices, housed them in a house that by today's standards would be inadequately small and primitive, and clothed them in clothing "suitable for their station," he had virtually no other expenses.

A chart provided in the nearby Custer newspaper in December of 1876 shows gold rush prices as follows, for purposes of comparison:

Flour (pound)	$0.10½	to	$ 0.11
Corn meal (pound)	0.08½		
Beans, white (pound)	0.18		
Salt (pound)	0.10	to	0.15
Bacon (side)	0.22		
Beef steak (pound)	0.15	to	0.20
Butter, ranch (pound)	0.55	to	0.65
Cheese, New York (pound)	0.21	to	0.33
Eggs (dozen)	0.75	to	1.00
Coffee (pound)	0.34	to	0.38
Sugar (pound)	0.27		
Chickens (each)	0.75		
Coal oil (gallon)	$1.25	to	$ 1.50

These, of course, were prices during the placer rush, and correspondingly inflated. By the time freighting outfits were well organized and movement to the Hills was undisturbed by Indian threats, prices were much lower, and lower still by 1890, when the railroads were running clear to Deadwood.[4]

There were no taxes to speak of, little insurance, medical expenses were low and worth it, the laborer had no automobile, no TV, no telephone, no movies, and although there were outside entertainments and quite expensive ones, he did not attend them often. At a guess, the worker of the 1880s probably *thought* he was doing better than the worker of the 1980s thinks he is doing—his wages then probably bought for him more of the things that he thought he ought to have than the wages of a similar worker (and of course nowadays more workers are skilled) do today, although such a conclusion about human happiness can of course be only a conjecture.

A survey of Collins's 1878 *Directory* shows that among Deadwood's businesses there were forty lawyers, five bakeries, five barbers, seven blacksmiths, six breweries, nine clothiers, six wholesale grocers, and seven hotels. Miners predominated, but various other entrepreneurs listed themselves as "speculator," an oddly popular profession, "capitalist," and "hotelist."

Deadwood in 1878 had an assessed valuation of nearly $500,000. Three years later the valuation had not gone up, but annual business had certainly increased:

Groceries	$904,000
Liquors, wholesale	285,000
Hardware	285,000
Drygoods	200,000
Clothing	188,000
Furniture	122,000
Saloons	252,500
Hotels	121,000
Restaurants	81,000
Meat markets	155,000
Sashes, doors, and blinds	150,000
Hides and pelts	100,000
Fuel	80,000

Total sales for 1881 amounted to $3,774,000, a huge amount for so small a town. Fifteen nearby sawmills poured out timber for the mines and lumber for the houses; 310,000 head of cattle grazed on the prairies to the north and east—Deadwood was only four miles from good grazing land—and farmers in the foothills raised three hundred thousand bushels of wheat and much other grain. By 1889 business had either fallen off or prices had gotten lower, for business amounted to only $2,540,000 for the year, with groceries, liquor, and hardware, as usual, leading the list. Fuel costing $52,000 had been burned, and freight bills of $361,000 had been incurred, which, taken in comparison with the cost of the goods consumed, gives an indication of the considerable part that shipping played in the cost of keeping house in Deadwood.[5]

Deadwood was an extraordinarily business-oriented community. A survey of the 1898 *Directory*, for example, shows that 20 percent of those listed were business owners, 371 of them, although of course one would expect businesses to make sure that they were listed in a city directory. Twelve percent were business employees, 18 percent were in skilled trades and professions, and only 18 percent were unskilled laborers, although, of course, it is unlikely that every laborer was listed. Missing from the directories are the less learned but more ancient professions, although a good many citizens listed themselves as "sport," "gambler," or as "Miss Such-and-so, boarding with Mrs. This-and-that," which gives some indication of the wide variety of employments available.[6] In addition, in 1898 the town had five architects, twenty-two lawyers, ten barbers, nine painters and paperhangers, thirteen physicians (one for every four hundred citizens), eleven restaurants, (seven of them run by Chinamen), twenty-two saloons, and two embalmers and undertakers. Odd trades and professions abounded: D. C. Baker was a "promoter"; L. R. Baxter a "speculator"; W. N. Boyce moved houses; Mrs. P. Casey was an artist, at what she didn't say; Caleb Daniels was not ashamed to list himself as a servant at the Hotel DeBedrock, on lower Main in the redlight district, employed by its proprietress, Mrs. Thomas Walter; Flossie Fields was an actress; Matilda Hansen a midwife; C. A. Rossingnol a musical director; and August Schedin a lime burner, one of those craftsmen whose long employment in the hydroscopic dusts of quicklime gave rise to the now-forgotten simile "dry as a limeburner's hat."

They were not poor people, these common and uncommon folks of Deadwood. Bank deposits of two hundred dollars per capita, 2.5 times the national average, attested in 1904 to their prosperity, and during the preceding six years South Dakota had each year produced more new wealth per person than any other state. This wealth of course was not evenly distributed, but even distributed unevenly there was more than enough to go around. Above all, Deadwood was a businessman's town. "The sterling men who fathered its economic life deserve the credit for what it was and for what it has become," as the Black Hills banker R. E. Driscoll put it in the memoirs he wrote in his old age.[7] Deadwood was in business, its merchants dedicated to making a profit and to building a town in which profit making was easy. They were the men who created and maintained the city and enabled it to make a lasting fortune from the gold mines by which it was surrounded. Each individual businessman had a tale to tell, a saga of hard work, sacrifice, good judgment, and good luck.

Among the leading grocers of Deadwood was P. A. Gushurst, who came into the Hills from Omaha via Cheyenne and Fort Laramie in the spring of 1876, and on the site of what is now Edgemont in the southern Hills bedded down in the dark with his companions, resting his head, as he discovered when daylight came, on the grave of a man killed by Indians a week before. He and his partner William Connors bought up general merchandise from men departing for the states, set up a tent on Deadwood's Main Street, and went into business as the Big Horn Store, which in a year or two they sold to Jake Goldberg and a Mr. Matthiessen, who in 1878 advertised themselves: "Jobbers and Dealers in Groceries—we make a specialty of miners's outfits and the supplying of hotels, boarding houses and families . . . warranted pure liquor." Goldberg's store is still in business on the same site in Deadwood. Still carried on its books is a bill for seven dollars run up on 10 October 1895 by Calamity Jane, and partially paid by means of a one dollar credit given for "a picture." I would have liked to have seen that picture! As Jake Goldberg's son told the present owner, "If the place burns down don't sell the lot until you sift the ashes!"[8] It is the kind of advice that made Deadwood what it was. By 1905 Goldberg's could advertise Christmas specials that still can make modern mouths water: a one-pound tinned plum pudding for ten cents; popcorn that pops; apple cider, fancy figs and dates; fancy raisins "in one pound cartons"; Caswell stub cigars, and turkeys, geese, and ducks for the holidays. Browning and Wringrose established their business, said to be the second grocery house to be started in town, in May 1876, and within a few years were doing a business amounting to one hundred thousand dollars a year, furnishing hot competition to Gushurst and his partner.

In 1876 groceries were not so plentiful. Supplies had been built up during the summer to such an extent that shippers stopped bringing in new food, and by mid-November flour was selling at fifteen dollars a sack, size of sack not designated but probably one hundred pounds, and thoughtful buyers were willing to pay that price, for supplies on hand were sufficient for only three weeks, and winter weather would soon block the trails into the Hills. Bacon was similarly in short supply, and sugar not to be had at all. With the price of flour soon up to twenty dollars a hundred pounds, "baker's loaves are a marvel of littleness," said the *Times*, and it was alleged that "two-bit loaves of bread can be delivered through the keyhole."[9]

Contributing, perhaps, to this shortage of food in the fall of 1876 was the arrival of General Crook and his command in town, at the conclusion of their disastrous "mud and horsemeat" march from the battles of the Rosebud and Slim Buttes. They had arrived in Deadwood in a starving condition and Capt. John Wilson Bubb, the commissary officer, had bought up all the bacon, flour, and coffee that was available at almost any price the sellers cared to ask. This boom in staples must have given (as the California gold rush did to the Mormons in 1849 and '50) a considerable boost to Deadwood's grocery business, but it doubtless both used up supplies and, when the troops departed, discouraged heavy restocking on the reasonable assumption that business would never be that good again.

William E. Adams, another dealer in wholesale and retail groceries and provisions, came to Deadwood in the spring of 1877, to form, with his brother James H. Adams, the Adams Brothers mercantile firm, and become the president of the First National Bank of Deadwood, a power in the town's financial circles, and highly respected, despite a suit against him, in the late 1890s, by his mother-in-law, who alleged, probably incorrectly, that he had neglected her and her property. The Adams Memorial Museum stands as a monument to both his memory and his generosity to the community he served so well.[10]

By the end of the century the grocery business had progressed to the point that the union of grocery clerks and deliverymen could insist that their employers close down at 8:00 P.M. each day, except on Saturday, when 9:00 P.M. would be permitted, and that on the miners' pay days (the sixteenth and twenty-sixth of each month) the stores could remain open until 10:00 P.M. The clerks believed that "all grocery clerks and delivery men have completed a day's labor at 8 PM each day" and that no work at all should be done on Sundays. The union believed that "Deadwood grocerymen have imposed long hours upon themselves and their employees under the mistaken notion that it was necessary to succeed in business." The members, they claimed, were not "agitators, dynamiters, or anarchists" but "part and parcel of the community," men who knew their rights and insisted upon having them. Apparently the grocers agreed, at least temporarily, for by the early 1900s Deadwood was in the grip of reform forces, and Sabbath-keeping was doubtless thought to be more meritorious than it had been in the gold rush days a generation earlier.[11]

The 1930s and 1940s saw the decline of the great Deadwood mercantile houses, their Hills-wide distributing functions being replaced by mercantile houses in Rapid City, which was more centrally located for both shipping goods in and distributing them by truck afterwards. An ill-fated attempt on the part of the Deadwood firm of Fish and Hunter to organize a sort of chain grocery system throughout the Hills, using existing retailers and banding them together to buy at lower prices, was too far ahead of its time to succeed during the Great Depression of the 1930s, and Deadwood's last effort to maintain its grip on the business of the Hills evaporated. It was a great pity, for as long as the railroads were the principal means of distribution, Deadwood was admirably located to serve the entire area, either up and down the center of the Hills on the Burlington, or up and down their populous east side on the North Western. Trucks, however, disrupted this structured flow of trade, and allowed Rapid City to intrude successfully upon it, and the tourist business, which also came to center on Rapid City, placed most of the consumers of Hills mercantile goods more nearly within the reach of Rapid City than of Deadwood.

Drugstores also prospered in Deadwood. Early in the gold rush C. M. Wilcox bought out a defunct Deadwood drugstore, starting, actually, with less than nothing, for the stock he purchased along with the store could not be sold, but by 1904 he had established "a handsome business, besides having accumulated considerable property and money," a feat not unreasonably considered to be unlikely in a similar situation in a more settled eastern city. K. G. Phillips, another gold rush merchant, began a drugstore in 1876, and soon dealt in drugs, medicines, chemicals, paints, oils, and druggists' sundries, and he was twice elected mayor of the city. Another, more modern druggist, who doubtless prefers to remain nameless, is said to have a trade of over five hundred dollars a month arising out of the "upstairs rooms" of lower Deadwood, dealing in merchandise designed to prevent or to cure the effects of those infectious businesses.[12]

The dry goods trade flourished, even before there were families and ladies to buy. In fact, three millinery shops were in business before "the first lady" arrived in town on the stagecoach, a news item which seems a bit ungracious toward Mrs. Tallent and any other respectable women already in the gulch, but it doubtless was meant only to imply that although there were *women* around, the supply of *ladies* was, in 1876, distinctly limited.

"And now cometh Geo. Stokes, with a choice lot of DRY GOODS, &c" reads the advertisement in the *Black Hills Times* in 1877. Stokes indeed had come, from Palmer Gulch where he made a few hundred dollars placering, but was soon convinced by that onerous experience that a merchant's life was much preferable. Stokes arranged with his friend Jim Doolittle in Denver to set him up with a dry goods stock, and Doolittle, unfamiliar with the needs of a predominantly if not entirely male mining camp, sent large quantities of Balmoral skirts, bolts of wool shirtings, flimsy bib overalls (a prospector would rather die than wear such a farmer's garment, although later they became popular with the hardrock miners), cheap broadbrimmed, low-crowned hats originally intended for the Mexican trade which surprisingly sold well at five dollars each (for any hat was better than none to a prospector who worked in the Black Hills summer sunshine), and thousands of yards of dazzling calico prints which could not be sold in Denver. Stokes sold out his entire stock of textiles and asked for more, for the miners used the cloth instead of wall paper to line the walls and ceilings of their cabins to keep the wind, the dust, and the bugs under control. "Glove-fitting corsets" were a staple in the business. Hoyt, Lowe, and Masterson advertised in detail that they had "Ball's coiled wire spring elastic section corsets . . . warranted to retain their perfect elasticity until the corset is worn out," and, unlike rubber, guaranteed not to "heat the person or decay with age." These vicelike contraptions came in four styles: "health preserving, self-adjusting, abdominal, and nursing" and were reputed to be "the only corset pronounced by the medical profession not injurious to the wearer." Modern experiments with a very large corset of those days and a very small girl of the present indicate that it must have taken a good many years of training in deformity to enable a woman to even get into one of these constricting garments, much less to wear it with either grace or comfort.[13]

By 1878 Wolf and McDonald advertised themselves as "Importers and Manufacturers of Ladies Suits, Cloaks and Mantles." D. Holtzman called himself a "Wholesale and Retail Dealer in Clothing: Gents Furnishings, Blouses, Overalls and Miners Patent Suits," and his prices, as might be expected from the tone of the ad, were "always the lowest." Holtzman's clothing "renders the most ill-looking and ungainly man nobby and graceful as an Adonis." One can envision a steady parade of ungainly louts making their way to Holtzman's, to emerge endowed by his skill with every appealing grace and nobby, that is to say, stylish, to the last degree. Osborne and McLary were merchant tailors, "dealers in cloths, vestings, &c" and guaranteed the best fit in town. A news item in the *Times* in

January 1880 was headed "Perished in the Storm" and dealt with the sad death by freezing of one John Smith whose party had that winter gone into camp, apparently near Rochford, where Smith had complained a good deal of the cold. "About midnight, as all nature shrieked and shuddered with the fury of the storm," Smith spoke his last words: "Joe, I can't hold out much longer. I feel that my life tide ebbs and flows toward the boundless shores of eternity. . . . What a fool I was for not buying my clothing at D. Holtzman's!"[14]

Prices for clothing were not high. In 1883 boys' overcoats cost from $3.50 to $5.00; men's from $6.00 upwards, and men's suits from $5.00, with the "prices in plain figures, right on the clothing" and a concluding cheer, "Hurraw for Chase's where they sell cheap." Liebmann's advertised, "San Francisco Bazaar, where a child can buy as cheap as a man, and 16 ounces make a pound." (The reference is to the days of the press gang and the Napoleonic wars, when on British naval vessels fourteen ounces of their rations were issued to the men, the remaining two ounces of each pound going as an added emolument to the captain of the ship.) They issued cards which when all punched out in token of cash purchases made entitled the holder to $1.00 in additional merchandise—it represented about a 4.75 percent discount if you spent $21.00. Munter and Lillienthal advertised "fancy and white shirts" and "collars, cuffs and scarfs" and indicated that the detachable cuff and collar, doubtless heavily starched to shed dirt and hold its shape, was popular at least among the leisured, professional, and clerical classes. Dainty lingerie, too, was available: nightgowns, chemises, drawers, corset covers, and such; and by 1899 Madame Mengetti, recently returned from Paris, was on hand at Lowe's, "Mr. Lowe having secured her at great expense" to bring the best of taste to the Bee Hive millinery parlors. Men too could be tastefully outfitted by the turn of the century, when the cyanide boom was beginning, if they went to the Zoellner Brothers store for dress and negligée shirtings, canes, umbrellas, "rich furnishings—things you positively must have to complete your wardrobe," and trunks and valises to put them in too, and hats, caps, and derbys, in short, "rich clothing at poor prices." The Panic of 1893 forced a good deal of retrenchment, and many of the clothing stores advertised that they would sell goods *at cost for cash*, but eventually the cyanide boom bailed them out in good style. One merchant dealing in gloves and mittens, J. W. Fargo, maintained a meat market alongside his clothing store, and the common supposition was that the hides from his cattle and pigs went to make up the gloves and mittens that he sold next door.

John Bourke, who came to Deadwood in the fall of 1876 along with General Crook, looked about him with a trained reporter's eye and noted that the goods for sale in town tended to be typified by "heavy and light clothing, hardware, tinware, mess-pans, camp-kettles, blankets, saddlery, harness, rifles, cartridges, wagon-grease, blasting powder, India-rubber boots, garden seeds, dried and canned fruits, sardines and yeast powders." Second only to the grocery business was hardware, as seems reasonable in a community of miners, and in which much of the life was lived, if not in a rural setting, at least so close to one as made no difference. George V. Ayres, of Ismon and Ayres, came to Deadwood in the spring of 1876, and established a business dealing in "heavy hardware, mine and mill supplies of all kinds, both wholesale and retail," which is still in business in the 1980s under the guidance of his son Albro, and is probably the oldest firm in the city.

In August 1876 a party of thirty-five western men from Bismarck came into town, bringing an appreciable proportion of names later to be famous in Deadwood history. Among them were Solomon Star and Seth Bullock, who went into business together on a corner lot at Main and Wall streets. Bullock later became sheriff and marshall and friend of Theodore Roosevelt, and Star postmaster and mayor, both of them remaining in the town as effective and adroit businessmen, politicians, and guiders of the economic destiny of the northern Hills. Together they established the Deadwood Flouring Mill Company at a cost of sixty thousand dollars, and together they invested and speculated in ranching and stock raising in the Belle Fourche valley. In 1878 they advertised themselves as "wholesale and retail dealers in Queensware, furniture, Hardware, lamps, Wall Paper, etc." For some reason known only to the devious minds of hardware jobbers one of the first shipments of goods that they received included a large assortment of chamber pots "of various shapes and colors," which Bullock auctioned off the evening they arrived in what must have been one of the high points of Black Hills oratory and enterprise. Neither man's many successes were achieved without now and then arousing some trifling animosities among their less successful neighbors in government and business, but in general, Star and Bullock's influence upon the town was, if turbulent, in the long run benign and beneficial.[15]

R. C. Lake too dealt in "hardware, stoves and tinware; mining and milling goods a specialty; iron and steel, belting and hose" and obviously catered to a specialized but demanding mining and engineering clientele. Curtis and Graves dealt in furniture, crockery, chandeliers (who could have wanted a chandelier in Deadwood in 1878?), window glass, carpets and bedding, and comfortable metallic burial cases, giving them the opportunity to advertise "Coffins by Graves" should the occasion ever arise. This may indeed have been the same Graves whose initials, "S. A. D.," did so much to convey local immortality upon him.

Mining is thirsty work, and entertaining miners is an enterprise which best goes forward glass in hand. Bullock wrote to his partner Sol Star that he had been to New York in February of 1877 and "secured an agency for Century whiskey," along with a supply of cigars, whiskey, tea, and condensed milk, items which do not figure largely in the stocking of a modern hardware store, and which must have brought him into conflict with many another full-time dispenser of malt, vinous, and spirituous beverages, among them John Herrmann and John Trebor, who began business as Herrmann and Trebor, wholesale and retail dealers in alcoholic goods, in the spring of 1877, and by 1884 were doing about $100,000 a year business. They held the agency for Anheser's (as they spelled it) Saint Louis beer for the community, competing with Hugh McCaffrey, who dealt in all alcoholic drinks and seems to have specialized in "bottled ale and porter." Eventually Trebor, whose business had grown to dominate the liquor trade of the Hills, was forced to move to Beulah, Wyoming, just over the border, by the wave of prohibition laws and sentiments which swept the state of South Dakota during the 1890s. Another liquor dealer, Harris Franklin, later a notable financier, mining man, hôtelier, and generally prime example of what could be done in the way of Deadwood business, also made his start in beverages and tobacco, and by 1884 his annual trade amounted to $125,000 a year, and his profits, invested wisely in the Golden Reward and several other mines, ended up building Deadwood's Franklin Hotel, which is still Deadwood's most interesting and imposing hostelry.

The life of the liquor dealer was not all beer and skittles. Moonshiners, supplying untaxed and hence low-cost but corrosive joy-juice, were often apprehended and their wares impounded, a process which continued on up into the early 1930s, for the Black Hills were famous, even as late as Prohibition times, for the sagacity and secretiveness of their bootleggers, and the zeal and diligence of their revenue agents. Liquor, always outlawed on an Indian reservation (and the Hills were of course in the very center of such a reservation in their early days) called for illegal producers, and these, in turn, summoned up officers whose duty it was to apprehend them. Within a couple of miles of my childhood home in the Hills there were at least three stills that I knew of at the time, and others that I learned of later on—and now and then, roaming nearby, I still come upon relics of isolated buildings and activities which seem much too secluded to have been entirely legitimate. Near Deadwood there was a still in Spruce Gulch that was broken up in March 1877, and another somewhere on the slopes of Terry Peak, and doubtless many another distiller throughout Deadwood's history stirred his mash and cooked his brew, boiled off his product, and hauled it to market without paying the liquor taxes in their entirety.

Mixed drinks and temperance beverages were apparently also in demand, for in the spring of 1877 Mr. S. H. Woods departed the Hills to return with a soda water machine and a supply of bottled soda water. Mr. A. Large a few weeks later established a competing business in Elizabethtown, producing not only soda water but sarsparilla and ginger ale. Beer was brewed by L. S. Parkhurst and Company as early as June 1876, and the famous Gold Nugget Beer was created in Central City. Rosenkrants and Werner's City Brewery on Main Street opposite Star and Bullock's sold quarts for a quarter of a dollar, and kept a cold lunch available, although their goods were not as healthful as Schlitz's, which "quenches thirst, tones up the system, prolongs life, and made Milwaukee famous," at least in the words of a local advertisement. By the turn of the century the Black Hills Brewing and Malting Company of Central City, in evident defiance of prohibitionary statute, was selling twenty-four quarts of beer for $2.50, about 10½¢ a quart, and Deadwood thirsts continued to be thoroughly slacked. Doubtless this enthusiasm for beer was due in considerable part to the large number of emigrants of German extraction who had come to Deadwood, for these emigrants were, except for those from the British Isles, the most numerous group of foreign-born citizens in town, and their enthusiasm for their beer gardens was notorious.

The line between saloons, dancehalls, rooming houses, restaurants, and the more formal and prestigious hotels was a narrow one, and many an enterprise that called itself one of these was, in actuality, another. The Grand Central Hotel opened in June 1876, with Lucretia "Aunt Lou" Marchbanks, a mahogany-colored (indeed, she was called Mahogany to her face) cook of remarkable talents in charge of its kitchen. Alas, the Father De Smet mine eventually lured her away to cook for the management of that coming enterprise, and still later she left to operate a roadhouse at Rocky Ford, between Belle Fourche and Sundance, Wyoming. While she was at the Grand Central, her sunny temper and outstanding biscuits set the standard for the culinary efforts for the whole town. During the gold rush of the 1870s the cost of room and board at the best of Deadwood's hotels was from twelve to twenty dollars a week; at a boarding house it ran eight to ten dollars, and a miner, batching in a tent or dugout, could support himself and companions at from three to five dollars a head, but it was no bargain, for any savings probably had to be later invested in patent digestive powders to soothe the stomachs corrupted by greasy pork and soggy flapjacks. These early hotels and restaurants went through a decorative mania, festooning fancy-colored cut paper trimmings around their walls, the fire hazards thus created being deemed a small price to pay for the added beauty thus bestowed. By 1880, toward the end of the rush times, the French Hotel was erected, where "Alphonso the polite presides over the bar," indicating that it was probably more of a saloon than a dignified hotel. Ben Hazen, in recognition of the dignity of hotel work, listed himself in the 1878 city directory as a "Hotelist, Lower Main"; but a hotel in that area could very well have been a bordello, although in individual cases it is hard to tell.

The Merchant's Hotel, built in 1879 by Jacob Wertheimer, had forty-five well-furnished rooms, billiard parlors and "sample rooms," these last being in the parlance of the times either rooms where commercial travelers could display their goods or barrooms where the public could sample, or even more stringently examine, the wares offered at the hotel. The appetites and tastes of the times are well demonstrated by the dinner bill of fare at the Merchants Hotel dining room:

SOUP
Vegetable Soup

BOILED
Brisket of Beef, Horseradish Sauce

Tongue with Egg Sauce
Corned Beef and Cabbage

ROAST
Loin of Beef
Saddle of Veal with Dressing
Rack of Mutton

ENTREES
Beef a la Mode aux Champignons
Chicken Fricassee, ala Mederia [*sic*]
Macaroni Forms, a l'Italienne
Baked Pork and Beans
Queen Fritters, Sherry Wine Sauce
Jenny Lind Pancakes, with Currant Jelly

VEGETABLE
Boston Baked Brown Potatoes
Green Peas
Asparagus with Cream Sauce

DESSERT
Mince Pie, Green Apple Pie, Strawberry Pie
Lemon Pie, Vanilla Ice Cream
Cakes, Candies, Nuts, &c.

French coffee, Buttermilk, Crackers & cheese,
Ice Tea, tea

This was for every day—on holidays they outdid themselves. Breakfast was served from 6:30 to 9:30 A.M.—the Merchants was obviously not a workingman's house—dinner from 12:00 to 2:30, and supper from 5:00 to 7:00. The diner, of course, did not partake of every dish, and there were probably days when not every dish was available had he wished to partake of all them; he ordered what he wanted from each category, and often would skip one or two. Still, it was a gastronomic display of considerable magnitude, and calculated to warm the cockles of the diner's heart clear down to the bottom, and send him from the dinner table in a somnolent and satisfied condition.[16]

The Overland Hotel, run by Pichler and Bartles, was in 1878 "a new house newly furnished." The building, which is still doing business, was three stories high, with twenty-six bedrooms and two large "parlors," or what would today be thought of as lobbies. Most of the rooms had stoves, and were also warmed by a warm-air pipe which went the length of the building. The kitchen was "presided over by a clean, neat, and intelligent white man," although considering the popularity of Chinese restaurants and the fame of Aunt Lou Marchbanks, it is hard to see why his color was necessarily a recommendation. No bar was kept on the premises, and any potential guest who appeared at the desk in an intoxicated condition was guided to a more suitable establishment next door.

The grandest hotel in town—and one which still serves the public—was not built until the turn of the century, but the efforts that went into starting it would probably have launched a battleship. In 1891 the Deadwood Board of Trade bought a lot on Sherman Street and raised twenty thousand dollars as a bonus to be given to the entrepreneur who would build a hotel on it. The Casey Company of Chicago began work but soon quit. In 1892 the Deadwood Hotel Company of Anson Higby, D. A. McPherson, and William Selbie (a famous promoter) took over, but without any noticeable results, and Seth Bullock, the hardware man, took over from them and in 1895 built the Bullock Hotel, a forty thousand dollar three-story sixty-room, steam-heated hotel on the spot, a building that still stands although now used for other purposes.

The Deadwood Business Club, as successor to the Board of Trade, raised money and subscriptions to the amount of $150,000 in an effort to build yet another hotel suitable to the dignity of the burgeoning city, one that would be a truly "metropolitan hotel." The building was named for Harris Franklin, one of the principal subscribers, and the four-story edifice of brick and stone opened on 4 June 1903, with eighty rooms, half of them with baths (a novelty for the times), electric lights, steam heat, two ladies' private parlors, elevators, and all rooms with brass or fancy iron beds supporting hair box springs and solid comfort. The grand ball given to celebrate the occasion found the musicians nearly obscured by potted palms, and the rank and beauty of the community all in attendance. Alas, in the 1920s the hotel put on an ill-timed addition, and never fully recovered from this financial burden at the time when the Great Depression was just around the corner. The Franklin, however, continues to serve the public with comfort and aplomb, and has added a motel, across the street, for those desiring more up-to-date accommodations. [17]

Odd names were then, as now, current as restaurant attention getters which use soon faded into the commonplace. Johnny Varne's eating place at Gayville was the X–10–U–8; R. S. Hukell ran the Eatephone at 109 Maine Street. A tiny lunch counter beside the Bella Union Theater was "Crumbs of Comfort Along the Crack in the Wall," and a news item in the form of a poem advised the potential diner:

> When you write home to your blossom,
> And want good news to tell,
> Say you had your Sunday dinner
> At the crowded IXL.[18]

As has been remarked, the line between hotels and restaurants was a thin one, the distinction being, then as now, that a hotel might provide both room and board, while the restaurant provides only the latter. The earliest facilities were limited: "When you have mentioned slap-jacks, beans, bacon and coffee, you were at the bottom of the bill of fare," said an early gold rusher.[19] By the spring of 1877, however, you could get a good Sunday dinner with ice cream for fifty cents at Delmonico's, and less ostentatious places would doubtless feed you well, but without the ice cream, for a good deal less, for there were twenty-eight eating places in town, and the Syndicate, a "first class short order house," would feed you at any hour for twenty-five cents, and provide more formal meals at 5:30 and 11:30 A.M. and 5:00 P.M., although the meals presumably did not come up to the level of the Metropolitan, in Central City, which advertised "everything *bon ton*" with "first class meals at low rates." The Palace Restaurant on Sherman Street "next to the Opera House" called itself the finest and largest in the Great West, and claimed "the richest silverware west of Chicago," while Chris Sasse's on Lee Street summoned, "All ye gluttons and all ye fasters [it was the Lenten Season] come and be happy," for Sasse's was the "place that puts Delmonico in the shade."

Gradually the cheap restaurant business tended to fall into the hands of Chinese proprietors, whose diligence and economy enabled them to serve a good meal and make money where another less careful host might either starve himself or his customers. These were not chop suey joints specializing in Chinese food, but simple American diners where "nice tables are set, and everything in the way of eatables is provided," as Wong Chong said of his Chicago Restaurant. Service and some of the cooking tended to be unconventional:

one Chinese proprietor habitually inquired, "What kind pie you want—we got apple," which kept the diner from having to make a hard decision.

Although agriculture, except for a couple of truck gardens, was manifestly impossible in the steep valleys and mountains around Deadwood itself, the surrounding meadows and the plains only four miles to the north provided ample opportunity for farming and grazing and thus provided the Deadwood grocers with many of their supplies. The mines and the lumbering activities provided a steady market for produce, and with the coming of the railroads in the late 1880s grain and cattle could also go economically to eastern markets. In 1879 the Spearfish Farmer's Union imposed a minimum price on its members, binding them not to sell grain for less than 2½¢ a pound in any of the mining camps, or 2¢ a pound in farming areas, indicating, perhaps, that crops did not always find a ready market that would keep up prices on its own.

Although the stranger to the Plains may suppose that when a rancher turns a cow out he has to pack her up a lunch to keep her from starving to death before she comes home again, the prairie grasses, although sparse, are nutritious, and by 1879, 150,000 cattle were grazing in and around the Hills, and by 1888 there were 80,000 head of cattle and 40,000 head of sheep in the six Black Hills counties alone. By 1925 there were 325,000 cattle in the area. The cattle trade headquartered around Belle Fourche, but a good deal of the money that it generated rubbed off on Deadwood, even though it became the custom among the range cattlemen not to sell to local butchers for fear that the meat in skinned-out sides, which could not be identified by a brand, would lead to rustling on the cattle ranges; they sold to distant markets instead, and fresh meat in the Hills came, if it came at all, from small grazing and ranching activities whose owners felt they could keep an eye on their own cattle.[20]

Such, then, was Deadwood's business: bustling, eager, optimistic, grandiose, fed by the gold of the mines, the harvests of the prairies, and the enthusiasm of its boosters and promoters. If the gold brought money, the merchants brought stability, and there are today a good many more businesses in Deadwood that date from the gold rush days than there are mines of similar antiquity. The miner knew that his mine, sooner or later, would play out; the merchant knew that there would be other mines and miners to supply when any single mine was finished. The miners brought in money, and they spent it, and called for goods and culture; the merchants and businessmen mined the miners, and seem to have made the better thing of it.

FOUR

The Professional Men

"Wisdom? Hell, we got more wisdom in Deadwood than you could find in an ordinary college.
Every other man you meet swells out and acts like
he's somebody."

An old-timer

"An ox, ma'am, is a bull that has gone to the dentist and had his teeth pulled, to keep him from
biting the heifers."

An old-timer

"A town is young just as long as it stays off the
railroad. . . . But Deadwood was young so long
that it will never quite forget its youth."

Buffalo Bill Cody

"Don't bite the hand that feeds the golden calf."

An old-timer

IN MARCH 1876 an eastern party headed for the gold fields of the
Black Hills "with all the various elements of good society represented—there being three teachers, one doctor, four merchants, *but
no lawyers.*" It was not a proportion that held good for long. By the
summer of 1876 nine lawyers were said to be in town, but the absence of courts and laws kept them from prospering, and one was
forced to deal faro at the Melodeon for a living, and another worked
as a common laborer on Claim No. 4 on Deadwood Creek. Within
a year, however, there were over fifty lawyers in town, a number
which thereafter seems to have been pretty constant throughout the
mining days, although considering the many and varied estimates of
the number of attorneys, it is hard to put much faith in the exactness
of the count.[1]

Notable among lawyers was Eben W. Martin, who came to
Deadwood in 1880 and formed the law partnership of Van Cise,
Wilson and Martin. Martin was later congressman for the district,
and a close friend of Theodore Roosevelt, whose sons romped across

the prairies with his son Paul, and he later moved to Hot Springs, where the nearby small community of Martin Valley still bears his name.

Chambers Kellar came late to the Hills, but his influence and that of his son Kenneth C. Kellar have long been felt especially in the legal prosperity of the Homestake mine, which they both served as chief counsel. Kellar, senior, came to Deadwood in 1898, and was examined for the bar of that city by Col. William H. Parker, who with that pompousness which in those days passed for dignity, inquired if young Kellar's conduct toward women was all that it should have been. Kellar pleaded the Fifth Amendment against self-incrimination and was forthwith admitted to the bar, whether legal or spirituous is not entirely clear, but it probably was both. Four times Kellar found it necessary in court to add physical violence to the merits of the cases that he represented, and indeed he seems to have made a virtue of a notoriously short temper which in a lesser man might have been considered a shortcoming. His tombstone is inscribed "Chambers Kellar—Distinguished Gentleman," a tradition in the law that his son Kenneth amply continued.[2]

The roster of the distinguished in Deadwood was not confined to the professions. In 1878 R. D. Jennings described himself as an "ex-internal revenue collector" and John Lawrence as an "ex-county treasurer." S. V. Chase was a "Black Hills infant," with whatever distinctions this title might convey. Oliver Cloud, doubtless some sort of factotum, was known to one and all as "Socks," and a good many citizens were distinguished by the title of "colored" as if it were an occupation or a trade, and in the case of Dan Hicks, who "will make flower beds, care for plants, clear yards, clean and lay carpets, wash windows, take down stoves, etc.," it seems to have been a full-time occupation. M. Liebmann hired a Mrs. Bemus, of New York, to superintend his cloak and dress department. F. W. L. Pieper made a business of "washing and renovating feather beds and pillows, making them as good as new" and promised one-day service. Miss C. E. Hinley, among many others, offered to the business world "stenography and typewriting" and would go anywhere to take dictation, promising to "return the work promptly and in good shape." Mrs. Alford gave lessons in "the new jewel chain decone work" and decorated linens and cushions, and a Mrs. Mellick provided "shampoo, massage, hair dressing and manicuring" at the same location in L. C. Miller's flats. Maude Warner MacPhetridge at 20 Denver Avenue taught both vocal and instrumental music, and the mortuary parlors of the Black Hills Undertaking Company framed pictures on the side. Horsehair work consisting of hatbands, bridles and watch fobs made in various penitentiaries was offered as an art form of interest to the public, and any man who could perform in this artistic line was therefore viewed with some trifling suspicion by his acquaintances.[3]

Other professions were also well represented. Doctors, of course, were present in Deadwood—five of them from the earliest times, and they will be discussed in more detail as an adjunct to public health. Rohleder and Smith, among many others, worked as civil and mining engineers and U.S. deputy surveyors, and announced in 1878 that "patent work was a specialty," the patents being not mechanical but those conveying title to federal lands to those mining upon them. Al Burnham, an architect, came to Deadwood with the gold rush and in twenty-one years built and designed most of the major business buildings of the town.

To be a newspaper editor is to be an optimist, else the constant exposure to the follies and foibles of mankind would drive the editors to despair; this ingrained optimism must be the reason that so many newspapers began in gold rush towns. A. W. Merrick's *Black Hills Pioneer* first appeared on 8 June 1876, and continues publication to the present. Later in 1876 the issues had to appear on dingy wrapping paper, and the next year it now and then came out on paper the color of which was "a shade between the Aurora Borealis and a new $13 saddle." The Deadwood newspapers all tried to make a custom of printing on brown paper (which is one reason microfilms of these early papers are so hard to read), calling it "El Dorado style," but fortunately this custom was short-lived. The early papers seem not to have been held in much esteem: "If a man wants gun wadding, he goes and pays four bits for a paper," said one observer, noting that "sometimes it's a daily, and then when the compositors get drunk it don't come out for several days. . . . Sometimes it comes out twice a week, and sometimes twice a day," which was not surprising, the newspaper offices being sandwiched "between two houses of peculiar traffic—a layer of virtue to two of vice," either of which may have served to distract the attention of the staff from its appointed duties. The *Pioneer* would be delivered, it was claimed, for eighteen dollars a year or two dollars a month, payment in *cash*, not "coon-skins, scalps, or watered bug juice," for the *Pioneer* intended to "prospect through the murky channels of literature solely for their colors."[4]

Porter Warner and W. P. Newhard's *Black Hills Daily Times* began publication on 7 April 1877, and both it and the *Pioneer* followed the common practice of offering a weekly edition which collected all the important news from the preceding six issues into one handy compendium. A partial list of Deadwood newspapers available at the South Dakota State Historical Society in Pierre shows the multiplicity of these journalistic endeavors. They changed names, merged one into the other, disappeared and appeared again, moved to other towns and came back, used different names or subtly altered the names they commonly used, so a true and accurate list is hard to compile, but basically these were the Deadwood papers that you could read from 1876 to the present:

Black Hills Daily Times, 1877–97
Black Hills Mining Review, 1903–1907
Black Hills Pioneer, 1876–91
Black Hills Weekly Pioneer, 1879–1923
Black Hills Weekly Times, 1879–1923
Deadwood Daily Pioneer-Times, 1897–present
Deadwood Weekly Pioneer Times, 1879–1923 on and off
Equality, 1899–1900
Evening Independent, 1897–1902
Evening Press, 1880
Independent, 1887–97
Lantern, 1905–1909
Telegram, 1908–27
Western Enterprise, 1879–80

All except the *Pioneer* and the *Times*, which eventually combined, were short-lived, their brief but tumultuous existences perhaps shortened by the excesses of spleen and partisanship which were so common in the press of the period.

"The Pioneer, our cheap-john morning contemporary," said an early issue of the *Times*, "is tooting its own horn in its usual maudlin manner." The *Times* claimed that it could fill its own columns "with the same character of lies that the Pioneer is regaling itself with from day to day," but the *Times* believed that *its* readers did not desire such trash in their daily paper. This style of editorial bombast popularized by Dickens's Eatanswill *Gazette* and *Independent* (in *The Pickwick Papers*) seems to have been for nearly four generations part of

the intellectual equipment of a newspaper editorial writer: "To de-
nominate the driveling brain-softened 'terrible example' of the
Spearfish Register a hopeless ass would be a gross injustice—to the
ass," said the *Times* in 1883, and "to brand him as a toady, and a
traitorous toady, an ingrate lickspittle, through predestination, inclination and natural selection, is to compliment him. . . . We will
not descend into this animal's congenial gutter to fight with it in its
natural filth for we abhor contact with vermin," the editorial continued, for the *Register's* editor was "an inborn Judas, a wretched and
irreclaimable journalistic prostitute, guilty of all crimes against journalistic nature, a practicer of all literary abominations unnameable
and nameless, [and his *Register*] endeavors to procure for itself the
dignity of our expressed contempt." It is difficult not to believe that
such editorials were produced by some sort of agreement between
the editors, each hoping to stimulate his own circulation by the ve-
hemence of his invective.[5]

Like the newspapers, the banks were many, varied, and influential, shifting and changing names, personnel, and activities as the
needs of the community and the skill of the proprietors dictated.
The first bank in Deadwood was a small private institution operated
by James W. Wood and bearing his name. It began operation in
April 1876, along with the gold rush. Its assets consisted of one iron
safe, in which valuables of all kinds could be safely stored for a
modest fee, and its banking activities consisted almost entirely of
buying gold from the prospectors at about two dollars an ounce less
than it was sold for at the Denver mint or eastern financial centers.
Profits on these transactions were said to be "coined," the assumption being that the gold itself had been converted at the U.S. mint
into golden ten dollar eagles or twenty dollar double eagles although
of course the difficulty of shipping gold generally resulted in the
return of credits to the bank in the form of paper currency or bills
of exchange. Obviously a bank that was doing well was said to be
"coining money," although it is doubtful that this phrase originated
in Deadwood, or that it ever referred solely to its transactions in
bullion.

The Miners and Mechanics Bank opened in July 1876; indeed,
Seth Bullock in his memoirs claimed it was "the first bank in addition to the faro banks" in the gambling houses, but in this he seems
to have been mistaken, unless this was a name given by Wood to his
own banking operation. The bank had a large safe, and would issue

paper money at a charge of 10 percent. Bank drafts from the East, the common way for an investor to bring his money to the Hills, would be cashed into gold for a 5 percent charge, and these drafts were also sold to those desiring money easily transported eastward for another charge of 5 percent—transactions which would make modern-day issuers of travelers' checks green with envy. In August of 1876 James K. Miller and James McPherson founded another private banking house, Miller and McPherson. McPherson was a major Hills financier, later financing the Deadwood Central Railroad, and dealing extensively in Deadwood real estate.

The firm of Stebbins, Post and Wood began operations in April 1877, and by September was conducting transactions at the rate of over one hundred thousand dollars a day, an astonishing business for a bank in so small a community. Business was so good that the firm hired a gang of armed guards to stand watch over the construction of their banking building. Many scurrilous canards have circulated about one of the founders of this firm, the most amusing of these being that he founded an orphanage in Denver and, in his idle hours, proceeded to fill it with his own bantlings, and that both his son and grandson went to their graves waiting for the old rascal to depart this world for a warmer, leaving them his money. Depart for a warmer he did, rumor has it, but for Africa, with two lissome damsels to provide such warmth as the tropic climes denied him, and when last heard from he was over one hundred and continuing to disport himself in a manner as pleasant as it was unseemly. Alas for the legend; it was doubtless based upon the old gentleman's will, which did indeed provide for a gift of five thousand dollars to found an orphan asylum, but when the will was probated, there was not enough money in the estate to fulfill the bequest, and the tale is mentioned here to lay to rest this happy but fallacious fable. By the spring of 1879 a new firm, Stebbins, Post and Mund had been created from the old, Wood becoming one of the founders of the First National Bank of Deadwood.[6]

Brown and Thum's Bank, a private partnership of George W. Brown and M. C. Thum, dealing in bullion and exchange, opened on 24 May 1877, with the event celebrated by a grand reception: "George Shingle says he will have a corps of attentive waiters to supply the wants of gentlemen who desire anything in his line of refreshments, and we do not speak wide of the mark when we say he can put them up right." Their advertisement in Collins's 1878

Directory announced that the firm would "transact a general banking business, issue drafts available in all parts of the United States and Europe" (many of the miners who came in with the rush were foreign-born), transfer money by telegraph, pay interest on time deposits, instead of charging for safekeeping as in the early days of the gold rush, make advances on ore and bullion, perform collections, buy gold dust, and buy and sell government, territorial and county bonds.

Stebbins and Post founded a new institution, the Merchants National Bank of Deadwood, in March of 1879, a bank which soon achieved an annual turnover of several millions of dollars. Seth Bullock, the notable marshal and merchant, was its vice-president, and W. E. Adams the merchant, J. Deetkin the druggist, and many others famous in the town were soon associated with it. Two other banks, evidently formed during the 1880s, were George Hickok's Deadwood National Bank and the American National Bank, founded by Harris Franklin and Ben Baer, and often called the Franklin and Baer Bank, both of which were absorbed into the First National during the Panic of 1893. Franklin, at least, does not seem to have suffered from the transaction—he was reputedly worth over $5 million.

The First National Bank, created out of Stebbins, Post, and Wood's earlier enterprise, went on through various permutations to become the Hills-wide First National Bank of the Black Hills, presently affiliated with the Northwest Bank Corporation. It began operation in 1878, with Samuel N. Wood as its cashier and L. R. Graves its president, and in August 1878 it underwent a reorganization which installed O. J. Salisbury as its president, D. K. Dickinson its vice-president, and D. A. McPherson (not the same man as the earlier banker James McPherson) its cashier, but Graves continued as a director, along with P. E. Sparks, and B. P. Dague (a name eminent in Deadwood history for many community services) as assistant cashier. Its officers formed what R. E. Driscoll denominated a "roll call of the wealthy men of the Black Hills, and names of nationwide renown." That may be stretching the truth a little, but the notion is a sound one, for bankers, when they succeed at all, tend to do well for themselves, the common, but one hopes erroneous, supposition being that with all that money passing through their hands it would be a dullard indeed who could not arrange for some of it to stick to his own fingers. Furthermore, banking, because it obviously deals with money, puts the banker in the know about any business opportunities which may be going forward in his community, and his bank connection generally provides him with the money or the credit to take advantage of them. R. H. Driscoll, for example, seems to have often invested in mines on the advice of Thomas J. Grier, superintendent of the Homestake, and he certainly profited immensely from a relatively modest investment in the highly profitable Wasp No. 2 gold mine at Flatiron on Yellow Creek.

Banks were not the only place to put your gold dust. The post office during the rush issued five hundred dollars worth of postal money orders every day, about as safe a way to send wealth back home as could be found. The frequent advertisements for Hall's safes indicated that a good many safes were sold in Deadwood, and that, if sold, it was because the populace in general had something to put into them. Sensitive gold scales too came into the Hills, for gold, in the form of placer gold dust, was for years the generally accepted medium of exchange, and this showy custom was maintained far beyond necessity for the aura of reckless and munificent abandon which it lent to the most mundane financial transactions. When a prospector tossed his bag of dust upon the bar for the bartender to pinch out fifty cents worth of dust for a drink, it advertised the mineral wealth of the whole area. Coined money was scarce, paper money carried a 10 percent discount, the smallest price for anything was twenty-five cents, and not much could be got for it; but gold dust, and later silver dollars, took the place of all of them. When the average citizen hung his britches on a hook on going to bed, the hook had to be a stout one, for one hundred dollars in silver would weigh close to five pounds. Both gold and silver continued popular in Deadwood as long as they were available, for such hard money always impressed the visitors.

The price at which placer gold would be accepted depended upon a variety of factors. Some of it was actually purer and of more value than the rest, depending upon the mining district from which it came. Some districts, too, produced more "black sands," iron or tin oxides, and although their gold dust was pure enough, it generally came to the market unintentionally adulterated with these impurities. The Deadwood merchants tried to set the price of a troy ounce of gold dust at a reasonable $18.00, but the miners howled so that the merchants had to attempt a system of gold values for each placering area: Deadwood Gulch $17.10 to the ounce, Bobtail $16.50, Nigger Gulch $18.00, and Little Rapid Creek $18.25. The miners, however, would not stand for it, and custom settled on $20.00 an ounce as the high but standard price. Merchants and bankers, of course, adjusted the prices of their goods and credits to match this inflated value. Such a practice was a bit hard on those miners who brought purer gold to market, but the ease of dealing with so pleasantly rounded a figure as $20.00 an ounce made up for the inconvenience.

With so much gold dust used as circulating medium the average business man became adroit at taking fifty cents worth from a miner's sack, pinching it out between thumb and forefinger. If his fingers were greasy, doubtless some of the dust stuck to them—bartenders, for example, tended to oil their hair, and run their fingers through it carelessly after each sale, and then wash their hair carefully and pan the bath water at the end of their shifts. The balances that weighed the gold for larger transactions often rested on a deep-piled piece of Brussels carpeting, and the carpet was shaken out into a gold pan at the end of every day. Bankers might be above such tricks, but merchants were not, and the saloonkeepers had probably invented them. Another device, the constant companion of the jeweler's balance, was the blower, a shallow, shovel-shaped piece of tin six inches wide at one end, with three turned up edges, narrowing to three inches at its narrow open end. Gold dust was poured from the sack through the air, its dirt and light sand blown out of it as it fell, and more vigorous puffs upon it as it lay in the blower might remove at least some of the heavy black metallic sands. A really enthusiastic puff might remove some of the gold too, but if it did, that gold fell upon the carpeting previously mentioned and became the property of the man who did the blowing. The blower also tended to remove any brass filings, which were frequently palmed off as gold dust upon the uninitiated, but being far lighter than gold, they could easily be blown away. In 1877 a gang of eight sharpers were arrested for trying to bring off such a swindle; "They certainly had brass," the *Times* commented.[7]

The banking business was a good one. Interest rates of from 2 to 5 percent *a month* prevailed during the gold rush; presumably a prospector would borrow at any rate if he expected he had a good claim and needed the capital to work it. If the claim paid out, the interest on his loan was negligible compared to his profits; if the prospect was a failure, the likelihood was that the miner would not remain in camp for the banker to collect his interest, or his principal either. Bankers, recognizing this risk, adjusted the interest rates to provide for a substantial number of bad accounts. In the 1880s interest of 2 percent a month was common—that was one reason why so many banks started up—but by the turn of the century the average merchant, at least, could get his money at 12 percent a year.[8]

Like most men who deal with matters of importance, bankers often disguised the seriousness of their endeavors with light-hearted jape and jest. During the 1896 "silver" election between Bryan and McKinley, a banker named Jack Gray, one of the goldbugs, took his pay in gold as usual, but saw to it that his silverite companion, Democrat Billy McLaughlin, was paid his $250 salary in ponderous silver dollars, to see if he liked "free and unlimited coinage of silver at 16 to 1" as much as his presidential candidate. McLaughlin, staggering under the burden of his silver dollars, which weighed about twelve pounds, admitted that he could at least see the weight of the Republican argument in favor of a gold standard. When paper money finally came in after the 1913 Federal Reserve Act, many an old-timer objected violently when a bank teller tried to palm off "printed ———— paper" on him, and insisted, as was his right until 1933, on receiving his money in gold. Many an executor clear down to the 1980s opening safe-deposit boxes even after possession of gold became illegal, found the boxes so heavy with coins that they could hardly be moved, for men who had dug the gold tended to save it for the future, no matter how much the law might dictate otherwise.

During the financial panic of 1907 the Homestake Mining Company deposited their gold in the Denver mint and, as was their right, demanded gold coin in exchange for it, which the mine officials then deposited in the First National Bank, providing that bank with a liquidity unknown in the financially depressed parts of the country, for not only did the bank have *cash*, it even had *specie*. During the 1933 bank holiday a similar scheme was employed to make sure that the Homestake payroll would continue uninterrupted. The Homestake could not demand gold coin from the mint in return for its bullion, but it could and did demand currency, which again was deposited in the bank, in the amount of five hundred thousand dollars; it took the bank's entire staff to count it when it arrived. Fearful that this large deposit might be frozen along with other bank funds during the holiday, the Homestake incontinently withdrew the money shortly thereafter, and again the whole bank staff counted it out. Two days later, when banks were permitted to open, the entire sum came back in again, and the mine's payroll was made up out of it, and for the third time in a few days the tellers laboriously received and paid out half a million dollars in small bills.[9]

Banking was less formal in those days. Among the loans accepted by the First National was one secured by collateral consisting of 35.5 cows. The half cow was not a side of beef in cold storage, but merely represented a portion of an undivided interest in 71 cows which the borrower had pledged as security to obtain his loan. Banks never paid in pennies before the turn of the century; they always rounded off to the nearest nickel. Real estate loans were invariably charged off as bad debts after a year or so, in order to avoid the state tax on undivided profits. These loans were perfectly good, and the payments on them were coming in steadily, but such assets were thought by the bankers to present too tempting a target for the tax assessors, so the loans were written off as if in default, no matter how good they were. Loans to gamblers were common, and they were almost invariably repaid, if the borrower lived that long.[10]

Loans to madams were not unknown, and a famous tale involves old Poker Alice Tubbs, who came to the Sturgis bank one day and asked to borrow two thousand dollars so she could build an addition to her establishment, make a trip to Kansas City to recruit some fresh girls, and in general improve her services to the community. She stoutly averred that she could pay the loan back "in a couple of years," and the banker in a light-hearted moment let her have the money. In less than a year she had paid it all, with appropriate interest. The banker, of course, was delighted to have the loan paid off—he had had some misgivings as to whether it would be paid at all—but curiosity prompted him to inquire of Mrs. Tubbs how she had been able to pay it off so quickly.

"Well," said Poker Alice, mumbling the dead cigar she habitually held in the corner of her mouth, "it's this way. I'd knowed that the Grand Army of the Republic was a-goin' to have its Encampment here in Sturgis—I knowed about that. And I'd knowed that the state Elks' convention would be here, too. But you know, I'd plumb forgot about the Methodist District Conference!"[11]

Postal services for the Deadwood mining camps was established on 25 September 1876, when the first Concord coach came galloping into town, drawn by six prancing horses, a part of the Gilmer and

Salisbury stage line. "Now," said a happy miner, "we will get out letters from home—the last one I got had more whiskers than I have, and *I* haven't shaved since I left home!" On 20 March 1877 the Post Office Department at Washington announced that regular triweekly service would begin between Kearney, Nebraska, and Deadwood on 1 May, and between Hat Creek Station, in eastern Wyoming, and Deadwood the following month. On 10 April the Deadwood post office was opened for business with R. O. Adams postmaster. He later absconded with post office funds, and was replaced by Sol Star, who was later, although perhaps unjustly, thrown out of his office for his alleged part in the famous "star route frauds," which in the 1880s wildly inflated the costs of mail carried under local contracts. Many letters went unclaimed for weeks, and newspapers habitually published long alphabetical lists of names of addressees who had letters waiting for them at the post office. Long lines commonly formed at the general delivery windows, and as it was not customary for the postal clerks of that day to hand out mail for more than one name to a single applicant, it was no use for a distant camp to send in one man to wait in line to pick up the mail for his whole outfit. Each man had to get his own letters, or at least wait in line in turn for each of his companions. It was a rule which brought more miners to town, and that may have been the purpose of it. Service was slow, and stamps were usually unavailable. "Everybody growls about the post office," said the newspapers, and letters of complaint filled the columns of the press. The *Times* scornfully asked its readers to "look at the character of timber that is generally selected for postmasters. The lunatic at Central and the 'hoodlum' at another place [obviously Adams]" were enough to discredit any postal system.[12]

The telegraph reached Deadwood, coming north from Cheyenne via Fort Laramie, Hat Creek, and Red Canyon Station, on 1 December 1876, with operator James Halley sending out the first message to the mayor of Cheyenne, who replied in florid terms that he hoped his "efforts will be recognized and appreciated by your people." A grand ball was held, with a bonfire, the usual libations, and the customary orations. To its users it appeared that the operation of the telegraph was not governed by the usual laws of physics and electricty, for the entire mechanism seemed to have a personality of its own. During the daytime it worked well enough under Halley and other skillful operators (and it is notable that to be a telegraph operator was one of the first steps upward in the business world—it was often, as it was for Halley, the first rung on the managerial ladder for young men of ambition). In the evening, however, when the instrument was run by Sam Kelley, communication tended to dwindle, for the line, it was said, "knows Sam, and don't like him," and somewhere around Hat Creek the wires would seize upon Kelley's arrival in the Deadwood telegraph office as an excuse to climb down off the poles for a good night's rest. The transmission of a ponderous Russian name—obviously invented—also served to disrupt the fickle telegraph, for as the foreign name progressed along the wires it kinked the wires, knocked at least one lineman off a pole, and blew out all the batteries along the way, or so it was claimed by those whose job it was to keep the line in operation.[13]

Few developments show as clearly the quality of life in Deadwood and the money available to sustain it at a high level as do the early coming of the telephone and the electric light. The first telephone lines were installed in Deadwood in 1879, just a year after the first telephone had been installed in the White House at Washington, and two years before the first commercial line, between Providence and Boston, in the East. By 1881 forty miles of telephone lines united the "upper camps" of the northern Hills with the central Deadwood office, which had 100 connections and a need to increase them to 150 to keep up with the growing and persistent demand for telephone service. By 1883 Deadwood and Rapid City were connected, and through the latter town the outside world could reach the mines. In December 1883 the first electric lights came to Deadwood, where two power plants worked together, one to supply electricity to the railway that ran between Deadwood and Lead and the other providing power enough to light the city. This kind of development required a public that was well versed in the benefits to be conveyed upon them by modern engineering, and one that had the money to support such technology as soon as it was available. The mining engineers and the mines provided both; it was a long time before the telephone, and longer still before the electric light, would follow the plow across the plains to the average farming community, but the Black Hills mines had the know-how, the money, and the technological orientation to install these new inventions as soon as they could get them.

A gold mining community does not ship much out, at least in bulk, but a tremendous amount of material has to get shipped in.

The heavy machinery and dynamite and timber for the mines, and the food and household supplies for the miners—and these are not much produced in the immediate area around a mine—combine to create a demand for transportation of all kinds. Early shippers fought their way past the Indians, nightly laagering their mule- or ox-drawn wagons into protective circles as they made their way toward the sheltering trees and valleys of the Hills. The early Deadwood merchant P. A. Gushurst was one such hardy pioneer invader who fought his way past the hostiles into the Hills. Capt. C. V. Gardner, who brought in sixty thousand pounds of merchandise in the spring of 1876, was another. He came into the Hills in March 1876 with a large party, and even so they had to be rescued from an Indian attack by U.S. troops under Capt. James Egan. The trail from Cheyenne into the Hills was another barrier to transportation—a quagmire half a mile wide in the springtime, and often only cloven-footed oxen hitched five or six yokes to each wagon could pull the three-ton loads, although in drier weather fast freight, at least, was hauled in more rapidly by nimble mule teams. Getting down Splittail Gulch into Deadwood itself was a major undertaking before formal roads were maintained, and individual wagons had to be half lowered, half skidded down into the valley.[14]

Although independent "shotgun" freighters continued in business until the railroads came, and even after until the motor trucks replaced them, the bulk of the hauling business was in the hands of some twenty well-organized freighting firms. Fred T. Evans, a notable character who once offered a reform-bound preacher a thousand dollars if he could drive a bull team one day without cursing, hauled in 7 million pounds of freight from Pierre alone during 1880. The Merchants Line in six months brought in over 5.5 million pounds; Bramble and Company 1 million. The Northwestern Express, Stage and Transportation Company of Saint Paul connected Bismarck to the Hills with one thousand wagons, sixteen hundred oxen, six hundred mules, and five hundred employees, and in 1884 hauled over 16 million pounds of freight. Cuthbertson and Young in 1878 brought in a shipment of five hundred thousand pounds of mining machinery for the Homestake, including two Blake crushers that weighed over eight thousand pounds apiece, eighty eight-hundred-pound stamps, a ten-ton flywheel in sections, and all of the other equipment for an eighty-stamp mill. Freight rates ran from three to five dollars a hundred pounds to bring in goods from any of the railheads—Cheyenne, Sidney, Fort Pierre, or Bismarck—which accounts for the inflated price of goods in the area: a safe, for example, could cost ten dollars at the manufacturer's and sixty dollars laid down in an office in Deadwood. It made a difference in the prices.

The bullwhacker, like the trucker of today, tended to be outspoken and forthright in his conduct. The oxen were controlled only by the whacker's voice: "Gee, Haw and Whoa" for right, left, and stop, and a peculiar "Eeee-ya-HAAAA" accompanied by a crack of the whip in the air to indicate that forward movement was desired. The long bullwhips were used only for popping over the team, or on one side or the other to guide them right or left, for only a fool would scar his cattle and provide lodging places for crippling grubs and maggots, which would annoy the oxen and reduce the value of their hides. Confined thus to controlling his teams mainly by vocal persuasion, the bullwhacker tended to have a vocabulary in which words and phrases both sacred and profane figured largely, combined, perhaps, with biological terms and comments upon the perversity and depravity of those who had built the road, constructed the wagon, or sold the ox. Reliable witnesses testified that the air over a bullwhacker's head, in rough going, was as blue as if he had been smoking a cigar, and that in a thunderstorm no God-fearing man would come within a hundred yards of him—or of her, for that matter, for Calamity Jane Cannary was said to have now and then handled a bull train, and Madame Canutson could drive and swear with the best of them, although admittedly not many other women took up the profession.

One well-known teamster on the Fort Pierre trail was more or less of ordinary size from the waist up, but had notably short legs, hence his nickname, Shorty. Standing in the muddy trail one day, Shorty noticed a long train of wagons swing out of the road and wallow into a nearby bog, there to thrash its way around him. Walking over to the wagon boss, he inquired what was going on. The boss looked him over, cursed long and loud, and replied, "I thought you was standing in a hole." Shorty always claimed he had worn his legs down following his wagon from Fort Pierre to Deadwood, and many of the Deadwood children, with whom he was something of a favorite, probably believed him.[15]

There is no question about the nature of the most famous cargo that was ever hauled to Deadwood: it was Phatty (he spelled it so)

Thompson's wagonload of cats. Thompson had met a dancehall girl in town who suggested to him that she would like a cat to make her place seem homey. Merchants may also have indicated that there were lots of mice and only a few mousetraps in town. Anyway, Phatty betook himself to Cheyenne, built a crate on his wagon, and let it be known among the boys of the city that he would pay twenty-five cents for cats in sound and merchantable condition. He got eighty-two of them, miaowing and caterwauling, and set out for the Hills. All went well until he got past Hill City, where, on the first crossing of Spring Creek, the wagon tipped over and the cats escaped, but kindly prospectors assisted Phatty in recapturing them in return for a cat or two for themselves. When he got the load to Deadwood, he sold the animals to the merchants and dancehall girls for a ten dollar minimum, with fine Maltese cats going as high as twenty-five dollars. Stories that he trained a sextet of tomcats to sit on a fence and yodel by feeding them Swiss cheese were invented by George W. Stokes. Phatty's success, however, aroused much jealousy in the community, and after his first day's business some rascal liberated his remaining stock of cats, and they were never recovered. South Dakota's self-styled cowboy poet lariat Badger Clark wrote an epic poem about the incident, "The Cat Pioneers," and how they civilized the community:

> The hairy miner on a spree
> Full of remorse and beer,
> Gazed at the kitten on his knee,
> And shed a scalding tear.

> Then vowed to quit the maddening cup,
> And mend his ragged life,
> And get a shave, and straighten up,
> And send and fetch his wife.[16]

Henry Keets coined the phrase "stagecoach aristocracy" and said, "Those who came in by stage had a certain flair of vision and a steadiness of purpose. They are the movers and shakers of the world—the aristocrats of the frontier." To be considered a real native of Deadwood even today, you have to have ancestors who came in before the railroads, and, presumably, who had money enough to come by stagecoach. It was a rough journey, for the big Concord coaches were mounted on leather thorough braces and swung in every direction known to man and a few known previously only to women, and it was a rare journey that some inexperienced passenger was not deathly ill, as much so as he would have been on an ocean voyage. Only the frequent stops to change horses afforded relief, and the dismal meals—whiskey, hardtack, beans, coffee, and pork— served at most of the stations did not do much to soothe the stomach. The shortest route, to Pierre, took about thirty-six hours on the Northwestern Express, Stage and Transportation Company's coaches, which provided "gentlemanly and experienced messengers [guards]" and in the winter months announced "buffalo robes furnished for passengers." The cost seems to have run about fifty dollars over the years, whether the route ran from Fort Pierre, Sidney, Cheyenne, or Bismarck, in order that the companies could stay competitive with each other. Customer attitudes were more or less on the same line as those of the tourist at the Sea of Galilee, who asked a native boatman how much it would cost to see the place where Jesus walked on the water. Hearing the price and seeing the boat, he remarked, "I don't wonder that He chose to walk!" [17]

Nobody except a masochist ever actually enjoyed a stagecoach journey, and an idea of the conditions to be met with can be got from the 1877 advice to travelers that was printed by the *Omaha Herald*. It urged the passengers to avoid tight boots in cold weather; to walk when the driver told them to, both to ease the coach and to warm themselves; to avoid liquor, which made people freeze all the quicker; to put up with the food at the stations; to avoid pipes and cigars in the coach, and if they chewed, to spit to leeward; if they did drink, to buy their liquor before they started as that available at the stage stations was not of the best quality, and to pass the bottle around in a neighborly fashion; not to shoot, which scared the horses; not to swear, or discuss politics or religion; not to grease their hair, for traveling was dusty; and above all, not to "imagine for a moment that you are going on a picnic: expect annoyance, discomfort and some hardship."

The roster of the stage drivers best known in Deadwood includes many notables: Dave Dickey, who drove the first coach into town; and Frank Hunter, who drove the last one; Johnny Slaughter, who was killed by Little Reddie McKimmie of the Sam Bass gang in a holdup; Frank Doten, later sheriff; Harvey Fellows, who went on to perform on another even more dramatic stage, as an actor; Russ Hawley, who later worked for the Homestake; Gene Barnett, who was driving when the treasure stage was held up at Canyon

Springs; and George Gates, who taught little Estelline Bennett to drive, and warned her that only a fool went close to the edge of the road. These were men who enjoyed a status similar to that of an airline pilot of today, and perhaps their spectacular activities, perched high on the box, handling six reins as an organist handles a bank of keys, made them even more conspicuous, for these were the men who brought the six-horse stage into Deadwood at a gallop, whooping and hollering with the joy and excitement, well pleased to be the object of so much attention. It was an honor to sit beside the driver—one that not every pretty girl desired, but she got it anyway—which is a good deal more than even an airline pilot can offer nowadays. The drivers had a language all their own, and when Handsome Harry Hansen lay on his deathbed and Judge Bennett tried to reassure him, he replied, "No, Judge, I'm on the down grade, and I can't reach the brake block," and it was that night he died.[18]

The paths the stage trails took have often been described. Almost every house or barn that was in existence during the stagecoach days is now claimed to have once been a stage stop, and it probably was, for the frequent stops for meals or for fresh horses shifted and changed as the trails found better paths or the station tenders moved away. Basically there were three routes into the Hills from the south: one from Sidney which came northward along the eastern edge of the Hills; and the trail from Cheyenne which divided at Hat Creek Station, one route going north through Red Canyon up the middle of the Hills. When Indians made that early trail (which can still be traced by the quarter-mile posts that marked it) dangerous, it moved westward to a second route to go up the western side of the Hills. The Montana trail came in from the northwest, the Medora trail from the north, the Bismarck trail from the northeast, and the Pierre trail from the east, and each of these enjoyed a certain prominence as trail or steamer connections varied. The Cheyenne trail was the earliest and most famous; the Sidney trail, because it was the quickest, probably hauled, over the long run, the most traffic; and the Pierre trail, because it connected with steamboats on the Missouri River, hauled the bulky goods.

The general tone of stage travel perhaps can be illustrated by Ken Kellar's story of the Englishman, doubtless full of beans from the previous station, who broke wind in a closed and cold coach, and moving to open the window, remarked, "I say, you know, this air seems a bit fixed," to which a demure blond passenger replied with feeling, "It sure is, and you're the son-of-a-bitch that fixed it."[19]

To go anywhere by stagecoach was synonymous with being robbed. Persimmons Bill and his gang infested an area in the southern Hills at the mouth of Red Canyon. Sam Bass, as has been mentioned, at least once invaded the Hills with his gang of outlaws, and dozens of others preyed upon the travelers. Nobody but a fool carried valuables with him on a stagecoach, and anybody with money to take out of the Hills took it in the form of Wells Fargo certificates—the ancestors of modern traveler's checks—or in nonnegotiable letters of credit issued by a bank. Now and then one of the dancehall girls would try to secrete her folding money about her person, but the robbers generally searched it out anyway, although one who wound it up in her back hair did manage to get through safely, the robbers presumably searching elsewhere. Gold was shipped in bricks weighing about two hundred pounds, which were just a bit too heavy for a mounted thief to carry and take to the woods, and if a thief tried to escape with a gold bar in a wagon, he had to stick to the roads and generally could be hunted down. The stage companies, however, soon began to employ shotgun guards seated beside their drivers, and on the trails most heavily infested additional armed outriders rode along to protect the passengers and the bullion shipments. These precautions eventually reduced robberies of the passenger coaches—which were pretty poor pickings anyway—to an endurable level. The bullion shipments, however, continued to offer a tempting target for the bandits even though these coaches were hardly ever attacked successfully. The stage companies charged 1 percent of the value to haul the bullion from the Deadwood mines to Sidney for shipment on the Union Pacific. It left Deadwood twice a month in a one-ton safe accompanied by eight armed guards, and only once, at Canyon Springs east of Four Corners, Wyoming, was this stage robbed, and even then the company recovered almost all of the loot.

The roster of the stagecoach guards is a long and an honorable one. Scott Davis, who survived the Canyon Springs shoot-out, took up ranching in Nebraska; Billy Sample went to Mexico and continued in the stagecoach business; Bill Lynn, who stood six feet, seven inches, remained in Deadwood; Dick Bullock continued as a guard for the Homestake when the stages no longer needed him; Paul Blum, like driver Harvey Fellows, entered the dramatic arts; Gene

Decker opened a curio shop in Billings, Montana; Gail Hill died after being wounded in the Canyon Springs holdup; Boone May, who was one of the rougher law-enforcement officers in the business, went to South America; Howard Scott became a mining engineer; and Jesse Brown and A. M. Willard, who perhaps had done as much as anybody to pacify the roads that lead to Deadwood, wrote down their recollections of two turbulent frontier lives in *Black Hills Trails*, a classic of frontier law-enforcement literature.

In and around Deadwood communication to the neighboring camps was made possible—though hardly ever convenient—by the construction of privately owned toll roads. Deadwood, Centennial Prairie, and Crook City were connected with a road constructed at a cost of seventy-five hundred dollars. A wagon and a span of horses could make the trip for a dollar, each additional team cost another twenty-five cents, and special rates were available for larger groups. Horsemen, who could easily bypass the road anyway, were allowed to travel for nothing. Another road, run by C. C. Tyler and Frank Green, between Deadwood and Gayville along Deadwood Creek, was a constant nuisance to its builders, who had to keep rebuilding it, as prospectors mined it away in their search for placer gold. A second toll road to Crook City, run by J. Chase and A. Thomas, went down Whitewood Creek to Montana City then across the hills to Centennial Prairie. A 12.5-mile road led from Gayville to Spearfish. Lead and Deadwood were connected by a road which ran from Cleveland up Gold Run, the route of the present highway. Nobody liked toll roads, which seemed to monopolize the only routes between the towns, and to offer little but permission to pass in return for their tolls, and with the coming of county organization they appear to have been abandoned, to be replaced by public highways.

For nearly fifteen years Deadwood was a stagecoach town. As Buffalo Bill Cody said when he came to Deadwood years later, "A town is young just as long as it stays off the railroad. . . . But Deadwood was young so long that it will never quite forget its youth." Even the people in Deadwood did not seem to clamor for a railroad in the early days, for "they have a theory that railroads kill out the life of a growing Western town, often by bringing in too much competition in all lines of trade, cheapening commodities and overdoing everything." Still, the lure of cheap goods, especially mining supplies, brought in by inexpensive transportation, eventually proved irresistible.[20]

A detailed study of Black Hills railroads has yet to be fully accomplished, and will not be attempted here, but some suggestion of their complexities may indicate their impact on the Deadwood community. After 1890 you can hardly put your finger on a map of the Deadwood area without smudging a railroad line or two; their influence was all-pervading, and the shriek of a railroad whistle could be heard almost anywhere in the northern Hills.

The first railroad in the Black Hills other than mining company tramways was the little narrow-gauge Black Hills and Fort Pierre, built by the Homestake to bring wood to Lead from Woodville, and eventually extended southeastward to Piedmont to connect with the Chicago and North Western, and to bring lime to the mines from the Homestake kilns at Calcite on Elk Creek. The railroad equipment was hauled in by ox teams beginning in 1881, and when one branch of the line washed out in 1907, another was built, looping into the logging country around Este and Nemo on its way down to the foothills.

The Deadwood Central, another narrow-gauge line, was begun in 1888, to connect Deadwood via Gold Run with Lead. It was eventually extended to the camps around Terry and Trojan, operating on a third rail laid inside the standard-gauge tracks of the Grand Island and Wyoming branch of the Chicago, Burlington and Quincy.

The Fremont, Elkhorn, and Missouri Valley (later the Chicago and North Western) came to Rapid City from the south and pushed up along the eastern edge of the Hills, more or less along the route of the old Sidney Stage trail, to Whitewood in 1887, and on up Whitewood Creek to Deadwood in late 1890, where the arrival of the first train connecting the town with the outside world created quite a stir, for as Judge Bennett remarked, "We'll have to lock our doors, now." This line also went on north to Minnesela, and then to Belle Fourche, and on to Colony to serve the bentonite clay beds northwest of Belle. Belle Fourche was also connected to the coal mines just over the Wyoming border at Aladdin, Baker, Hay Creek, and Barrett Town by the little Wyoming and Missouri River line, traces of which can still be followed along South Dakota Highway 34.

The central portion of the Hills was served by the Grand Island and Wyoming branch of the Chicago, Burlington and Quincy, which entered the Hills at Edgemont, about where the old Cheyenne stage trail had come in. It then clawed its way northward through Minnekahta, where it sent a branch eastward to join the North Western at Hot Springs. It continued northward to Custer, Hill City (where it branched off to Keystone and the Addie tin mine), Mystic (where the Black Hills and Western "Crouch Line" joined it from Rapid City), Rochford, then Nahant (where the McLaughlin Tie and Timber Company railroad branched off), and on to Deadwood. In the northern Hills this rail line had still more branches—to Hanna, to Galena, and over the side of Spearfish Canyon to run down the canyon to the town of Spearfish—and it was perhaps the most pervasive railroad in the Hills.[21]

The railroads were of course a commercial blessing, and a building and mining boom followed their arrival in the Hills. The engineers who surveyed the railroad routes and supervised the construction of the tracks and the operation of the lines were, like the engineers who built and ran the mines, educated and progressive men, and they too brought with them to the Hills an inclination toward culture and the mechanical improvement of life; for they, like the mining engineers, had both the knowledge and the money that would make Deadwood a comfortable place to live. The many excursion trains that each major railroad ran to take Black Hills citizens to state fairs, Grand Lodge meetings, Odd Fellows conventions, and other such cultural events kept the people of the Hills from becoming provincial; it is hard to be a hick when you are earning good money and the North Western Railway will take you to the International Exposition in Portland (1905) in seventy-one hours. Nevertheless, with the coming of the railroads, something passed out of the life of Deadwood, and the town took one more step away from being a gold rush community and one step nearer to being the service, shopping, distribution, and social center for an industrial area whose product happened to be gold.

FIVE

A Boom in Cyanide

"Mine: a hole in the ground the owner whereof is
a liar."

Bill Nye

"It's a lot easier to put money down into a hole
than it is to get it out again."

An old-timer

THE FREE-MILLING GOLD ORES which were so generously susceptible
to amalgamation played out by the end of the 1880s. The complex
chlorine process with its attendant high expenses could only operate
on ores containing an ounce or more of gold to the ton, and the
matte smelters similarly required rich ore for their continued operation. Mines which had seemed promising in the 1880s were closed
down by their disappointed owners as their ores dwindled in productivity, and others, located near more successful operations,
merged with the mines that still kept going in the hope that the
economies brought about by joint operation could keep both in the
business. The combined grip of high milling costs and dwindling
supplies of high-grade gold ore was squeezing the Black Hills mines
out of business, although as each new milling process was introduced to the area, the mining industry received a new, albeit brief,
infusion of success and optimism. The silver mines of Galena and
of Carbonate Camp were never productive enough to bring more
than passing prosperity to the northern Hills, and even these mines
were eventually forced to close by the falling prices for silver which
swept the West during the 1890s. It was upon this scene of inter-
mittent mineralogical successes punctuated by periods of thoroughly justified gloom that the cyanide process arrived and with it
a renewed wave of profitable mining operations which was to last
until the First World War, and in the case of the mighty Homestake
mine at Lead, clear down to the present day.

By the end of the 1890s five major mines—the Homestake,
Golden Reward, Mogul-Horseshoe, Bonanza, and Wasp No. 2—
were producing most of the $6–$7 million worth of gold that came

out of the Hills each year, with the Homestake producing about half of it. In 1894, 1,281 men were employed in mining in the Hills; by 1903 there were 3,500, with many new mines opening in every valley, and the gold production of the Homestake had doubled. In the words of the Deadwood Business Club, "New life and vigor have been infused into mining affairs all through the Black Hills." The cyanide process had reduced gold mining and milling to the "simplicity and security of manufacturing."[1]

The cyanide process of removing gold from its refractory ores had been developed in the late 1880s by J. S. McArthur and R. W. and W. Forrest. As employed in the Black Hills it was used to extract gold from the tailings of the mercury amalgamation processes, although later on cyanidation was used alone. The process depended upon the ability of potassium, sodium, or calcium cyanide, in an extremely dilute solution and in the presence of air and water, to convert gold into a soluble gold cyanate, the chemical equation being generalized as $Au + KCy + O_2 + H_2O = KAuCy + KHO$. The problem of cyanidation was thus to subject the finely ground ores to the action of a 0.027 percent cyanide solution while maintaining sufficient air in intimate mixture with the whole in order to permit the process to go forward. In the Hills huge vats of either wood or steel were used, and mill engineers devised intricate methods for draining them to admit the air, and to bubble the cyanide solution up from underneath, or trickle it down from above, to dissolve the gold. Once the cyanide liquor was charged with gold, it, like the chlorine solutions used earlier, was run over zinc shavings and the gold precipitated out onto the finely divided zinc, to be later washed off, dried, melted, and cast into the one- or two-hundred pound bars that were so popular at the time. It was said that if you could lift one of these bars, you could have it, the gold having a slightly slippery texture which was hard to grasp, but very few companies made good on this jocular offer, which was generally made only to youthful visitors. The heavy bars, in addition to providing this meager jest, were extremely hard for a robber to steal and carry—he could do it, but as previously mentioned, they would slow him down considerably.

Cyanide, to be sure, was closely related to the deadly poisonous hydrogen cyanide, or prussic acid, into which it would turn if exposed to a strong acid, as in the present-day California gas chamber, or in a human stomach. It was commonly supposed that the tailings from the Homestake that flowed down Gold Run Creek and into the Whitewood were reeking with poisonous particles and that even to breathe too deeply of their villainous contents would stifle the sniffer, but apparently this was not so, for the solution was too dilute to be harmful, and as it tumbled in the sunlight and flowing water it tended to break down into its component elements and become harmless after flowing less than a mile. Calcium cyanide, unlike the cyanides of potassium or sodium, could more easily produce deadly hydrocyanic gas, and although it would work in the cyanide mills, it was probably not much used because of this dangerous property. Poisonous or not, diligent search has not revealed the name of a single person ever accidentally poisoned unto death by the cyanide process, either in its mills themselves or by exposure to the outflow. Now and then a miner might be somewhat sickened by the fumes and have to leave the mill to seek fresh air for a few minutes, but the effects seem to have been noncumulative and transient, and no deaths appear to have occurred.

A further complication encountered by the Homestake in its use of the cyanide process was that its runoff of ground ore and water from the mercury amalgamation tables consisted of both sand and muddy slimes. The porous sand could be treated easily enough in tanks and vats of cyanide, but the slimes—and they contained a significant amount of gold—packed too closely for the air and cyanide solution to dissolve the gold out of them. In 1899 young Charles W. Merrill, a mining engineer, was brought to Lead to solve the problem, and was promised a percentage of all the gold that he could save. Working eighteen hours a day, Merrill developed the clarifying filter and the slime press, which by drying the slimes enabled air to get into them, and allowed the cyanide to work. Merrill also developed a sluicing system to clear the spent slimes from his filters, and the use of zinc dust rather than shavings to precipitate the gold out of his cyanide solutions, and when his contract with the Homestake expired in 1908, he went his way a wealthy man. The Homestake could afford it—he had reduced their cost of cyanidation to seventeen cents a ton, and his slime plant built on McGovern Hill in Deadwood is still in operation.[2]

An interesting mineralogical notion—and one that on the whole was true enough, and much used in the limestone ores around Spearfish Canyon—was the idea that the gold was not evenly distributed throughout the peculiar ores of that area, but lay instead in the interstices, the tiny cracks and crevices, of the rock, and that only enough crushing to cause the ore to fracture along these natural cleavages was necessary for a well-conducted cyanide bath to remove most of the gold that the ore contained. The method worked, leaving behind huge mounds of gravelly tailings on the sites of such operations, but it by no means got all of the gold, and by the time this was recognized, these shallow deposits had been pretty well worked out anyway, but while they lasted these ingeniously economical mills gave a considerable boost to Deadwood's business.

With the refinement of the cyanide process into a system which could extract almost all of the gold from all but the most refractory deposits, Black Hills mining, to quote Maj. J. A. Simmons, an eminent mining engineer and promoter, was relieved of risk "and elevated to a first-class standard of business and financial investment, with stability and profits far above the ordinary manufacturing enterprises; the finished product commands an unvarying price." The development of huge deposits of low-grade ore, some of which yielded as little as $1.60 in gold to the ton, in some cases became practicable, and Black Hills mining promoters noisily trumpeted and touted these new opportunities to the investment world.

> Now if you talk bonanza high-grade ore to these men [conservative bankers and merchants] you might as well talk to a sphinx, but the moment you talk "low grade ore and lots of it" their ears move around in your direction. Why is this? Well, it's because they've "been there" on the $10,000 per ton proposition before they began to bank profits on $5 ores; they know the latter are reasonably safe if good ordinary sense is used in buying first and manufacturing afterward; and you'd be surprised to know how few failures these men make.

It certainly sounded just fine: "You can't overstock the market, don't have to curtail production in dull times, and always have a fixed price for your goods and sell them to a pretty good institution—Uncle Sam."[3]

Cyanide mills became all the rage in Deadwood—the Rossiter on the north end of the city was run to its seventy-five-ton a day capacity by its manager Bryan Rossiter and did mainly custom work for mines that did not have their own mills. The Imperial Mill was just below it, and the Consolidated, and then the great Golden Reward Reduction Plant, next to the now declining Golden Reward Smelter. Smaller operations all through the northern and central Hills added their endeavors, though rarely a large share to gold production, and the presence of Murray, Phillips and Company's Machinery Clearing House advertising "bargains in second hand machinery" indicates a considerable turnover among these lesser mining enterprises.

Brief histories of the major Black Hills mines can hardly do them justice, for it is hard today, knowing by hindsight that the Homestake would one day surpass them all, to share the avid interest that the speculator and the investor of the 1890s and early 1900s took in these, and many other lesser, mines. The Horseshoe, for example, which later combined with the Mogul, had twenty-one hundred acres of mineral land at Bald Mountain and in the adjacent Ruby Basin, and a few prospects far to the west around Bear Gulch. The mine by 1904 had produced $2.5 million from its Kildonian chlorination plant at Pluma, and in 1902 this plant was changed over to a three-hundred-ton per day cyanide operation. Their five-hundred-ton plant at the Mogul Mine near Terry was immense—and a second plant the same size was projected, to be built beside it. Two hundred men were at work, and as the major stockholders also had a controlling interest in the National Smelter works in Rapid City, they did not seem likely to run out of milling facilities.

The Homestake Extension, apparently near the more famous mine, was in 1905 busily driving an 826-foot tunnel into its ore, and took pride in the fact that its ore and that of the Homestake itself were "difficult to tell apart," which often was an indication that the two ores were indeed the same, the ore of the better mine having been brought in to artfully enrich that of the poorer. At any rate, the optimism of the promoters and their faith in the new cyanide process led them to boast of ore that ran only three dollars to the ton, a value which in earlier days would have been considered laughably negligible. A one-hundred-stamp mill was proposed, exemplifying a common fault of Black Hills mineral promotions: overexpansion of plant facilities before the ore was in sight. Indeed, with custom milling so easily available in Deadwood, only a promoter eager to pass as much money as possible through his own hands in the hope that some of it would remain would build a mill before making a good many custom-mill test runs on his ore. It was this sort of grandiose promotion however which, over a good many years, gave the Black Hills a bad name in those circles interested in mining investments, for those mines which were not outright swindles tended to be grossly overbuilt and scandalously mismanaged.

The Golden Crest at the head of Two Bit Creek was another example of this entrepreneurial optimism, for it figures frequently in the mining news from the earliest days until the 1970s, when its huge mill burned to the ground. There was always somebody digging ino the Golden Crest, or improving its mills so as to "get the values" or otherwise provide excuses to mulct the stockholders into still further investments to "enhance and protect" their interests.

The Lexington Hill, in Spruce Gulch, in 1905 was one such mine, declaring a "Dutch Dividend" by soliciting loans from its stockholders to carry on diamond drilling in order to fully locate its ore shoots. For a loan of $100 a stockholder could get 1000 additional shares of stock as collateral for his loan, and when the company repaid the loan, it was hoped within six months, 100 shares of stock would be given, along with 6 per cent interest, as a return. It sounded to the thoughtful a good bit like selling additional stock for $0.10 a share. Nevertheless, this mine continued, on and off, in its development work, up to World War II, and the ruins of its huge Belle Eldridge mill still stand to mark its many endeavors.[4]

The Wasp No. 2, on Yellow Creek at the town of Flatiron two miles south of Lead, began producing gold in late 1896 and continued a steady producer to 1917. One Deadwood banker, R. H. Driscoll, invested $15,000 in Wasp stock, and received $350,000 in dividends before the mine closed down. It was one of the most economical operations in the Hills, its manager John Gray making a profit for the investors on ore that produced only $1.60 to the ton. The secret lay in quarrying shallow beds of ore largely by opencut methods, and running the ore through the cyanide process entirely by gravity. A spur railroad from the Burlington line was hauled up to the mine by a winch, and the heaps of tailings from the mill were sold to the railroad for track ballast. In 1927 a storm caused the tailings piles to slump down onto a loading train, and folks are still digging out tracks and cars from the resulting rubble, but no gold has come from the Wasp No. 2 since the First World War.[5]

The Hidden Fortune had a tumultuous existence. In 1886 Otto Grantz located it as a claim, and for years put in a little work each day upon it, until in 1899 "with a few blows of the pick in the mountain side a fortune stood revealed: a single piece of ore assaying from $1,000 to $68,000 to the ton. Was he flurried? Not he; it was what he had expected." Assays like that *could* be expected if the prospector selected his assay samples judiciously. Grantz shipped eight carloads of ore to Denver and came back with sixty-eight thousand dollars in his pockets—presumably in bills, for gold in that amount would have weighed over two hundred pounds—and went on to become the president of three large mining companies.

The Hidden Fortune operated its mines, which included the Durango, Harrison, Sula, Grant Reddy, Golden Crown, St. Patrick, and Swamp Eagle claims around Lead, and sent their ores to a huge mill built on the east side of Whitewood Creek a mile or two north of Deadwood and connected to the mines themselves by the Burlington and North Western Railroads. Some tungsten production resulted, but the only recorded gold production, in 1904 and 1905, amounted to $188,000, after which the operations were closed by litigation. The Black Hills Mining Men's Association unanimously passed a resolution expressing confidence that "the affairs of the Hidden Fortune Company are being honestly and justly administered and the interests of the stockholders are and will be fully protected by the present management." A Mr. Egbert, evidently conceiving himself to be one of the less protected stockholders, protested that the "conduct of the Hidden Fortune affairs is something outrageous" and urged that the association not bring discredit upon itself by taking a stand on a situation in which they did not know the facts. The tangle was sufficient to tie up the mine thereafter, as stockholders and management continued to bicker over who owned what and how it should be managed. Nowadays a dredge operating in Whitewood Creek below the mill site makes what profit it can dipping up the gold and amalgam which was lost from the fruitless mill of the Hidden Fortune and its unfortunate investors.[6]

By 1904 the Deadwood area had 9,900 tons of ore-processing capacity, 700 of it in smelters and the rest in cyanide plants, and 2,400 tons more were being built, for a total capacity of 12,300 tons a day.

Alder Creek	100	stamps	cyanide
Columbus	80	"	"
Dakota (Trojan)	120	"	"
Deadwood-Standard	200	"	"
Golden Reward	500	"	smelter
Golden Reward	200	"	cyanide
Golden Crest	50	"	"
Hidden Fortune	250	"	"
Homestake	1,000	"	"

Horseshoe-Mogul	500	"	"
Imperial	150	"	"
Jupiter	100	"	"
Lexington Hill	100	"	"
Lundberg, Dorr & Wilson	100	"	"
National Smelting	200	"	smelter
Penobscot	150	"	cyanide
Rossiter	75	"	"
Spearfish Mining Co.	200	"	"
Wasp No. 2	125	"	"

Not all of these mills were in operation at any one time, and not all of them operated profitably, but their presence—and the list omits many of the smaller mills—is an indication of the scope of mining activity during the cyanide boom years of the early 1900s.[7]

Black Hills gold production boomed from 1898 to 1917, with production running just short of 400,000 ounces of gold a year in the best years, although there were years when fires or strikes markedly reduced that figure, which with gold at $20 an ounce would have been about $8 million a year, a figure which was reached in 1912. The coming of World War I, with increasing costs for labor and supplies, produced a dramatic slowdown, production falling to $4,978,000 in 1919 as all of the mines except the Homestake were forced to close. The major mines, their periods of operation, and their gold production were about as follows, rounded off to the nearest $1,000:

Dakota Mining and Milling	1902–1906	$544,000
Gilt Edge Maid	1905–1909, 1930s	749,000
Golden Reward	1887–1918	21,000,000
Hidden Fortune	1904–1905	188,000
Homestake	1878–1976	(31,510,612 oz.)
Horseshoe-Mogul . .	1894–1919	7,000,000
Imperial	1902–1906	(not available)
Lundberg, Dorr & Wilson .	1904–12	872,000
Maitland and predecessors .	1903–1906, 1930s	(91,681 oz.)
Portland–Trojan–	1908, 1912–23,	
Bald Mountain . .	1930s, 1946–59	12,000,000
Reliance and New Reliance	1902–16	610,000
Spearfish-Victoria . .	1901–1905, 1912	972,000
Wasp No. 2	1897–1917	$2,767,000[8]

The Homestake's production, which by 1980 had probably brought them close to $1 billion, and that of the Maitland-Penobscot-Canyon

Company are given in ounces of gold because the amount sold at any given price is not known, although the Portland-Trojan-Bald Mountain group seems to have been able to come up with a dollar figure despite the varying gold prices.

Many other mines, of course, did development and exploratory work and ran test mill runs now and then, but the bulk of the Black Hills mineral production during the early 1900s came from those listed above. The billion-dollar production of the Homestake to 1980 of course makes it appear overpowering in relation to any of the other mines. Its production to 1918 was about $120,000,000, which is still sufficiently larger than all the rest of the mines together to attract attention. It would be a mistake, however, to view the operations of this large and long-lived mine as dominating the psychology of Black Hills mining. The Homestake was big, but in the thinking of the investor other, smaller, and riskier, but for that reason possibly more promising, mines were uppermost. The Homestake was a big business, with the virtues and the shortcomings (from a speculative point of view) of stability; the other Black Hills mines, it should be remembered, played more flamboyant parts upon the mining stage.

The mighty Homestake, according to Moses Manuel (apparently pronounced, at the time, "Manwell" in the Portuguese fashion, although his descendants pronounce it "Man-u-el") got its start when he and his brother Fred came to Lead and on 9 April 1876 found a chunk of very rich quartz ore. They built an arrastra, then a ten-stamp mill, to work their claim. L. D. Kellogg, sent by the California mining investor George Hearst, bought the Manuel claim for seventy thousand dollars, then found that one-fifteenth of it had been already sold to H. B. Young in return for ninety dollars worth of groceries. Hearst later had to buy out Young for a considerable but undisclosed sum, cursing and swearing all the while. The mine and its adjoining claims seemed promising, there was good bit of valuable ore in sight, and Hearst at once began to bring in large quantities of cash and mining equipment to work his purchase, and to buy up other nearby claims: the Golden Terra, Old Abe, Golden Star, Giant, Deadwood, De Smet, Caledonia, and Highland, along with many lesser claims, were eventually absorbed into the Homestake, although the De Smet, at least, put up quite a struggle. The Oro Hondo was purchased in 1920, when the Homestake had nearly run out of ore, and the Oro Hondo owners were unaware that they were sitting on top of a huge amount of it—at least that is the local story, and it is said that when the Homestake miners, underground, worked the Oro Hondo they found diamond drill channels a few feet from, but never quite touching, these important ore bodies. The Oro Hondo owners must have been a dull lot, however, for they had done over 3,000 feet of diamond drilling on their property, extending outward from a shaft down 2,165 feet, explorations which led their mining engineer John Tait Milliken to report in 1919 that the drills showed large quantities of very valuable ore. Perhaps the owners of the Oro Hondo had heard the story too often, for the mine, despite its shaft and drilling, never seems to have had any significant production until the Homestake got a hold of it.[9]

By 1888, to use a single year as an example, the Homestake was bringing up ore that yielded $3.68 in gold and $0.03 in silver to the ton, and mining, hauling, and milling it at a cost of $2.51, leaving profit of $1.17 to the ton, and that year they processed 243,355 tons of ore, for a profit of about $292,000. The mine was said to be the financial foundation of the Hearst newspaper empire, which it supported in good years and bad, giving William Randolph Hearst, George Hearst's son, a degree of editorial independence not common in his profession.

The Homestake was not without its tribulations. The timber props that held up the mine decayed in from two to five years, and when they rotted away, it was only a matter of time before huge areas fell in. In 1883 a cave-in dropped part of the town of Lead into the two-hundred-foot level of the mine, nearly taking the home of the superintendent, H. M. Gregg, along with it into the abyss. Indeed the whole business section of Lead eventually had to be moved, for parts of it, at least, rested upon what is now the open cut, a man-made canyon on the northern edge of the city. Nowadays the sands and slimes from the mills are run back into the mine and the water that carried them pumped out, leaving a concrete mass that keeps the entire area stable, but in the early days the expense of preparing the underground works to receive such backfilling and the cost of pumping out the water was considered prohibitive, and it was thought to be easier to move the town than to stabilize the underground workings.

Fires too were the bane of every miner's existence, but particularly so in the workings of the Homestake, where deep shafts and good ventilation provided a draft that made a fire, once started, extremely difficult to get under control. In 1893 the underground workings of the Deadwood-Terra caught fire, and all attempts to seal off the blaze by working toward it from the Homestake were driven back by the poisonous gases. Finally the Terra works had to be sealed off at some distance from the fire and flooded down by pumping water into the open cut. In 1907 another fire broke out on the five-hundred-foot level, and red-hot molten rock ran in the Homestake drifts and prevented any approach to the flames. Again the mine was flooded down, and it took seven weeks to get the water back out again, for it had taken 643,453,000 gallons to drown the fire. Again, in 1919, fire broke out, this time at the seven-hundred-foot level, and again it could not be fought under ground and the mine was flooded to seventy-seven feet above the six-hundred-foot level, this time using 700,000,000 gallons of water. Skips, which were mine cars designed to lift water like big fire buckets, pumps, and an air lift, much like a modern jet pump, again took about six weeks to get the water out, and production, of course, was seriously diminished, although work for all of the underground employees was found on the surface during the fire and flooding, so labor expenses went right on.[10]

The pollution produced by the Homestake—and indeed by all of the mines—first stained the creek waters red with the rust of the cement ores and placers, then gray with the slimes of the mills, and the reek of cyanide hung over the valleys of Deadwood and the Whitewood like a curse. The territory of Dakota had, in 1881, provided by law that the Homestake had a vested right to dump its tailings into Whitewood Creek (which runs down through Deadwood, downstream), and that creek ran gray to the Belle Fourche River, and ranchers along it complained bitterly that every flood deposited dark banks of noxious and infertile tailings on their land. The Homestake, with a good deal of forethought, habitually settled such claims for small sums, and obtained along with the payments a release running as a covenant with each rancher's land, permitting such tailing deposits ever after. One case, a classic of its kind, involved a rancher on the Belle Fourche with the improbable name of Howdy Jenks, who sued the Homestake for ruining his ranch: his trees died, his horses and cattle bogged down and were poisoned by the slime, his crops were ruined, and the fish went away, or so he claimed. He sounded irritable, and of course other ranchers along the creek waited attentively, contemplating additional damage suits if Jenks's should be successful.

The Homestake, not content to stand on its statutory right to pollute the water of Whitewood Creek, went to court guided by its attorney Chambers Kellar. Kellar proved that as many trees died on the Belle Fourche above the Whitewood as along the polluted water below its mouth. He obtained photographs of dairy cattle drinking in the Whitewood a mile below the Homestake outfalls, and apparently prospering on this sanitized, enriched and nutritious gruel, so unlike the pallid and insipid waters which coursed in most Black Hills streams. He proved by experiments and testimony that crops actually grew *better* on land which, like the lands of Egypt, was enriched by the silt from above, and that the gumbo clay of Jenks's ranch was much aerated and improved by the Homestake's gratuitous addition of sand and silt to its otherwise sticky and obdurate nature. Kellar even had an ex-sheriff, Whitey Helmer, his general factotum, catch a string of healthy catfish on Jenks's own ranch, to prove that even the fish could prosper in the cyanide slimes. The judge directed a verdict in favor of the Homestake. More recently, however, the U.S. Environmental Protection Agency has forced the Homestake to build a $10 million system for impounding, settling, and recovering the slimes and treating the water of the Whitewood so that it at last flows purely to the Belle. Unfortunately, both Lead and Deadwood emptied their untreated sewage into this stream, and cleared of the slime and cyanide, it stank and smoked like the pot of Acheron, until in the late 1970s a joint sewage system was installed for the two towns.[11]

Homestake gold production slumped badly, to just over 200,000 ounces, in the years following World War I, then rose to close to 300,000 ounces—about $6,000,000—in the 1920s, then jumped rapidly upward in the 1930s, particularly when the price of gold was raised from $20 to $35 an ounce in 1934, and from the 1930s to World War II production climbed well above 500,000 ounces ($17,500,000) a year. Closed down by law during World War II in order to conserve steel and manpower, production dropped to practically nothing in 1942, 1943, 1945, and 1946, as stockpiled ore and accumulations were used up but no mining except pumping and maintenance was carried forward. In the late 1940s and on into the 1960s production again climbed up to over 500,000 ounces a year, reaching a peak of 601,000 ounces in 1967, after which increasing cost of operating the mine at depths below seven thousand feet slowed down production. When in 1974 the price of gold was allowed to fluctuate on the open market, production became even smaller, either to wait for higher prices, or because the resulting higher prices enabled the mine to get by with less production, and by 1978 only 285,000 ounces were produced, but they sold at an average of over $176 per ounce, for a total income that year of over $50,000,000. The wealth of the Homestake was of course the backbone of much of Deadwood's business prosperity, although by this time a discouragingly small amount of it found its way into the coffers of Deadwood's merchants.[12]

Despite the successes of well-trained mineralogists in the Homestake, the disrespect of the prospector, or "practical miner," for the professional engineer, or "rock sharp," was proverbial. The scorn heaped upon Professor N. H. Winchell, who managed to accompany the 1874 Custer expedition without discovering any gold, and upon Professor Walter P. Jenney, whose praise of the Black Hills gold deposits were restrained but just, was enough to blight those good men for life, but it didn't.

Equally repelling to the sensibilities of the practical prospector were the arrogant pretentions of the self-styled experts. One such bloater, a Professor Underwood of Chicago, arrived in the Hills to investigate a claim for his clients. The claim, alas, was well known as a barren prospect, and Richard Hughes, a local editor and miner, consulted with his friends, and they agreed together that the Professor should be at least warned of what he was up against, and cautioned that the mine's values might have been artfully augmented by the mind of acuity and the hand of guile. The Professor swelled up like an offended turkey-cock, and announced, "When *I* have completed the inspection of a mine and made my report upon it, it is *final*; if I recommend the purchase of it it is purchased; if I advise against it there is no further consideration." The professor then proceeded to take out twenty tons of ore, crush and amalgamate it, ship the amalgam to Deadwood, and use the resulting gold bar to judge the value of the entire mine. The claim was sold for fifty thousand dollars, but luckily only ten thousand dollars was paid down—it was the only amount that changed hands, for the operation of the mine on its own unaided merits proved to be totally unjustified. No one ever quite figured out how the mine had been salted, but the

"Calamity Jane" Cannary Burke, in the 1890s, and presumably a picture of herself which she sold while performing at the World's Columbian Exposition at Chicago. *Centennial Collection—Deadwood Public Library*

"Calamity Jane" Cannary Burke and the photographer pose in front of Wild Bill Hickok's grave around the turn of the century. *Centennial Collection—Deadwood Public Library*

Jack McCall, the murderous nobody who shot Wild Bill Hickok from behind in Nuttall and Mann's Saloon No. 10, 2 August 1876. *Centennial Collection—Deadwood Public Library*

The Gem Theater, said to be "an infamous den of prostitution under the guise of being a dance hall." *Centennial Collection—Deadwood Public Library*

Deadwood's volunteer fire-fighting companies combined civic service and social festivities with the chance to dress up in uniform. *Centennial Collection—Deadwood Public Library*

A Deadwood fruiterer presides with scowling aplomb over his displays of local and exotic goods. *Centennial Collection—Deadwood Public Library*

A bull team or two in downtown Deadwood, with the signs of many well-known merchants and the Deadwood bathhouse well in view. *Centennial Collection—Deadwood Public Library*

Stebbins, Post and Company got into the banking business at a time when interest ran as high as 5 percent *a month. Centennial Collection—Deadwood Public Library*

The Smith Block was built in 1890 as a livery stable with a stone horse's head to advertise the business and provide a perch for the little birds that made a living following the horses. *W. Parker photo*

Liebmann's San Francisco Bazaar was one of Deadwood's early dry goods stores. *Centennial Collection—Deadwood Public Library*

seller is said to have claimed that the buyers never even got half the salting that he had put in to fool Professor Underwood and his employers.[13]

More to the taste of the pilgrims and miners of 1880 was Professor John Murphy, whose "wisdom was not derived alone from books" and who "had a hard, horny fist and did not part his hair in the middle" and had never heard of the German mining school at Freiberg. Naturally Murphy praised the Black Hills mines and urged the inauguration of cheap mining and milling processes. The skilled engineers, Bowie and McMaster who ran the De Smet and the Homestake, added lustre to the profession, and eventually convinced the practical miners that not only professional praise but possibly professional advice could be of use to them. With the coming of the more complex ore-treating processes, with their intricate chemical and mechanical manipulations, the need for skilled mining engineers became ever more apparent. In 1885 the Dakota School of Mines was established at Rapid City, and there seems to have been marked satisfaction with its staff and its performance throughout most of the mining community, although the 1916 *Report* of the state inspector of mines sniffed a bit and urged a "more strict adherence to the purpose of the school" and more "willingness on the part of those connected with it to cooperate with mining interests." The work of this great technical institution has continued to the present, and it has consistently added stature to the intellectual reputation of the state. The role of Professor Carpenter in developing matte smelting has already been mentioned, and the school's role in developing the "blue ores" worked during the 1930s did much to keep it in the public eye. Indeed, the history of the Black Hills mines spans, with considerable accuracy, the transition of American mining from an art practiced by grizzled prospectors to a science carried forward by the lace-boot engineers, skilled metallurgists, and the stolid but effective chemists who never see the dark side of a mine at all.[14]

For the most part labor-management relations in the Black Hills were friendly, peaceful, and profitable to all. The most notable strike, though by no means the most important, was the miners' sit-down in the Keets (or Aurora—the record is not clear) mine in the fall of 1877. A group of miners, doing contract mining under the direction of one Connelly were simply not paid at all, Connelly having divested himself of their money in recreation and deviltry. The irate miners led by their foreman, Matt Plunkett, took over the mine, holed up inside it with their supplies, bedding, and a cook-stove, used an air shaft for a chimney, and said they would stay in place until someone—they didn't care who—paid them what was owing. As the mine was, prior to this take-over, taking out eighteen thousand dollars a week, the interruption of work was a serious matter. Cavalrymen from Fort Meade, under the command of Lieutenants Winfield Scott Edgerly and Horatio Gates Sickel, Jr., surrounded the mine and bawled threats into the entrance, but the miners remained unmoved. Judge Granville Bennett summoned Seth Bullock and gave him a free hand in removing the miners, just so long as nobody got hurt. Bullock, smiling craftily, made his way to the miners' air shaft and dropped a noxious substance—some say asafetida, others claim it was burning sulphur—down the shaft, and the strike collapsed and its revolutionary tendencies were for a time suppressed. The miners were never paid, but the sanctity of private property had been upheld and a "riotous assembly" suppressed, in accordance with the prevailing attitudes of the day.[15]

Doubtless one reason for the peaceful labor-management relations of the times was the high wages, $3.50 for a ten-hour day, paid to most of the miners. Although this wage had to stretch around Lead and Deadwood prices which necessarily were higher than at home in the states, the thoughtful miner could often enhance his income by high grading, or taking home such evidently valuable jewelry rock as came to his notice. The inclination of miners employed in a mine with identifiable values to take these home with them was ineradicable. The resulting gold could be sold to venal assayers, or, more commonly, alleged to have come from the miner's personal placer claim—the number of such claims always was high, and their productivity astonishing, and the speed with which such profitable placers were discarded when their owner left the employment of a rich mine was notably precipitant. Even today it might be possible to find a high-grader complete with pick and pan prospecting some obvious spot where his activities can be noticed without being observed too closely, and if questioned, he invariably reports considerable success: "There's still a lot of gold in this here country, ifn' a man knows how to go for it," but upon his retirement such activity usually ceases.[16]

Another reason for the peacefulness of Black Hills labor relations was undoubtedly the presence of the "Cousin Jacks" and "Cousin

Jennies," the Cornishmen and women whose hard-won experience in the tin mines of Cornwall made them miners the world over. Staunch Methodists, virulently antiunion, and diligent high-graders, they firmly believed in the Ten Commandments, the Methodist Church, and the notion that "gold belongs to him wot finds it first." Their descendants may still be identified by their names, for as the old proverb has it, "by Tre, Pol, Per, and Pen, ye may know the Cornishmen." It was said that in shaft sinking a Cornishman would climb down any number of ladders rather than hang at the end of a rope, and the unkind said that this was because they hoped to defer this eventual but inevitable end as long as possible. They lived on a diet of strong tea and pasties (pronounced "past-eez"), the latter being an infamous combination of pie and stew consisting of a firm, not to say impervious, crust folded into a half-moon enclosing meat and vegetables. Made small, it tends to run pretty much to crust, and bears out the legend that the pastie was made sturdy so the Cornishwoman could bake it in the morning and drop it hot but unharmed down the shaft to her man for nooning. Executed with more liberal measurements, say, a foot across the diameter, the ore and the values get into more harmonious conformity with each other and make a tender and excellent meat pie, the like of which can still be bought in Lead and Deadwood on Payday Thursday and other times of celebration.

Even the Panic of 1893 did not seriously diminish the Black Hills miner's salary, and falling prices, as later in the Panic of 1907, markedly increased his buying power. Company unions without outside affiliations in Lead, Terry, and Central City accumulated funds, built their own halls, paid benefits to unfortunate members, and were cordially accepted by the mine operators. The boom in mining employment, rising from 1,402 men in 1893 to 3,207 in 1902 and 3,808, its peak, in 1912, also kept the miners happy, but of course led, as times when the management can afford to pay so often do, to strikes and labor troubles, for in 1909 the miners in Lead agitated to keep out all nonunion labor, and the Homestake, followed by the mines on Bald Mountain, refused to hire anybody who belonged to a union. The strike ended in January 1910, after a two-month work stoppage, with the complete defeat of the union. Even the encouragement provided by a sister organization, the Black Hills Working Girls Union, of women employed in laundries, factories, and stores (the omission of housework, the main employment of young women at that time, apparently weakened the girls' united front), was not sufficient to gain the miners' union a victory.[17]

Mining, like most active physical employment, and indeed like active bodily sports, was dangerous. Basically, men fell *into* the mines, the mines fell *down* on the men, and the men blew *up* with gunpowder or, later, with dynamite, and in addition those accidents incident upon vigorous industrial work of any kind took their toll. A few examples set the tone of mining accidents: In 1878 in the Pecacho a block of rock weighing one hundred tons fell on James DeLong. He was unrecognizable when they dug him out from under it. The same year a heavy timber being hoisted into position slipped and crushed Robert McCarl, who was killed, and badly injured his companion. James Bryant was killed by a premature explosion in a tunnel. In 1880 John Oleston, charging a hole with black powder, thought that the powder was spoiled, damp perhaps, and in sifting it through his fingers to dry it, some of it fell into his candle. It was hoped by his friends that his injuries would not prove fatal. In 1883 the management of the Esmerelda in Blacktail Gulch noticed that their old workings were about to collapse, and warned the men to stay away from them. Fred Ehler, Joseph Griffin, and James McKee were in an adjacent tunnel when about an acre of the old workings fell with a crash, and the blast of air generated by the falling mass of earth and timber blew them through the tunnel and against its walls with fatal results. The men were newly employed, and should have heeded the warnings given them, and the management was not believed to be to blame.

The management never *was* responsible, apparently, for inquest after inquest assigned the accidents to the carelessness of the miners or to acts of God beyond the control of anybody. The Homestake provided a hospital, and the miners in other mines tended to contribute a dollar a month from their wages for the relief of the injured, but that was about as far as anybody's liability was assumed to go.[18]

Boys (the bane of human existence!) now and then got into the machinery or equipment with lamentable results. One young crew of ruffians released the brake on an ore car at the Old Abe, and rode it to the end of the ore chute, where it stopped with a suddenness that injured them all. It was hoped that this taught them to "let things alone with which they have no business," but it probably didn't. Dynamite, stored in a blacksmith shop, of all places, blew up and killed young Professor Willis B. Bower, principal of the Terraville school. In another Terraville mine two hundred pounds of giant powder (this is sometimes the name given to dynamite, sometimes to blasting powder generally, by those who do not know the difference) went off underground and shredded Philip Weyman, a miner named Rosevere, and one other man who could not be identified. It was caused by one of the men insouciantly smoking his pipe while preparing a blast. By the 1890s the *Reports* of the South Dakota inspector of mines record, year by year, the details of accidental deaths and major injuries. Falls into shafts were frequent; apparently when a miner began to push an ore car, he often didn't notice whether there was a skip in the shaft to receive it, and when the ore car started to fall into the shaft he, like a ninny, would attempt to hold it back, and failing, fell into the shaft along with it. Rocks fell and crushed miners, in spite of vigorous attempts to "bar down" loose ore overhead after every blast. Dynamite charges that failed to explode were drilled into later, and went off then, usually driving the drill through the driller.

Black powder, or blasting powder, was the old gunner's explosive first compounded by Roger Bacon out of sulfur, charcoal and saltpeter (potassium nitrate). Each ingredient was ground fine, then moistened, and the whole mixed together while damp, then pressed into thin strands which were cut up into grains, dried, dusted with graphite, and sold loose in wooden kegs or metal canisters. The larger its grains, the slower would be the resulting explosion, and the effect of such blasting powder was generally a heaving, moving, one which, by judicious choice of powder and placement, could be made to shove rocks just about where the miner wanted to put them. Dynamite, on the other hand, was developed by Alfred Nobel in 1867, in an attempt to control the ferocious power of nitroglycerine. Basically, dynamite consisted of nitroglycerine mixed with an inert absorptive substance such as clay, chalk, sawdust, or diatomaceous earth. In lower concentrations like the miner's usual 40 percent mixture, it is thoroughly stable, resistant to shocks, and can even be burned in small quantities if proper provision is made to dissipate the heat that its burning generates. In higher concentrations, or if old, so that the nitroglycerine migrates and concentrates in the lower portions of the individual paper cartridges in which it is wrapped, it is extremely touchy, and in any case the nitroglycerine itself, which is easily absorbed through the skin, gives the user terrific headaches until he becomes accustomed to it.

The effect of a dynamite blast, unlike that of black powder, is a shattering and disruptive one, pulverizing rather than merely moving the rock upon which it acts, and it took a great deal of painfully acquired skill to place dynamite so that its power would move rock with economy and precision. It did require a special cap containing fulminate of mercury at the end of each fuse to provide the necessary shock to set it off, and these tiny but powerful explosives had a way of going off in a miner's hand, or under foot, or elsewhere where they would be a nuisance, but the dynamite itself was so much safer than black powder that it eventually became the staple explosive in the mines.

Both dynamite and black powder, to reach full effectiveness, had to be packed tightly in the hole. Attempts to tamp down charges with a metal crowbar eventually result in the tamper becoming a statistic, as did efforts to tamp charges with a hammer handle. Powdermen sometimes left the site of a blast too late and were involved in it. Ideally, a powderman cut his fuses to precisely calculated lengths, shorter and shorter, so that they would go off from the center outwards, but more or less all together. The center, or "relieving," charge opened a gap in the face of a drift or tunnel so that successive charges around it had some place to push the rock, and "trimmers" at the edges shaped the tunnel, and if all went off in succession as planned, the effectiveness of a blast was much enhanced. The precision reached by Black Hills miners in these operations is on visual display at the Mount Rushmore Memorial, where local miners from Keystone blasted to within two inches of the finished surface of these gigantic mountain carvings. The powderman, once his fuses were in place, cut a "spitter," or fuse shorter than the shortest fuse that he had to light, and lit the others from it. When his spitter burned his hand, it was time for him to depart with all deliberate speed, but sometimes he didn't. He was rarely blown out of the tunnel; instead the rock caught and buried him, and he entered into a column of that year's *Report* of the state inspector of mines.

Dynamite, in spite of its fearsome power, is, if in good condition, relatively stable and unlikely to go off under ordinary shocks. When old, however, or frozen—and it freezes at above the temperature of ice—it is sensitive in the extreme, and likely to go off if it is tickled. Frozen dynamite (or "powder" as it is still called in the mines) had to be thawed, preferably in a sort of double boiler, in which the sensitive frozen substance could be heated by bringing warm water to it, rather than by setting the device upon a stove. Those who did set it on a stove tended to need a new stove afterwards. Some miners buried dynamite in the ground and built a mild fire over it to thaw it. The results were often spectacular but not dangerous unless the miner happened to be stoking the fire at the time.

The engineer who ran the hoist that pulled the skip up and down the shaft needed to be a man of maturity and precise judgment. To match up the rails on the skip with the rails of a tunnel a couple of thousand feet below called for experience, for the temperature of the steel rope, the wear on the rope and on the hoist drum, and the tendency of such a cable to stretch, bobbing up and down when at full length, all made it difficult to hit each landing with precision. The state inspector of mines repeatedly called for a standard code of bells, so that there would be no misunderstandings between the hoist engineer and the men below. If the skip came down on men at work, it tended to ruin them, and if it rose while they were loading it, it tended to cut them in half against the roof of the tunnel. Many miners were sensitive to these slights, and in 1902 a system of bell signals was imposed by law upon the mines at the recommendation of Inspector Thomas Gregory:

1 bell	. . . . . .	. hoist, if standing
1 bell	. . . . .	. stop, if in motion
2 bells	. . . . .	. lower men ⎫ men on skip
3 bells	. . . . .	. hoist men ⎭
4 bells	. . . . .	. blasting—engineer must raise and let back bucket or cage to acknowledge blasting
1 bell	. . . . .	. hoist men away from blast
5 bells	. . . . .	. steam on ⎫ steam signals
6 bells	. . . . .	. steam off ⎭
7 bells	. . . . .	. air on ⎫ air signals
8 bells	. . . . .	. air off ⎭
3–2–2 bells	. . . .	. send down tools
9 bells	. . . . .	. danger (fire, accident, and so forth), then ring station number

It does not sound like a very flexible means of communication, and apparently it wasn't, for eventually the Homestake installed two-way radios between hoist and skip tenders.[19]

As was mentioned earlier, the employment of cyanide in the mills does not seem to have resulted in any industrial poisonings that were recorded. One suicide, however, made use of cyanide to shuffle off this mortal coil, and it was said, probably incorrectly, that he hit the ground before the glass did, but of course he was drinking prussic acid rather than the dilute chemical employed in the mills. L. D. Graves, visiting a Deadwood jewelry store where prussic acid was employed for cleaning jewelry, helped himself to a drink out of a bucket, supposing it to be water, and he too departed quickly from his earthly troubles. Nobody else seems to have been bothered, and as has been mentioned, even the dairy cattle were able to drink the noxious batter that flowed in Whitewood Creek and prosper on it, although it was said by the sceptical that the milk they yielded was so thoroughly sanitized by the cyanide that there was no need to pasteurize it.[20]

The highest recorded annual death rate for mine employees in the Hills seems to have been 6.2 per thousand in 1894, but that was exceptionally high, for thereafter the rate varied between 1.0 and 3.0, averaging, at a guess, less than 2.0 per thousand as a general rule. As a comparison, in 1912 the death rate in the Hills was 1.57 per thousand miners; in Idaho, Arizona and Montana it was much higher, and in Nevada it reached 9.4 deaths per thousand employees per year. It may have been the prospect of a dark, dank, miserable death underground that made so many miners turn to a life of crime, or at least chicanery, up on the surface.

Not every miner who had a prospect or a mine to sell was entirely honest. If a seller had the misfortune to drop his gold watch into the ball mill, he considered himself to be amply recompensed for his loss by the added values that the mill run might show to a prospective buyer, and it was even said that it was in general useless to ask the time of day of a mineral promoter because nine times out of ten he would not be in a position to enlighten you, his watch having long since been sacrificed to his cupidity. Prudent selection of ore for assaying, as has already been remarked, could work wonders in a glowing assayer's report, and the assayer who wondered if the sample was truly representative of a mine's entire ore body tended to keep his doubts to himself, or go quietly out of business.

The coming of the cyanide process, which could profitably handle ores of a very low grade, made the process of artificial enrichment of an ore body much less burdensome to a seller, for an indication of values of only a few dollars a ton could indicate a saleable mine, whereas the earlier milling processes needed ores containing at least an ounce or two of gold to the ton in order to be profitable to a buyer. It was much easier to make barren rock look like six-dollar ore than to make it look as if it ran forty dollars to the ton, and consequently salting, during the cyanide days, boomed right along with the mining industry.

The ways of making a mine look more heavily endowed than it had been by nature were limited only by the imaginations and ingenuity of the sellers and promoters. The edge of a gold coin could be drawn over the surface of the rock, or if the prospective buyer was green down to the ankles, the brass from an old cartridge could serve the same purpose. A shotgun loaded with gold dust instead of shot could be fired into the tunnel, and in any of these cases the prospective dupe was then invited to help himself to whatever gold-spangled ore he wanted. Rich ore, usually selected with an eye to its evident values, could be brought in from a paying mine and distributed about the bottom of a shaft, or on the floor of a tunnel where it would mix with fresh ore brought down by a blast. Gold coins could be chopped up or filed into the rock—although it was a good idea to have the quality and alloy of the gold matched to that which might be expected in the area, and not mix the yellow gold of Uncle Sam with the reddish gold of Castleton or Rapid Creek. Panning a placer, gold dust could be concealed under fingernails, if the prospector had any left after dabbling in the gravel, and heaps of gravel awaiting panning could be dusted with just enough gold dust to make them appear preternaturally attractive. Ore samples could be collected in a hat, that carryall receptacle of the West, and gold nuggets concealed under the hatband added to the samples. In milling, solutions of gold chloride or gold cyanate could be surreptitiously added to more straightforward chemicals, and as a well-known proprietary cure for venereal disease contained gold chloride, it was often possible for a miner to personally contain enough mineral values to largely augment ores which were intended to undergo treatment by chlorination.

No mining engineer worthy of the name believed an assay submitted to him by a seller, nor did he accept for assaying ore which he had not blasted down himself from a fresh and unmarked face of ore. Indeed, he generally provided his own drills, fearful that gold might be added to those supplied him on the site, to contaminate with unmerited values the holes that he drilled, and he generally provided his own dynamite also, for the seller's powder might be similarly enriched. The thoughtful engineer generally took home some samples from rock known to be without values, now and then, and if such rock showed value later on, he surmised that it and all his other samples had been tampered with on the sly. It was a precaution worth taking, for it was easy for a hypodermic syringeful of gold chloride or gold cyanate to be injected through the canvas of a sample bag while the seller and buyer rode together in a buggy toward Deadwood and a fruitful assay. A drunk waving a bottle of putative liquor might fall against the mill machinery, break his bottle, and go his way a sadder but richer man. The buyer did well to recall Bret Harte's words:

> The way of a man with a maid be strange,
>   yet simple and tame,
> to the way of a man with a mine, when
>   selling the same.[21]

The well-known tendency of the miner to yield to temptation accounted for some otherwise strange behavior in the management of the mines. At the De Smet, for example, the amalgamating tables were laid out face to face at considerable inconvenience, so that a single guard could keep his eye upon all of them to prevent unauthorized removal of their values. A seventh of the cost of the mill went to pay for men to guard the product as it passed through. Even in the early days when prospectors were presumed to be bound together in the band of camaraderie and loneliness, suspicions tended to arise, and two brothers nearly killed each other before they found that the gold each suspected the other of taking had actually been stolen by a nimble packrat to ornament his nest. One old prospector, smitten by disease, lay upon his deathbed, and Mr. Molyneux the minister, summoned to the scene, inquired reasonably enough if there was anything he could do to ease the mind of the departing miner. "My partners—git my partners, and have them set here, beside me, Bill there, and Lem on t'other side," gasped out the sufferer, and the preacher brought the partners in, and placed them as directed. A look of ineffable peace and satisfaction spread on the face of the departing miner as he said with heartfelt contentment, "Now I kin die just like my Savior—between two thieves!"[22]

By 1923 all of the major Black Hills mines except the mighty Homestake had closed down, strangled by rising wages and costs and the increasing costs of working their steadily deepening or diminishing ore deposits. In 1926, however, the U.S. Bureau of Mines began experiments at Reno Station near Deadwood with an intricate process of first roasting, then cyaniding the highly refractory blue ores west and north of Deadwood at Bald Mountain and the Maitland District, and when the price of gold rose to thirty-five dollars an ounce in 1934, these mines opened again, along with many lesser prospects, to take advantage of the higher price, the depression-lowered costs, and the easy availability of otherwise unemployed labor. Over fifty mines up and down the Hills resumed exploration and development work, and most of them set up modest—and in some cases not so modest—mills to test the ores they found in the light of new metallurgical developments. The Anaconda, at Roubaix, operated part of its huge mill; the Bald Mountain Company, encompassing most of the claims in that area, operated until 1959; the Canyon Corporation, at Maitland–Garden City, built an imposing roaster and mill and employed eighty men; fifty men were building a huge mill for the Gilt Edge Maid, south of Galena; the Holy Terror (named for the wife of its locator), in Keystone, was pouring a gold bar every now and then; and theatrical personalities Sid Grauman and Al Jolson were the officers of the Black Hills Exploration Company, which had mines three miles south of Lead and offices in Hollywood.

Almost all of this depression-inspired mineral activity had dwindled away by the time a wartime order closed the gold mines early in 1942, and only the Bald Mountain and the Homestake reopened afterwards. Various mineral efforts during the war involved the Belle Eldridge, in Spruce Gulch, which hunted for zinc; the Spokane, southeast of Keystone, that went after lead, zinc, and arsenic; the various tungsten properties; and the Tinton tin mines, which struggled manfully to produce something of value to the war effort but without much real success. The rising price of gold since 1974 also occasioned much exploratory work, usually undertaken, nowadays, by diamond drilling crews from other mineral areas, and every now and then a rumor leaks out that the Homestake is about to open mines in Keystone or Bald Mountain or around Rochford or

Spearfish Canyon. Even gold at modern-day prices has not proved
to be sufficient to offset the rising costs of discovery, mining, and
milling, and even the Homestake, which could easily afford to mine
a graveyard for the gold in the fillings, has not by 1980 dared to
tackle some of the Black Hills' minor mines again. The Homestake
continues to bring prosperity to Lead—it sold $55 million worth of
gold from the mine in 1978 alone—and this enormous payroll continues to provide business for the stores and entertainments in
Deadwood, but the great days of the mining boom are, as in the
1920s, temporarily over.[23]

The whole life of the miner and his mine is aptly summed up in
a Biblical parody published in the 1880 *Black Hills Daily Times*:

> Behold the prospector, who wandereth over the face of the earth.
> He traverseth the hills and picketh the barren mountains with his
> pick.
> The pangs of hunger gripe his bowels in the morning, and at night
> he lieth down with only a blanket to cover him.
> And the gray-backs come forth and rend him.
> And he lifteth up the voice of lamentation in the wilderness and
> cries aloud to heaven:
> "Why has this affliction come upon me, and why do the terrors of
> hell compass me round about?"
> And while he sleeps the wolves devour his substance.
> And when he findeth the croppings he diggeth in the ground and
> tacketh up the location notice on a board.
> Then he hieth to the valley and saith to the capitalist:
> "Hearken unto me, for I have struck it big."
> "Here are the samples from the ground, and behold the gold mak-
> eth lousy the rock with richness."
> And the twain return, to find others toiling upon the claim.
> And the prospector graspeth his gun, saying—
> "Get ye gone from here, for it is holy ground."
> And a fire coming out of the bush smites him on the hip and he
> calls with a loud voice—
> "I am done for, pull off my boots."
> And they hasten to take off his boots and the fragrance of his socks
> reacheth unto heaven.
> And he giveth up the ghost and is gathered to his fathers.
> And behold, others work the mine, and they float the stock in the
> cities of the valleys
> And all buy thereof. The washerwomen who worry the raiment of

the wealthy, the clerks who measure tape, and the impoverished devils who write for the press.

"Let us get in before the boom cometh," saith the buyers, and the assessment is levied and they cry aloud:

"What is this thing that cometh upon us?" And no one can answer them.

And with one accord they all pungle, saying, "This is the last."

And in another sixty days another call from the main office comes unto them, and they rend their clothes and blaspheme mightily,

And the insiders make merry, one with another, saying:

"Behold this hole in the ground will bring great riches." And the superintendent writeth another letter, proclaiming the wealth of the west cross-cut:

"Behold, the breast is in ore, and the stones drip fatness."

"The bonanza comes in on the south side, and the chlorides proclaim their greenness."

And the stockholders lifted up their noses and said:

"Behold, we smell the dividends close at hand."

And they held on even until the voice of the caller in the board proclaimed not the name of their stock unto them, and they are sore worried, and say among themselves:

"Are they not deceivers of men?"

And they curse the day that they were born, and cry aloud—

"Where are these men? Let us lay hands upon them and smite them."

And they search diligently among the habitations of the money-changers and find them not.

Because they are in the country of the Gauls, making merry at the chief capital thereof, and passing many shekels of gold and silver unto the artificers and dwellers therein.

And they return not, and the mine remains a hole in the ground, two fathoms deep, unto this day.

Hearken ye to the voice of wisdom, and observe diligently the words of the prophet.

That thy name may be great in Israel, and thy possession increase upon earth. [24]

There is no question that Deadwood was linked, economically and socially, with Lead. "The Homestake Mine," as the engineer Merrill said, "operated as the chief civilizing influence on both Lead and Deadwood, and it was of course indisputable that the mine's steadily expanding operations and increasing payroll provided the principal economic foundation on which both towns grew and thrived." The two towns are called the twin cities of the Black Hills, yet it is hard to imagine two more dissimilar twins, for the wealth and ethnic diversity of Lead, with its dozens of cohesive foreign groups, and the overall domination of the Homestake, which keeps a benevolent and paternal eye on everyone, is markedly different from the more ethnically unified but socially diverse Deadwood. Lead was merely an industrial town which happened to have a mine; Deadwood was where all hell broke loose.[25]

SIX

Refractory Ore

"The cowards never started, the weak died on the
trail and the fools went on to Wyoming."
                                        An old-timer

"Where are the friends of earlier years,
    The fond and faithful-hearted;
With whom we shared the smiles and tears,
    Of days long since departed."
                                    Black Hills Pioneer

"There were giants in the earth in those days."
                                        Genesis

THE PIONEERS who attended the Black Hills gold rush of the 1870s
were not like other men; there was a spark in each of them that set
him apart from those who formed the more settled populations of
the East. Some were western miners accustomed to follow each rush
as it erupted, and to abandon it if fortune did not immediately smile
upon their prospects. Others were young men out for a few months
of vacation in the mines—a good many came to the rush and never
even looked for gold to speak of—and who hoped to strike it rich by
some miracle, but mainly hoped to have a little time of irresponsibility before they went back home to settle down to steady labor.
Many another pilgrim was a mature working man who had saved
his money and saw in the rush to the Hills his last chance to really
get ahead in life and who was willing to gamble his energy and
savings against the mountains. There were speculators (the title had
no contemptuous overtones in those days) and capitalists (who today
would be called investors) who saw in the Black Hills—as Hearst
saw in the Homestake—an opportunity for advantageous investment, a chance to get in on the ground floor of a new edifice of
mineral excitement. There were the scoundrels and swindlers,
thieves and hoodlums, real and would-be desperadoes, loose women

and honest ones; and all of them, living in a new, raw, wild country, were anxious to live up to its possibilities and eager to portray the new land as they saw it themselves.

It has always been the custom in such a country for the inhabitants to make it appear by deed and gesture, tale and rumor, more wild and woolly than it actually was. Like the pinch of gold that the pilgrim preferred to a coin or shinplaster, the gun on the hip, the raucous laughter and casually abandoned stance all served to advertise new and profitable and exciting ways in a new and promising land. Many an observant and literary visitor—and newspaper correspondents were a small but important part of the emigration to any new gold field—received a dose of frontier exaggeration that lasted him clear back to Boston, and when he wrote his column on Deadwood, it was of exaggerations foisted upon him rather than of reality, for the pilgrims generally put on an act, and the more curious and gullible the spectator, the more outrageous the act was likely to be. All actors on life's stage, the gold rushers played their parts before whatever audience they had, actors on a stage that they built themselves, in a play that they wrote as they went along.

There is no doubt that the more refractory element in Deadwood society tended to get the most publicity and thus tended to be taken as repesentative. Even Deadwood's solid citizens joined in perpetuating this myth of a wild frontier town, although for business purposes they now and then officially denied it.

> In song and story and by legend the world hears much of the rougher, more picturesque characters whose memories have been much enhanced through the passing years . . . but more sober reflection recognizes that it was not the picturesque character with the long hair, nor the wandering miner, nor the gambler nor the painted lady who founded the region. They were incidental to its life and its surroundings,

said R. E. Driscoll in his recollections of seventy years of banking in the Black Hills, and he is probably correct, for the western miners, the tenderfeet from the East, the farmers and businessmen from the Midwest, the Civil War veterans (and there was many a man who honestly could be called "General" in the Hills) gave the community its ability to survive and prosper, while the inhabitants of the Deadwood badlands only gave the town something to talk about. Whoever they were, and whatever their background, most of the Deadwood pioneers had that combination of grit and insouciance that was then called "sand in the craw," and those who had it most were most successful and soon became the leaders of the city.[1]

Adverse comments on the general population of course were common: "I never in my life saw so many hardened and brutal-looking men together," wrote the reporter Leander P. Richardson in 1876. It was "a disorderly, sinful, sickly city. . . . a queer place," which "the man who ventured the remark that a fool and his money are soon parted must have had in his mind's eye" when he coined the apothegm—"a sharpers' paradise" for "the ingenious bummer, the slick confidence man, the claim jumper, the land shark and the desperado" who dominated the bustling main street and infested its saloons. In short, a country where a man had to be "of more than usual alertness . . . not to get taken in somehow or other before he has been 24 hours in this sinful city." It is bad news that makes news, however, and newspaper correspondents have always been more prone to criticize than to praise the new scenes which they examine.[2]

The population of the gold rush days of '76 was almost entirely composed of young men; children were a rarity, even middle-aged men, despite the occasional grizzled prospector, were few, and women amounted to between 100 and 150 for the entire Black Hills area, perhaps constituting between 1 percent and 2 percent of the pilgrim population, although of course estimates of both total population and of women are necessarily rough, with a maximum population in Deadwood of up to 10,000 at the outside, although some of the estimates, depending on which communities they included, ran higher. The rushers tended to be raucous and noisy but otherwise well behaved, for the norm of gold rush behavior had been long since established in countless other mining camps throughout the West, and those who did not conform were urged or aided to move away. Honesty, reinforced by the ready availability of deadly weapons in almost every hand, was taken for granted during the early days of the gold rush. Claims, tools, and even gold, if left in plain sight where bystanders could observe a thief, were thought to be safe, for the entire community looked after property when its owner was absent. Miners sorted through the early, unofficial mail deliveries and took what they wanted of it for their partners and themselves, and to arrive in camp was to share the food and fire of those already there, for to be a pilgrim was, in the early days, to be a friend. Even the miners, of course, had their peculiarities:

The smartest Alecks on all subjects here are men from Montana. The best miners in lean ground are men from California. The men who demand the highest wages, and earn the smallest, are from Utah. . . . The ones most given to contemplating the cocktail come from Colorado. The weakest knee'd, no account growler generally comes from down east.

The stereotypes may have been thus established, but the miners all worked together anyway, and those who were there during the rush remember it as a happy, if not for everyone a golden, age.[3]

As Deadwood grew from a gold rush camp into a mining city, the "true western man" who had "subsisted for several consecutive weeks on bacon, beans, flapjacks and black coffee, and slept at least a month on the ground floor of a tent" using his back for a mattress and his stomach for a bedspread again began to take on the rudiments of civilization. The transition from "pilgrim," or tenderfoot, to "pioneer" was hastened by being chased by Indians, held up on the stage, and "gone bust" on a likely prospect or two, and when the process was completed, it eventually produced, as one enthusiastic booster put it, an "irresistible aggregation of brain-directed force that distinguishes Deadwood from the ordinary frontier or western town," a town in which the visitor would "come face to face with culture and refinement" and where a stranger would "have to search for rudeness and incivility," a town in which one had to do with "men of brain, and men whose knowledge of the world, and of the ways of the world, is thorough and complete." This transition, from mining camp to city—and it was a transition which retained many of the mining camp ways almost to the present day—was the result of a boomtown gold rush atmosphere combined with business acumen, educated businessmen and engineers, determined wives and a general tone of Victorian gentility. It was quite a combination.[4]

By the 1880 census times had changed. Only 29 percent of the population were miners—the next largest identifiable group, 16 percent, was wives. Laborers were 12 percent of Deadwood's population, and the ratio of males to females was 80 to 28, that is, 35 percent, which meant that over half of the women in town were *not* wives. The median age aided by the passing years had gone up to thirty-three. Foreign-born citizens outnumbered native-born in Terraville and in nearby Fort Meade, and would come to do so in nearby Lead. The population obviously contained many highly mobile families, for many are listed as having each of several children born in a different state or country. By 1908 the town could claim, without blushing, to be "inhabited by a hospitable, generous and well-informed people, who live well, dress well, and while they are very attentive to business, always find time to cultivate the higher intellect and are well versed in literature and art," a people who had built "fine palatial residences on the hillsides, and elegant business structures down town," a town which bore "marked evidence of a cosmopolitan little city." Even today Deadwood flaunts her happily combined heritage of gold camp and Victorian commercial center. The people are genuinely tolerant of almost anything—they have much of which they need to be—and they do not ignore, but neither do they condemn. The modern "upstairs girls," the motorcycle gangs, the earnest skiers, and bedizined tourists, are all observed, considered, profited from, and sent their way with an amused and tolerant smile; Deadwood has seen so much by now that she can stand just about anything.

Deadwood people of today may well be called "the people of the book," and in their case the book is Estelline Bennett's tolerant and perceptive *Old Deadwood Days*, a delightful compendium of her childhood memories of the days before the railroads came. Judge Granville Bennett, Estelline's father, was a power in the community, her mother a blessing to it, and Estelline's pen as a reporter and writer and editor shaped the town, though neither father nor daughter escaped criticism, one of her friends writing in 1890 that "if she had only been *quite clean* she'd have looked very nicely," and the judge now and then being accused of trifling irregularities. Still, her book has done more to shape Deadwood's conception of itself than any other literary influence, and if this happy work, now long out of print, is misquoted and garbled by those Deadwood citizens who know it only secondhand, still it works its wonders in the way that Deadwood thinks and feels about itself.[5]

Many others less distinguished but more notorious left their impression on the town. The list of gaudy nicknames that were remembered evokes the image of a community in which unconformity was tolerated and probably encouraged as the norm: Cayoose Laura, Big Tim, Homestake Harry, Texas Frank, Colorado Charley Utter, Lame Johnny, Swill Barrel Jimmy, Jerry the Bum, Gunboat, the whole crew "that was always watching around for one thing or another." Johnny the Oyster, Club Foot Frank, Cheating Sheely, Laughing Sam, Pink Bedford, Bloody Dick, and others of their stripe peopled the badlands, as the shabby underworld north of Wall Street stairs was called, and though their lives only occasionally impinged upon the lives of the respectable folk of Ingleside or Cleveland, the racket from their doings drifted easily up to Forest Hill, whose houses were hardly fifty feet above the badland's raucous misbehavior.[6]

Justin "Old Frenchy" Cachlin the Bottle Fiend—the town seems to have had more than one character of this name—collected bottles as a hobby, until he found that he could sell his thousands to the local brewery. He lived pretty much on the wrong side of the law, having once gone so far as to steal Sheriff Manning's pants and overcoat; one wonders what the situation was to allow such a theft to go even momentarily unnoticed. Alas, Old Frenchy fell and injured himself in his lonely cabin on Thanksgiving morning of 1880, and after lying in a stinking and loathsome condition for weeks, he died on Christmas Eve. A second Old Frenchy, Hannibal Morris, had come to Deadwood with the rush of 1876, labored at chores around town, and was considered to be "one of the most law abiding citizens." He had been born in French Guiana, from which he took his nickname, about 1819, was sold five times as a slave, and still bore the marks of his servitude upon his body. The charity of the city supported him in his tiny cabin during the concluding months of his existence, and his passing was greatly mourned.[7]

Swill Barrel Jimmy wore a long, frayed, faded frock coat, a derby as aged, and, astonishingly, a clean white collar. He lived quite literally from hand to mouth, begging the leavings from the restaurants, bars, and bawdy houses, and living tucked into the corner of a hospitable saloon when the weather was cold. He had a story, but no one knew what it was, although it was rumored he had been a Confederate officer and, broken in spirit by the war, had come to the West to smother his troubles.[8]

Nigger General Fields listed himself in the 1878 *Directory* as a "cosmopolite" who lived at the Arcade. He carried messages, ran errands, acted as a procurer, and lived a life of shabby notoriety, being perhaps best known for having carried the note that led a young man to an assignation, not with his inamorata but with Bill Gay her irate husband, who shot the young lothario dead.

Henrietta "Madame Henrico" Livingstone, who considered herself a "clairvoyant physician," lived on the Gayville road at the east end of Forest Hill, where she worked a mining claim on her little lot and threatened everyone who bothered her with a shotgun, a reclusive and quarrelsome crank who now and then was hauled before the police courts for threatening to disturb the peace. For some thirty years her quarrels and scoldings perturbed the otherwise staid households in her neighborhood.[9]

Old Billy Wilson ran a four-horse stage line—it must have been a pretty small one—southward to the Union Pacific at Sidney and was making money until his drivers became frightened of the many stage robbers and quit on him, leaving Old Billy to drive for himself. Alerted to a pending ambush, he whooped up his horses, took the reins in his teeth, a revolver in each hand, and galloped through, leaving five of the robbers dead behind him. On the way back the same band of singularly determined highwaymen again attempted to waylay him, this time losing eleven of their number to this implacable jehu. Cured of attacking Old Billy in bunches, the robbers attempted, one after another, to stop him individually, each with some new device or stratagem, and one by one Old Billy weeded them out and left them lie for the vultures to dispose of, until he had laid to rest forever the shadow of the highwayman across the trail of the Deadwood stage. By 1880, however, he had retired to Carbonate Camp in the limestone country, where his speculations ended in disaster, leaving him only the happy recollections, perhaps somewhat embellished by the passing years, of his long career as a liberator of the Sidney-Deadwood trail. At least that was the story that he told an inquiring reporter who was hard up for news, and it was doubtless as true as many another tale which is nowadays taken for gospel truth by modern readers who do not fully understand the verbal extravagances inherent in the oral traditions of a mining camp.[10]

Who has not heard of Deadwood Dick? A whole succession of diligent old gas-wells have assumed this title, worn it as a cloak in the parade of life, and gone to well-deserved graves wrapped in its mysteries. The last of these synthetic heros was buried in 1930, bizarre, beloved, derided, and admired. The truth of the matter is that there never was a real Deadwood Dick—he was a creation of the fervid mind of the dime-novelist Edward L. Wheeler, who produced a series of tales each including the name "Deadwood Dick" in their title, each one a marvel of the slam-bang, shoot-'em-up,

"Which way did they go, Scout?" brand of literature so dear to generations which had neither movies, radio, nor TV for their boyhood entertainment.

The first to claim to have been Deadwood Dick was Nat Love, a black cowboy whose published autobiography seems to be almost entirely a figment of his ornate imagination. Banjo Dick Brown, who played and sang in the Melodeon, was another who wore the title, but never pretended to be anything more than what he was, a talented performer in the local burlesque house. Richard "Little Dick" Cole brought the first stagecoach into Deadwood, and indeed did have a few encounters with bandits in the course of his profession, and in his declining years he let it be known that it would gratify him to be known as Deadwood Dick, and kindly friends humored him in this innocent conceit. Dick Bullock (not to be confused with Seth), another stagecoachman, was indeed a valiant and proficient "messenger" who guarded the bullion shipments for several years, both on the stage and later on the railroad. Either Bullock or his friends for a time promoted the idea that he too could be called Deadwood Dick, and once the custom was established, it gratified him immensely to wear this nickname along with his own honors.

A fifth Deadwood Dick, Richard Clark, arose in the 1920s, the creation of Fred Gramlick, who felt that as the mines declined the Black Hills could use all the publicity that they could get, and he encouraged Clark to assume this notorious title. Clark, so ornamented, tried to ride in one of the first Days of '76 parades but incontinently fell off of the prancing stallion provided for him, and thereafter he marched afoot, armed with rifle and shovel. A tourist inquired what the shovel was for, to which Clark replied, "Lady, I always aim to give the men I kill a Christian burial." It set the tone of his pronouncements from then on. The whole notion of Deadwood Dick seems to have brought out the worst in those who, one way or another, have come in contact with this enduring legend. When I was wee I had my photograph taken—for a small fee— standing beside Deadwood Dick Clark with a look of absolutely bilious adoration in my infant eyes, so I suppose I will, in my declining years, tell my descendants that "*I* once shook hands with Deadwood Dick" and thus enhance an already well-established reputation for mendacity.[11]

Deadwood Dick was a fabrication; Seth Bullock was as genuine as the West that made him, and his activities flavored the whole of Deadwood history. A pioneer law officer in Montana and in the early days of the gold rush to Deadwood, an eminent businessman and politician, a soldier in the Spanish-American War, and a good friend of Theodore Roosevelt—it is, perhaps, in this last capacity that Bullock is best known, although it was his activities in the other areas which won him TR's affection and regard. He first met TR when that worthy was bringing a horsethief, one Crazy Steve, into Deadwood for trial, and from then on their friendship ripened rapidly, for Roosevelt believed that Bullock represented—and indeed he did—the best that the West had to offer. Bullock was appointed captain of Troop A of Grisby's cowboy regiment, but sat out the Spanish-American War in training in Louisiana. In 1900 President McKinley, undoubtedly advised by his vice-president, appointed Bullock supervisor of the Black Hills National Forest, and in 1905 Roosevelt appointed him U.S. marshal, an appointment which was continued by President Taft and for a year under Woodrow Wilson. Bullock often rode herd on Roosevelt's turbulent sons, escorting them on various exciting hunting and camping trips across the plains to the north of Deadwood in pursuit of antelope and adventure. Roosevelt even brought Bullock to London, to show off to "those Britishers my ideal typical American." Perhaps the most characteristic indication of the happy relationship between Roosevelt and Bullock is shown in Bullock's letter regarding the Republican convention of 1908, a letter which shows Bullock as both a shrewd politician, a good friend, and a westerner who enjoyed playing the part:

> As you know the Western States in my bailiwick have all had their roundups and selected delegates to the Chicago Convention each delegate being branded with a circle T, the Secretary's brand; they would only stand for a hair brand, however, and it will be necessary to have them counted quickly at the Convention on the 16th of June, for if they 'mill around' much . . . the hair will shed off and disclose the Maltese Cross brand burned into their hides by the people and there will be trouble about the ownership. The people want and will insist on the President holding his position for another term so you may expect many bad half hours at Chicago.

What Bullock meant by all this western jargon was that the western voters might follow the Republican party line and vote at first for the nomination of William Howard Taft, but their allegiance to Taft was minimal, and given much opportunity to discuss the matter with each other, they would quickly turn to their preferred candidate, Teddy Roosevelt.[12]

Bullock's role in bringing the railroad first to Deadwood, and later on to the area around Belle Fourche where he had a ranch, have now and then been criticized as bordering on sharp practice, but the undoubted benefits conveyed upon both areas compensate for any alleged chicanery. His own dealings with the railroad were by no means contented: one of his prize horses was damaged by a passing train, and in answer to his complaint the railroad officers replied that they could legally sue *him*, for allowing his horse to get in the way, but inasmuch as their engine did not seem to be injured, they were willing to let the matter drop. By that time they apparently figured that the railroad could get along without Bullock's support. Seth Bullock died in 1919, soon after assisting at the dedication of a stone tower on top of Mount Theodore Roosevelt, a monument to the friend who had long regarded him as the truest westerner available.

Each community—and particularly one like a gold rush mining camp—tends to develop its own peculiarities of speech and address. Some of these are merely western, some were peculiar unto Deadwood itself. The Black Hills, for example, were now and then referred to as "the Colored Elevations," a bit of jocularity which fortunately did not become well established. "Montenegro," a latinized form of "Black Hills" was also suggested for the area, again fortunately to be discarded. Shine Street, in downtown Deadwood, was named by somebody who wanted to call it *Cheyenne* street but didn't spell very well. The phrase "Whoa, Emma!" was common during the rush, capable by varying inflections of conveying almost any meaning that the speaker had in mind. It referred to a poem by Matthew Prior, but probably no one knew that. Most notable of all the local phrases was the wistful, echoing call of "Oh, Joe!" which would begin about dusk in the camps down below Montana City, and work its way upward through the gulches, passed on from mournful mouth to mouth, until it died away in the upper mountains around Gayville or Gold Run. It was said to have originated in the plaintive calls of a miner who fell into a shallow shaft and spent the night bawling for assistance, but whatever its origin, the miners took it to their hearts, and indeed used it not only in the evenings but as an awakening cry when dawn's rosy fingers tipped the western edge of Deadwood Gulch with the golden hues of day.

When the last call for Joe had faded away into the dusk of evening, a final note was sounded by one Smokey Jones, whose specialty was to give forth with a long and mellow howl of a timber wolf, a call which rang through the valleys like a final bugle call of peace summoning the weary miners to a well-deserved and well-guarded rest.[13]

The assumption of titles both military and civil was so common throughout the West as to excite comment from visitors from areas less liberally endowed with such honors. Ten men, for example, came together late in the Deadwood rush, in 1879, the party consisting of two judges, two colonels, two majors, two doctors, and two professors "and," said the reporter, "there was not much law, little medicine, hardly any metallurgy, and scarcely any military in the whole crowd." A foreign visitor, looking into a Fort Pierre directory published in the 1880s found that out of fifteen hundred names there were eight hundred colonels, and two to three hundred majors or judges; all the rest were captains. This is probably an exaggeration. The same observer also commented that "you must always tell an American that he is the *pioneer* of something, or the *prominent citizen* of some place" if you want to establish cordial relations with him; it was a custom long continued in the multitude of laudatory "mug books" containing biographical sketches of supposedly eminent citizens.[14]

Miners, of course, as well as westerners, had their own language, their own professional jargon, in addition to a large amount of slang, the whole studiously elaborated both as a folk art and as a means of obtaining distinction and notice from those who were not parties to this new conversation. If they referred to everybody they had met before as "pard," this was not only an indication of a frontier friendliness and usage, but to show off before those who had not yet joined the magic circle of pard-ship. The frontiersmen often called upon the Almighty for divine assistance; indeed, a visitor might have supposed himself to be in a theological seminary, so often was the name of the Lord brought into their conversations. A plucky or courageous man was said to have a liberal supply of "sand," a contraction of the Civil War phrase "plenty of sand in his crop," a phrase truncated, as mentioned before, into the single pithy word "grit." A skillful man was a "sharp," as in "rock sharp" for a mining engineer or geologist, or "gospel sharp" for a preacher. A truthful man was said, in reference to the infant Washington, to "carry his little hatchet right along with him." A wide-awake and enterprising man was a "rustler," a title also bestowed upon those who did their rustling among their neighbor's cattle. The word "sir" as an intensifier was never omitted, as in "he's a white man, yes, sir," the adjective "white" referring more to purity of soul than to actual color. The salutation "Howdy!" was invariably followed by the question, "What do you know?" and generally got a conversation started. A bald man "had his head above the timberline," or was giving visual signs of having a "boss" intellect which had worn away the fringe from his thinking apparatus.[15]

Doubtless some of the men had read the dime novels, and imitated their supposed conversation—life imitating art, so to speak. Others, as previously pointed out, talked the way they did for effect, and others merely from habit. Bullock's letter to Roosevelt about the election of 1908 is perhaps typical of the long-continued effects of such habits; Bullock could and did write better English than that, but in his letter to Roosevelt he wrote what he assumed was expected of him; it was the custom of the Black Hills citizens not to disappoint those who expected them to be fantastic.

Deadwood has always been proud of its ethnic groups, although by no means as blessed with them as Lead, a city in which more than half of the population was foreign-born and which reveled in the variety of its various foreign clubs and societies. It is notable that 41 percent of the members of the Society of Black Hills Pioneers—those who had come to the Hills before 1877—were foreign-born, although, unlike the "new" immigrants of Lead, the bulk of them came from the British Isles, Germany, and Canada. An influential Jewish community was in evidence in Deadwood from the very first, and as early as 1883 "the finest mazzos [sic] ever seen outside the Holy Land" could be purchased during Passover at the Vienna Bakery on Lee Street. Sol Star, Harris Franklin, Ben Baer, Jake Goldberg, Fred and Moses Manuel, Adolph, Louis, and Max Fischel, Charles and Jonas Zoellner, Sol Bloom, and about thirty others took their place in Deadwood's social and economic life without arousing the slightest comment—indeed, their religious affiliations can only be discovered by reference to the roll of the now defunct Deadwood synagogue.

Anyone who doubts the tenacity and vigor of these early-day Jewish merchants, often itinerants who carried their goods in hundred-pound back packs to their rural customers, has only to visit the "Jew Peddler Trail" on Rapid Creek between Canyon City and Mystic, where these hardy peddlers, to save a three-mile walk along the creek, took to the mountains and crossed a narrow but precipitous gooseneck of land between the loops of the stream. It was their regular trail, more or less over the Volin Tunnel, as they came westward from Rapid City, and today as in the past a casual hiker without a burden has to be in good health to negotiate it at all.[16]

The black population was of about the same size as the Jewish one; thirty-eight Negroes were listed in Deadwood in the 1900 census, but because of their supposedly comic possibilities they aroused a good deal more jocular comment in the newspapers of the day. Edmond Colwell ran a saloon in 1880; another black man, name not known, ran a newsstand near the telephone building. Charlie Brown, as Isadore Cavanaugh was known, murdered a Mrs. Stone and was hanged for it. Most of the black population seems to have been male, and single, although Lucretia "Aunt Lou" Marchbanks and Sarah "Aunt Sally" Campbell, who had cooked for Custer during his 1874 expedition to the Hills and later lived in Galena, were notable exceptions. The appellation "aunt" or "uncle" was a common title of courtesy applied to mature black people at that time, "Mr." or "Mrs." being contrary to custom, and yet the newspapers needing some honorific title with which to indicate a respectable social status. The black people of Deadwood had a "picnic and festival" on Spearfish Creek in the summer of 1879, and appeared to a white reporter "to be an industrious, enterprising, and frugal group." In 1880 a certain "Colonel John Lawrence" of Silver City, "a town composed of one deserted log cabin somewhere at the head of a small gulch in the Bald Mountain district" was busy trying to work up black support for his favorite political candidates, although neither he nor his candidates had "ever been known to do a disinterested act for the good of our colored citizens." Racial distinctions were clearly shown when in 1883 the *Times* happily recorded a fight on lower Main (the badlands district) "in which a colored and a plain man participated," the latter being the aggressor. A notable black citizen, Bo Williams (his nickname was a corruption of *Beau*, that is, "handsome") summoned many of his friends to help celebrate his birthday at the National House in April 1883, where he engaged an orchestra, brought in many of his friends of the Twenty-fifth Infantry from Fort Meade, and attempted to collect an admission fee at the door, but so few of his friends paid that Mrs. Marie Bernard, the proprietress, was obliged to collect from them herself, after kicking Bo several times around her dining room in retribution.

One black citizen arrived as the valet of a mining promoter who came to town in a private railroad car but went away under his own power, leaving his valet behind to become a respected citizen. "Cutting Affrays" were commonly reported in the paper—John Roberts was sliced in several places by Homer Calley, who resented interferences with his acquaintance with Jennie (or Lizzie) Venerable of the notorious Green Front. Calley was discovered also profusely bleeding and comatose, Roberts having not only operated on him, but, to quiet him for the procedure, had tapped him on the head with half a brick. The whole outfit was distributed between jail and the hospital until sufficiently recovered to testify, at which time both of the combatants were sent to prison, thus settling to everyone's satisfaction a typical badlands ruction.[17]

Considering that the Indian War of 1876 had left many scars upon the psyche of the Black Hills body politic, it is astonishing how amiable relations with the Indians appeared to have been thereafter. The Indian appeared as a sort of natural phenomenon to be watched out for, and in many cases interest in him far outweighed fear of him. The arrival of Mapa Chatka ("Left Hand") to testify in a law case in 1883 led to astonishment on both sides: the telephone amazed the old gentleman, and when he spoke over it to Crow Dog, "his wonderment was indescribable and only equaled by his pleasure." He was described as "a splendid specimen of his race—tall and well proportioned, and as yet untrammeled by civilization and the ways of the white man. . . . the beau ideal of the noble red man."[18]

Events arising out of the trial of Crow Dog for the killing of Spotted Tail in 1890 did much to improve relations between the races. Crow Dog had been tried and the case settled in an Indian court on the reservation, but the Deadwood courts also got into the picture and again tried and convicted Crow Dog and sentenced him to hang. Crow Dog took the sentence stoically enough, but requested permission to go back to the reservation to settle up his affairs. Permission was granted, and Crow Dog, unguarded, cheerfully went home, to as cheerfully return to be hanged on the appointed day. Fortunately his lawyers had appealed his conviction, which was reversed by a higher court on the ground that as he had once been tried by an Indian court, his second trial had put him twice in jeopardy for the same crime and his conviction by it could not be sustained. The straightforward and stoical dignity of the Indian, and the obvious determination of the white man's courts to do justice, whatever justice in the case might be, won the admiration of both peoples.[19]

Far less amiable was the trial of Cha Nopa Uhah ("Two Sticks") for killing four young men on the Pine Ridge Reservation. The Deadwood courts having jurisdiction at that time of course presided, and Two Sticks was convicted, and though he maintained his innocence, at least of any intent to do murder, protesting to the last, "My heart is not bad," he was hanged in February 1893. The jurors presented the presiding judge with an inscribed cane in token of their esteem for his conduct of the trial, which had been a thoroughly tangled and contentious one.[20]

The interest that the people of Deadwood took in the Indians whenever their business brought them up from their reservations into the Black Hills was phenomenal, and the Indians reciprocated by stalking about their camps muttering "Ugh!" or "How!" with immense éclat, presenting to their gaping visitors the traditional image of the grim and silent warrior. The Indian women were more outgoing, and welcomed visitors—if not too many or too unmannerly—to their tents and tipis, but they too were not above a sly jest, muttering, as they reached for a long-handled spoon, "Stirrum up pot—puppy on bottom," as they went about their cooking. Indian dances were common and did much to please both groups—the white men got the show and the Indians got an audience—and by the 1920s the Indians made regular pilgrimages to Deadwood (I can remember as a child being often driven by their camp by the side of the road near Hill City) to participate in the parades and celebrations connected with the Days of '76.

Of all the ethnic groups in Deadwood, the one that attracted the most comment and interest was the Chinese. From the start of the rush in early 1876 the *Cheyenne Leader* noted their arrival from the West and their departure for the Hills, unkindly recording that an apocryphal group composed of "Hop-Lee, Ding-Dong, Heap-Wash, and Hang-Jeff, Celestial chuckle-heads from the Flowery kingdom" had pulled out of town for the new mines. Many found profitable employment reworking abandoned placer tailings, for with care and hard work they could extract enough of the gold which the original miners had missed to support themselves. Others went into the traditional Chinese laundry business, still others ran cheap but excellent restaurants. Their cleanliness was proverbial, although their proverb also had it that "he who would enjoy his dinner should not look over the kitchen wall." Others operated stores dealing in imported goods attractive to both Americans and Chinese, and as they came to be known and trusted, many of them found employment as cantankerous but efficient household servants. When Judge Bennett twitted his cook on his entertainments, saying, "Where did I see you last night?" Wang replied without a blush, "Humph . . . where did I see YOU?"

Population figures for the Chinese of Deadwood are no more reliable than those for the rest of Deadwood's people, and probably considerably less so due to the secretiveness of the Chinese who feared various anti-Chinese laws or hostilities if it were known how many of them there actually were. Estimates run from 164 in 1880, to 100 in 1892, a guess of "upwards of one hundred" in 1898, and 400 around 1900, but in the census of 1900 only 67 Chinese are actually recorded. The census records probably did not include all of the Chinese, but the boasts sometimes heard that Deadwood had the largest Chinatown east of San Francisco are certainly unfounded. Nevertheless, a visitor coming into the lower, or Chinatown, end of Deadwood Gulch in the 1880s would have imagined that he was entering a Chinese village, for "at every house signboards are hanging out recommending to the public Ah-Chin as a linen washer, or Wan-Loo-Ting as tailor, and at every door, notwithstanding the late hour, the 'Celestials' are bawling and gesticulating," and a slight odor of opium pervaded the circumambient air. By 1902 the city directory listed many Chinese: Flam Wing, cook at the Elegant; Woo Wing, his boss; Ho Ching, at the Lincoln Restaurant; S. Y. Woo, proprietor of the Lincoln; Ki Yee, Wah Lee, Toy Wong, and You Quong all in the laundry business; and Yang Ching, a clerk in a Chinese store. The 1910 directory listed businesses run by Hi Kee (groceries and drugs), Sing You (restaurant), Iwong Wing Chong and Company (merchandise), and laundries operated by King Lee, Hong Lee, Yee Gee, Yee Lee, and Yee Sang, as well as the famous emporium managed by Wing Tsue Wong at 566 Main Street, long a landmark in Deadwood.

Wing Tsue, as he was commonly known, sold Chinese groceries, chinaware, herbs, Chinese novelties, Japanese curtains, wastepaper baskets, intricately hand-carved work boxes, napkin rings, fancy inlaid bread knives, "and hundreds of other appropriate gifts" in surroundings advertised as "unique, neat, and appreciative." An early arrival in Deadwood, Wing Tsue was soon entangled in charges of opium selling, and was at least once fined for that crime. His struggles for political power in the Chinese community were well known, for he was the head of one of the tongs (those turbulent combinations of secret society, chamber of commerce, and hooliganism), the other being governed by Ki Kee, the merchant next door. Wing Tsue brought his wife to Deadwood and invited his many friends to call upon her: "the lovliest bit of exquisite china I ever saw," said Estelline Bennett, "painted and mascarra'd in a way no nice American women could understand in those days but on her the effect was charming." Mrs. Wong served tea, little almond cakes, candied limes, and Chinese bonbons, and even though she spoke not a word of English she made her visitors delightfully at home. In 1902 Wing Tsue took his wife and children back to Canton, and in 1919 he joined them there for good. Several of his children, however, returned to the United States—one of his sons achieved distinction in the U.S. Army during World War II—but none of the family lives in Deadwood now.[21]

The customs of the Chinese were always a source of interest and amusement to the people of Deadwood. The incense—or the opium—from their joss house could be sniffed a block away; their polite but secretive manners, and their cheerful mangling of their new language made them objects of both interest and admiration. Tales like that of the Chinaman (they were always so called, perhaps because so few of their women came to the United States, and fewer still of those came to American attention) who had learned English at the Congregational Church's Chinese school, and wrote upon a wedding cake he had decorated, "God made the world but Wong made this cake," were common. Similarly, Colonel Steele's servant, Yee Murk, left a note for his employer, "Mr. Chicken Pot Pie, he sawen wood. Us to him two dollars'n half," which, all things considered, was pretty good English for somebody who had only recently learned the language. Their ten-day celebration of the Chinese New Year, in February, was prepared for weeks in advance, and their signs, fireworks, music, and parades attracted enthusiastic audiences to the strange doings of "the rice destroyers." Their opium dens were regarded as hellholes of iniquity, for "if there is any enjoyment in its [opium's] effect," one reporter wrote, "it must be in

the imagination of the smoker," and anybody could surmise what
would likely be in the perverse imagination of a Chinaman. The
same reporter noticed in his visit to the Deadwood opium den
"many who we had met in better circles of society," for this particular vice tended to spread beyond the confines of the Chinese community, and in addition to Deadwood, Lead, Central City, and Sturgis all had their opium houses.[22]

Chinese funerals were an open and public display of strange oriental customs. The Chinese always raised a fund for a respectable
funeral for their poor, and indeed never did ask the community at
large for charity or assistance. Oddly, the Lawrence County *Record
of Deaths* for 1878–98 lists only a single Chinese death, but the large
number of Chinese graves on Mount Moriah indicates that this record must have been defective. Red papers full of holes were scattered about, the notion being that the devil had to wind his way
through all the holes before he could reach the soul of the departed,
which certainly gives the Evil One credit for less ingenuity than he
usually is presumed to have. There was a fireplace and oven in the
Chinese section of Mount Moriah Cemetery, where the Chinese
roasted pigs for the funeral festivities. One spectator inquired when
the departed would arise to partake of the roast pork. The Chinese
replied, "Same time 'Melican man comes up to smell the flowers."
Dr. H. von Wedelstaedt, who belonged to the Chinese lodge of Masons, often walked in their funeral parades, and attended the subsequent banquets, but he never learned to use chopsticks, and always carried a spoon in his pocket. The Chinese, however, did not
confine themselves to their own foods, but had a positive addiction
to American bread, if they could buy it hot from the baker's oven.
Baker Bob Howe took advantage of this predilection and put out hot
bread during the Chinese dinner hour, when it was generally
cleaned out with a rush, each Chinaman buying a whole loaf for his
noonday meal.[23]

Not everybody was completely entranced by the oriental oddi-
ties of the Chinese. Attorney Henry Frawley, for example, defended
a white client who had murdered a Chinaman by alleging that there
was no law against it, and he urged the judge to fine the murderer
twenty-five dollars for "cruelty to animals" instead. The judge, apparently anxious to impose some punishment less than a capital one,
agreed. It is likely that in such a case there was some uncertainty
about obtaining a conviction on a capital charge, and the judge ac-

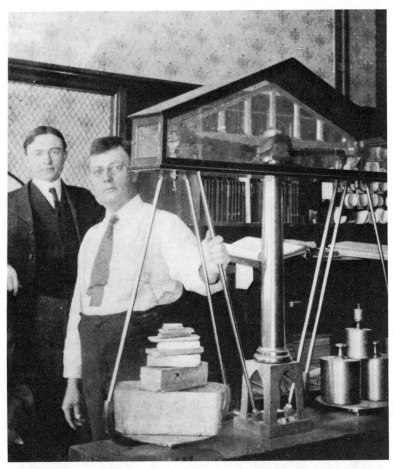

Col. W. J. Thornby keeps a watchful eye on 75,000 ounces of gold bullion on a heavy-duty scale. *Centennial Collection—Deadwood Public Library*

An ancient log cabin still marks the area near Four Corners, Wyoming, where the Deadwood stagecoach was held up at Canyon Springs. *W. Parker photo*

The last run of the Deadwood stage, 1890. *Centennial Collection—Deadwood Public Library*

The Chicago and North Western Railway Train, near the Whitewood Tunnel about 1890. *Centennial Collection—Deadwood Public Library*

The mills and railroads at Blacktail, with Terraville high atop the mountains in the background. *Centennial Collection—Deadwood Public Library*

The Golden Reward Chlorination Plant, a milling process around the turn of the century. *Centennial Collection—Deadwood Public Library*

The great Deadwood and Delaware Smelter at the northern end of Deadwood, already perched upon a growing pile of slag from its many furnaces. *Centennial Collection—Deadwood Public Library*

The joys of the local saloon were many. *Centennial Collection—Deadwood Public Library*

The Green Front Theatre, a long-enduring oasis of dissipation in Deadwood's badlands of iniquity. *Centennial Collection—Deadwood Public Library*

George V. Ayres, pioneer Deadwood merchant, and founder of the hardware store. *Centennial Collection—Deadwood Public Library, from S. J. Clarke's "South Dakota" (1915)*

Seth Bullock, pioneer merchant, marshal, sheriff, forest supervisor, and friend of Theodore Roosevelt. *Centennial Collection—Deadwood Public Library*

Teacher Dottie Smith, about 1903. *Centennial Collection—Deadwood Public Library*

Robert H. Driscoll, the banker. *Centennial Collection—Deadwood Library, from S. J. Clarke's "South Dakota" (1915)*

Winters are cold in the northern Hills, and the fur coat—here doubtless from the hide of a buffalo or two—was both stylish and convenient for the stage or an open buggy.

Centennial Collection—Deadwood Public Library

cepted this form of plea bargaining in order to inflict at least as much punishment as possible. Tormenting a Chinaman was a common form of entertainment for the city's clodpolls. The youthful George Hunter (later a most respected citizen) used to fill a grape basket with small rocks and slide it down the telephone wires from Williams Street into Main, timing it to impinge upon passing Chinamen, who of course knew better than to waste time trying to catch pestiferous small boys. An 1882 news story tells of "a couple of hoodlums" who assaulted a Chinaman, but John (the generic name for the Chinese, as "George" was for a sleeping car porter) seized a stick of cordwood (that would be about four feet long) and cleaned up on the two, and "for a wonder the Chinaman wasn't arrested," said the newspaper, which would imply that in the ordinary case he would have been, an indication of the customary arbitrary treatment of the Chinese by the officers of the law.

The Chinese themselves frequently quarreled and fought in internecine battles but dimly understood by those unacquainted with their tempestuous internal affairs. Giant powder blew the porch off of one Chinese house—whether an outrage committed by other Chinese or by whites is not clear—but the Chinese skill with explosives was proverbial, even though none of them worked in the mines, and they were blamed for it. Tong Hay and Ton Lem Sang attacked Ching Kee Lang, who was said to be "a good man, a Mason, a man who reverenced the maxims of Confucius; a law abiding man, a man who loved the starry banner of the free" and chopped him up so thoroughly with a hatchet that when he recovered it gave rise to the novel anthropological "opinion that a Chinaman cannot be killed." The attackers were arrested. The murder of the China Doll, a young and beautiful Chinese prostitute, who was chopped to pieces, presumably by some of the more reclusive Chinese citizens, was never solved, and remains a mystery, commemorated nowadays by a Chinese restaurant named in her memory. Times changed, and by 1905, when some cheap thieves murdered old Mak Gib of Portland to steal ten dollars from him, there was a considerable outcry to hunt down and lynch the murderers.[24]

Although the Chinese were of interest to the Deadwood community and were individually respected, the desire to expel Chinese cheap labor was always lurking in the back of the minds of the rougher laboring men. In 1878 a "Caucasian League" was organized to "protect the interest of the white miners," and action was taken to "prevent the employment of the Celestials," but not much seems to have come of it, except that in that year four Chinese houses were burned and Frout Hop's damaged by an explosion. Hop not unnaturally came out the door like a shot, cursing with great vigor "Helly dammy 'Mellican man!" Resolutions aimed at running out various individual Chinamen were now and then passed by miners' groups, as much, perhaps, in response to individual crimes as from animosity against them as a group, although the notion that any man who would work as hard for as little as a Chinaman would probably steal also was doubtless present in the miners' minds. "The Chinese Must Go!" was a common enough cry in the 1880s, yet their cheap prices for laundry and labor kept them employed and to a degree essential to the community. The last Chinaman in Deadwood, employed as a janitor, was Ching Ong, commonly known as Teeter, who lived in Deadwood for forty-five years, and when he departed in 1931, a large crowd assembled at the railroad station to bid him an affectional farewell. Ching Ong departed, but the Chinese heritage remained, and Deadwood still likes to think of itself as a town that once "had the biggest Chinatown for its size in the country."

Living conditions and social customs in Deadwood were for the most part about like those in any other small Victorian city in America, but there were of course a few exceptional variations. The presence of a large group of technically educated engineers, a larger than usual number of bustling businessmen, and the availability of far more than the usual amount of wealth to put their schemes into practice made Deadwood far more up to date than most cities of its size or age. The presence of an enormous criminal class—something like a third of the town made a living from saloons, gambling, and prostitution—also distorted the staid Victorian ways which the respectable classes wanted to create and maintain. And the presence of a frontier tradition long-lived and pervasive kept Deadwood a frontier town long after it ought to have become a merely industrial little city.

Sunday, at least during the early gold rush and hardrock mining days, was not only a day of rest and relaxation, but one of active business. And although white shirts and polished boots might be a rarity, now and then a dude like Bill Gay strutted through the day decked out in a boiled shirt with a two-foot watch chain made of nuggets the size of hickory nuts stretched across his ample bosom, with two or three even larger chunks of gold dependent from it to give tone to what might otherwise have been considered a garish and ostentatious display. Jeweler E. F. Heinze would make you a ring out of your own gold, with your initials worked out upon it in jet, and this too was thought to be the height of stylish good taste during the boom times of the 1870s. Whittling, a southern notion of entertainment apparently invented by someone not overly familiar with worldly pleasures, was widely prevalent, the sole object of it being to take a piece of wood in the left hand and with a "pocket-knife, razor, or bowie knife" in the other reduce it to the size of a matchstick. In a community of smokers it must have been a considerable fire hazard, but sensible storekeepers and bartenders usually provided suitable whittling sticks for their customers because it saved wear and tear on their furniture and premises. Chewing tobacco and cigar smoking were popular, but the cigarette, then viewed as an introduction of dissipated criminality, made quicker headway in Deadwood than it did in the rest of the nation. Drunkenness was common, not only because Deadwood was a town devoted to both business and entertainment, but because the 4,630-foot altitude lent a horrific jolt to the low-country effects of hard liquor, a factor which doubtless resulted in markedly increased misbehavior, at least among the tenderfeet.

The number of servants employed would astonish the housekeeper of today. The Chinese men, well trained to cook in Chinese restaurants, often took such positions in private homes. Deadwood housewives, in the 1880s, thought of banding together to send an agent east to recruit fifty servant girls "and do away with much of the impudence and impertinence with which they now have to put up." The *Times* editorialized that "several dozen modest and industrious girls could find employment in our best families at much greater salaries than are paid in the states," but cautioned that "loud and gaudy girls shouldn't apply, the woods are full of that stripe now."[25]

Forest Hill, one of the elite sections of town, consisted of several streets that clung precariously to the northwestern side of the valley, looking directly down on Main Street and on the badlands of Lower Main. Its most prestigious section was on Williams Street, the so-called Iron Hill Row, a nickname derived from the profits its residents had supposedly harvested from investing in the silver mines at Carbonate and its Iron Hill Mine. Ingleside, farther up the gulch on the other side of the valley, was less precipitous, some houses had yards of a sort, and there was not quite so much danger, there, of falling, physically or metaphorically, into the badlands. The grocer, W. E. Adams, had a handsome home in Ingleside with a tower, five staircases, electricity, and hand-painted canvas walls, a home still preserved by his widow in his memory. There were, however, very few real mansions in Deadwood; for one thing, there wasn't room, and for another it did not seem to be the custom to build a house that would require large numbers of servants—always temperamental on the frontier—to run it. It was one thing, apparently, to be a cook or housemaid in a small house, almost a member of the family, and quite another to labor as a cog in the machinery of a household staff for a mansion. At any rate, the wealth of Deadwood did not manifest itself in building large or ornate houses, and most of those which still stand on their cramped hillside lots seem unpretentious compared to those built in more spacious cities. Deadwood nevertheless maintained an air of formality, of self-restraint and urbanity, all out of proportion to its modest size, a degree of social sophistication that oddly continued side by side with its bawdy and raucous and all too evident underworld. Indeed, it may well be that respectable Deadwood cultivated its airs and dignity in order to be distinguished from the less respectable badlands with which it subsisted cheek by jowl. The Deadwood ladies, for example, all stayed away from the downtown stores on Monday afternoons, for that was the time when the "upstairs girls" did their shopping. On the other hand, as late as the 1960s, Deadwood ladies, when they did go shopping, dressed up to do so, for Deadwood shopping, like many of its other activities, was a social as well as a commercial affair.

It is hard for readers nowadays to understand the sickliness of ordinary people a hundred years ago. Unbalanced diets (and too much or too little of them), polluted food and water, totally inadequate sewage and garbage disposal, lack of screens, lack of refrigeration, lack of effective medical care—all resulted in constant indispositions, long sicknesses, and frequent deaths. Although Deadwood bragged of its healthy climate, and probably was, at least for the phthisic, healthier than a smoky eastern city, Whitewood creek was for a hundred years an open sewer, and if the people in town seemed healthier, it probably was because the weakest of them had died of "summer complaint" (diarrhea) or other diseases in their infancy, leaving only the sturdiest behind. Lugubrious poetry on death and departure was a staple item in the papers:

> Rest, dear one; no sorrow, no care
> Can reach you, sleeping there.
> No sickness, grief or pain.
> All is past. Never again
> Will you suffer, languish and die
> Rest, dear one, there on high.

There were some who said that such poetry probably contributed to the death rate, or at least to the incidence of "summer complaint" among the reading citizens.[26]

If Whitewood Creek was a sewer, the streets of Deadwood were a cesspool. The mud between Deadwood and Gayville, for example, was said to be "of a rich quality, it's adhesive qualities are rare, its depth unfathomable, its color indefinable, its extent illimitable, and its usefulness unknown," and the man who made his way on foot from one town to the other in 1877 was advised to offer up a prayer for divine assistance before making the trip. The mud of the roads so covered the stagecoach teams that the Sidney stage, one day, came in with six horses so completely covered that their colors could not be determined. Even the sidewalks were inches deep in mud, and wooden crosswalks only dammed up the drainage of the streets. Sheriff Manning kept a ball-and-chain gang of city prisoners hard at work trying to improve the streets, and the *Times* suggested that if the peace officers would enlarge the gang by additional convictions, it would improve both the streets and the morals of the town. Garbage and slops too were thrown into the streets as a matter of course, and only old Frenchy and a few hogs were available to clean up the resulting mess. The mud and garbage combined with the manure from the horses, mules, and oxen to produce a remarkable slush and stench, "a reeking cesspool of rottenness." One rowdy brawler, thrown into the street by a saloon bouncer, sank beneath the surface of the mud, and there was hope that he was lost for good, but he eventually clambered out, and was "absolutely unapproachable, he stank so."[27] The same year a reporter noticed a hat and part of a raincoat protruding from the mud on Main Street a short distance below Lee, and although a reward was jocularly offered to anybody who would risk his life to find out if a man was underneath them, nobody could be found with sufficient nerve to attempt the rescue.[27]

In the 1880s abandoned houses—a sure sign that the placer boom was over—along Sherman Street were used as privies by passersby, as was the surrounding area in general, through which many children had to pass on their way to school. Similarly unsanitary conditions were particularly noticeable along Lower Main and in Chinatown and Elizabethtown, where "in perambulating these thoroughfares one is almost compelled to think that he is walking between two rows of privy vaults for the stink emitted is equal to that emanating from such caverns." Property owners were urged to clear the gutters in front of their premises in order to permit the runoff of rainwater to wash away the filth, but the habit of throwing and sweeping refuse out the front door and into the street continued. Efforts to flush out the gutters in Chinatown with fire hoses could not overcome this long-standing custom of using the public streets for sewage and garbage disposal. In 1883 the mud on Main Street was from two to ten inches deep, "the consistency of batter," and not high quality batter, either. Deadwood's sanitary conditions improved very slowly, for as late as 1950 the city council and the Chamber of Commerce combined to pay one hundred dollars a month for a washroom attendant at the Franklin Hotel, that being apparently the only public facility in town, and the gas stations not wishing "to provide restrooms for the entire city."[28]

With conditions like these prevailing in the streets, it is not surprising that the first governmental body in Deadwood—aside from casual miners' meetings—was the Board of Health and Street Commissioners, set up in 1876 to combat communicable diseases. An epidemic, apparently a mild form of smallpox, swept through the community, and C. L. "Red" Clark, James Vandaniker, Thomas Short, James Matkin, and Seth Bullock were elected to investigate sanitary conditions and to establish a pesthouse for the afflicted. The original site for this useful edifice was on Spring Creek upstream from L. G. Parkhurst's brewery in Elizabethtown, but as this was deemed likely to damage an essential industry through pollution, the crude hospital was soon moved to the Spearfish road, where at least one death in it led to protests so vigorous that the pesthouse was moved again, to the settlement newly named South Deadwood at the junction of Deadwood and Whitewood creeks. Admirers have claimed that Calamity Jane nursed some of the small-

pox victims, and she probably did, being a woman of generous inclinations and noted for her disregard of any and all of the dangers
of her profession, but her detractors murmured that if indeed she
cured any smallpox victims, she probably gave them the great pox
in return.[29]

Other diseases of course resulted from the uncleanliness of the
prospectors' environment. The Civil War soldiers who came to the
mines were thoroughly acquainted with lice—the carriers of many
a low fever—but still they hated them with a passion born of long
experience. One old bullwhacker claimed that for six years he had
been infested with these pests with but a single twenty-four-hour
intermission. The bathhouse in Deadwood advertised "Hot Baths,
cold baths [one would think that the average prospector got enough
of them!], dry vapor, sulphur, alcohol, and SHOWER BATHS" as a sure
cure for rheumatism, mountain fever, and all skin diseases, with
"accomodations and charges same as the states," but a visitor remarked that although the bathhouse was there, nobody seemed to
know what it was for and "the hinges on the door have grown rusty
and a look of total desertion pervades the entire establishment."
Other diseases, doubtless spread by the town's defective sanitary
arrangements, included "diarrhea, typhoid fever, epizootic and six
shooters," the last, said a visitor from Manitowoc, Wisconsin, being
the most usually fatal. By 1877 the ladies of Deadwood had organized a society to care for the destitute sick, and Jack Langrishe, the
impresario, staged a theatrical benefit for the aid of the hospital
fund, which seems to have needed all the help that it could get.[30]

Insanity was not common. A Mrs. McCleod wandered for four
days in a deranged condition through the Hills between Deadwood
and Spearfish until search parties found and restrained her, but she
was thought to be an unfortunate exception. Yankton, the home of
the state asylum, later alleged that an epidemic of insanity was
sweeping over the Hills—perhaps a result of 1890s disappointments
in mineral speculation—but the *Deadwood Pioneer-Times* demurred,
saying that out of a population of twenty thousand in the northern
Hills only three persons had been adjudged insane during the twelve
months preceding the spring of 1899. The Hills rejoiced in this reputation for mental stability and told with glee the story of the sor-
rowful farmer from the eastern part of the state who had hauled his
wife to Yankton, and in explaining the sad case to the asylum's superintendent dolefully remarked, "I don't know what would drive

her crazy, Doc; she ain't been off the farm in twenty years."[31]

In 1880 one of many successive epidemics swept the town; it was variously described as diphtheria, pneumonia, or "fever," and the town's unsanitary condition was generally blamed for the disease. It was so severe that the *Times* joked with unseemly levity that "Patton's hearse is worth about fifty dollars a day just now!" The sixteen-bed hospital was full, and an additional ward for twenty more patients was planned. The patients were either charity cases, without friends to care for them, or moribund, for anybody who had a home of his own preferred to be cared for in it. In the 1890s a ferocious epidemic of diphtheria wiped out whole families, and was especially fatal to the children; many a mother and father lost every child in a large family, and sorrowfully began again to build up a line of descendants.[32]

Despite this record of sickness and death, it was breezily claimed that when Deadwood laid out its Mount Moriah Cemetery (the name is from Masonic ritual) and applied to the federal government for a patent on the land, the town was so singularly healthy that they could not get one, for they had not a single corpse on hand to give the proposed new burying ground an official status. The city fathers, it is rumored, eventually had to send out an official to kill an undesirable character so they could get the cemetery legitimately started. It is a tale that smacks somewhat of frontier exaggeration. Mount Moriah today constitutes one of the major tourist attractions of Deadwood, for in it are buried the martyred Preacher Smith, Calamity Jane, and Wild Bill Hickok. Tourists often inquire, "Where's Wild Bill?" and the customary reply is, "Well, yesterday he was up to the cemetery, but I don't know where he is today."[33]

Of course, there were doctors in Deadwood. Dr. F. S. Howe has left a delightful memoir of his practice in the early 1900s, and there were many others, including Dr. H. Wedelstaedt, who treated the Chinese, and a couple, nowadays, who still augment their income by the weekly inspection of the "upstairs girls." In the 1880s a Dr. Spinney advertised that those "who may be suffering from the effects of youthful follies or indiscretions" could come to his office in Denver, possibly in order to conceal their visits from the prying eyes of their Deadwood neighbors. During the epidemic of 1880 Dr. E. Sick was laid up for months, and of no help to the other sufferers. In 1882 R. R. Buchanan, next to Post and Mund's bank, advertised that he was able to extract or fill teeth "without pain by the use of nitrous oxide gas or vitalized air—the only apparatus of the kind in the Territory." The problems involved in having teeth attended to *without* the aid of some such anesthetic are so horrific that they don't bear much thinking about, but these could be prevented by caring for the teeth with the proper dentifrice:

> If health and beauty you'd maintain,
>   And keep your breath a perfect charm,
> Use SOZODONT with might and main,
>   For it alone prevents the harm
> That mars a woman's teeth and breath,
>   And leaves her mouth as dark as death. [34]

It was a period of odd and fanciful medical notions, especially among the less educated. One old miner on his deathbed was restless and dissatisfied until after his repeated requests those attending him brought a chair and placed it at the bedside, where it remained, empty, for some hours. At last one of the bystanders got up courage enough to inquire just exactly what this chair was for, and the old fellow, possibly with a twinkle in his dying eyes, muttered, "It's . . . it's, for *rigor mortis* to set in." [35]

No matter how many doctors were in town, people seemed to dope themselves with patent medicines to a considerable extent, and perhaps more than they do today. Bent and Deetkin's drug store advertised "That Linament [*sic*]" for burns, scalds and wounds, "That Pain-Knocker" for internal and external pains, aches, and stomach complaints, and "That Pile Cure" for "instant relief and cure of acute piles; relief [only] for chronic piles." They also handled paints, oils, and fancy goods, and were the agents for organs and pianos, which may indicate that the drug business was insufficient to keep them fully occupied, or merely that they were exceptionally enterprising businessmen. [36]

The dread disease of "torpid liver" seemed to figure largely in the hygenic thinking of the Deadwood community, at least judging by the advertisements for nostrums designed to alleviate this somewhat obscure complaint. The symptoms of this dreadful bane (in case the reader may fear himself afflicted) were "loss of appetite, bowels costive, pain in the head with a dull sensation in the back part, pain under the shoulder blade, fullness after eating, with a disinclination to exertion of body or mind, irritability of temper, low spirits with a feeling of having neglected some duty, weariness, dizziness, fluttering at the heart, dots before the eyes, yellow skin, headache, and . . . constipation." Fortunately Tutt's Pills could save the sufferer, if administered in time. Phosphoric Air, another cure-all, could further rectify his general debility and alleviate "sperma-torrhoea, seminal weakness, loss of vitality, impotency, and all diseases arising from the errors of youth or the excesses of adult age" which, in a town with as many opportunities for waywardness as Deadwood, must have been a considerable comfort to a large segment of the male population. "Blood disease" (as syphilis was generally referred to, when not mentioned as a product of youthful indiscretion) could be cured by Hood's Sarsaparilla, especially prepared "under the personal supervision of educated pharmacists who know the nature, quality and medicinal effect of the ingredients," and it was also advertised as a great "spring medicine" and "true blood purifier," in order to include the female sufferer among its customers. [37]

For those just generally run down Dr. King's "New Life Pills" were each "a sugar-coated globule of health," a veritable "surprise party for the stomach and liver" busy working night and day to transform "weakness into strength, listlessness into energy, brain fag into mental power," and giving to the user "the appetite of a goat." According to other ads "ladies tell each other" of the "comfort and security" afforded by Williams' Pink Pills for Pale People. . . . Wise mothers give them to growing girls." For the man of affairs (in a business, rather than a social, sense), H. T. Helmboldt's Fluid Extract of Buchu was claimed to cure "debility, loss of memory, indisposition to exertion or business, shortness of breath, trouble with thoughts of disease, dimness of vision, pain in the back, chest, head, rush of blood to the head, a pale countenance, and dry skin" and promised to "stimulate the torpid liver, bowels and kidneys." A full dose of Helmboldt's memorable drench must have been a moving experience and one which caused all other sufferings to diminish in comparison to the rigors of the cure. [38]

Many of these patent medicines of course were nationally advertised, and any newspaper of the times will yield similar advertisements for them. Nevertheless, in a mining city—and one with so many opportunities to become afflicted with the result of what were obliquely referred to as "excesses"—these nostrums doubtless drew more customers than in a less disease-ridden and eruptive community, and few of them were any worse than the standard prescriptions of the day, most of which leaned heavily on purgatives and opium. There is little doubt that those who took these potions were for the most part indeed endowed thereby with a considerable sense of the spirit of "get up and go" which, at least metaphorically, typified the miners and businessmen of Deadwood.

Deadwood has had more than its full share of natural disasters, having so far avoided only earthquakes during the hundred or more years of its existence. During the winter of 1876–77 blizzards and snows fell upon the city repeatedly, and James W. Watson's poem about a freezing prostitute—

> Beautiful snow! It can do nothing wrong.
> Flying to kiss a fair lady's cheek,
> Clinging to lip in a frolicsome freak;
> Beautiful snow, from the heavens above,
> Pure as an angel and fickle as love

—was on every lip, and imitations of it appeared in every edition of the papers, until the *Cheyenne Leader* claimed it warmed its premises by burning proffered poems on beautiful snow. Jack Langrishe, the Deadwood actor-reporter, wrote a parody for the *Pioneer*:

> Oh, the stove, the beautiful stove,
> Heating the room below and above,
> Broiling, roasting, and keeping warm,
> Beautiful stove, you can do no harm.
>
> Fill her up to thaw your toes,
> Fill her to thaw the end of your nose,
> Open the damper, and let her go,
> She'll soon knock hell out of beautiful snow![39]

On 7 March 1878 the day opened fair and warm, and in the afternoon a gentle rain began to fall, a rain which soon turned to a snow that fell for three days. Prairie land was covered seven feet deep on the level with snow twenty feet deep where it had drifted. In Deadwood the snow reached to second-story windows, and many roofs were broken in by its accumulated weight: a platform scale used to weigh hay wagons measured a weight of 3,165 pounds of snow upon its surface. Soon, however, the weather turned fair, and the snow melted and produced a flood, and April produced yet another storm, from the sixteenth to the twenty-second, which washed out bridges, cut roads, isolated mining camps, and suspended all placer operations. Such weather, of course, has since become the basis for much of Deadwood's modern prosperity, as skiers swarm into the northern Black Hills to take advantage of the snows which so annoyed the early residents. Violently fluctuating temperatures are typical of the Black Hills: Spearfish, a few miles from Deadwood, went from minus four degrees to forty-five degrees in two minutes during one notably erratic storm, and then fell from fifty-four degrees to minus four degrees in less than half an hour. Similar dramatic variations are common throughout the Hills, bearing out the old-timers' often repeated advice: "If you don't like the weather in the Black Hills, just wait a few minutes, and it'll be considerably different!"[40]

Tornadoes, which are especially vicious and visible in the mountains, where the swaths they cut among the pines can be seen for years, repeatedly visited the Hills. In June 1881 one swept down City Creek to McGovern Hill, killing Nora Wilcox and injuring several other citizens; the fearful hid in mine tunnels until the storm had passed. Many other tornadoes have struck the hills near Deadwood, and the scars that they have left are often nowadays attributed to the excesses of commercial lumbermen, much to the amusement of the old-timers who know better.

In a narrow canyon like that of Whitewood Creek on which Deadwood is located, a canyon which is fed by streams draining a considerable area, floods are of course common. In 1883 a disastrous one roared through the gulch doing $250,000 worth of damage. Many mercantile establishments were washed away or so badly damaged that they had to be demolished, and three people living in the tollhouse on the Gayville road were drowned. At least one house of ill repute was washed away, and many other "female seminaries" were disrupted, but the moral lesson implied in their destruction was somewhat vitiated by the fact that the city school and the Methodist church were also destroyed, while the Gem Theater and most of the saloons survived—it brings to mind the later poem about the San Francisco earthquake and fire:

> If the Almighty shook old 'Frisco down,
>   Because she was too frisky,
> Why did He burn the Baptist Church,
>   And spare Hotalings whiskey?

On Thanksgiving Day in 1896 a violent blizzard swept the whole area and several lives were lost. In 1899 floods washed out most of the railroad bridges, and train service to Deadwood was seriously disrupted; in 1908 tracks were washed out again. In January 1949 seventy-seven inches of snow fell, forty-three inches of it from January 1 through 5. In May 1965 thirty-four inches of snow followed by seven inches of rain produced another major flood, doing $4 million damage to the town. In Deadwood, as one old-timer put it, "It just don't pay to build in the bottoms."[41]

A great legal battle between the Homestake and Father De Smet Mines over which of them should supply Deadwood with water for drinking and firefighting raged with peculiar venom as the partisans of both factions saw their own interests involved in the outcome. Each of the mines had surreptitiously obtained the other's water supply, and to retain this advantage, each had to find some use for the water, and each offered a share of it to the city. A long court and political battle resulted in the defeat of the De Smet interests, and brought Deadwood a supply of relatively pure and ample water, although in the words of an early booster, "in its passing through the flumes, which are somewhat cheaply constructed, fine particles of mica find their way into it and these produce irritation of the bowels and kidneys." Actually, of course, the water was polluted and corrupt, and it took a good deal of getting used to. As late as 1899 a *Pioneer-Times* editorial called for "more water—less mud," and pointed out that "nine months of each year the supply is short and the other three it is wholly unfit for use." The editorial urged that the city spend fifteen to twenty thousand dollars to build a water supply sufficient for the next ten or fifteen years, at which time "we will then be either rich enough to put in other water works or so poor that we won't want any water," a sentiment which summarized the frontier booster's sentiments exactly. The water from the flumes was supplemented by shipments of bottled drinking water from the Kidney Springs at Hot Springs, water which would not "endanger your health, ruin your disposition, or make sand paper of your throat, as is the case with the water you buy of the city." Purveyors also shipped in a somewhat less medicinal water from Piedmont, that of Kidney Springs being said to be a well-named diuretic. The water came in one-, two-, and five-gallon bottles, the latter costing only twenty-five cents delivered to the door, and it was a considerable improvement on the gruel served up by the city's water utility.[42]

The city water supply was in other ways unsatisfactory, for in the spring of 1899 the water broke out of the old City Creek ditch, which supplied the storage tanks on Forest Hill, and "cut a slice out of the side of the hill the size of a church" much to the confusion and dismay of those whose houses were in the way of the rushing torrent. As can be imagined, the flumes and, even worse, the open ditches which brought water from as far up stream as Englewood were generously polluted with mud and trash, offal, and dead cats whenever a heavy rain swept such muck into them. When the Horseshoe Mill at Terry burned and its cyanide vats collapsed, the cyanide solutions too eventually ran into Deadwood's water supply, much to the discomfiture of the citizens, who had to wait until the lines had been thoroughly flushed before they felt the water was safe to drink, and even after a considerable lapse of time a few sensitive souls complained that the city water was dissolving their gold and silver fillings.[43]

Despite the unsanitary conditions, epidemics, and patent medicines, the Deadwood area seems to have been a healthy place to live to a ripe old age. In 1883 the Lawrence County coroner reported a total of 105 deaths out of a total population of 16,000, or, including suicides, murders, and executions, a death rate of 6.56 per thousand population. Comparable figures for Chicago come to 16, Philadelphia 18, and New York 23. Over the period 1877–98, the book of Lawrence County deaths, now in the Deadwood Public Library, noted, out of 1,929 deaths (many seem to have gone unrecorded, and the book itself may be more a record of burials than of total deaths), the following percentages of the more dramatic forms of departure from life's cares:

Alcoholism	.1%
Accidents (all kinds)	10
Murders and killings	3
Executions (hangings)	0.33
Suicides	3.33

Many of the causes of death recorded were probably unusual then, and would certainly seem unusual today. Cholera infantum (infant diarrhea), diphtheria, and similar childhood diseases were common, though not as common as they would have been in a community with the usual number of children. John Crummins died of eating fourteen hard boiled eggs. Richard Freudenburg died of complications of a wound given him by a buffalo, F. L. Graham some-how managed to die of a broken thumb, and Silvester Green of a "fractured hump bone." A Frenchman died of "dissipation," and one John Klass was "leaded," whether by inunction, ingestion, or injection is not made clear. Louise Phillips died of "nervous prostration," and the fairly common "froze to death" probably means, in many cases, that the unfortunate victim collapsed in an alcoholic stupor during chilly weather. James Watkins was "killed by a bear," and Nora Wilcox, as has been mentioned, was killed by a cyclone. Julia Laundy and Etta Linderbawen seem to have jointly committed suicide, and in several cases the cause of death is recorded as "God knows!" although this may imply either that God alone knew the cause, or that everybody did, but didn't want to mention it. The incredible disparity between Deadwood and more civilized communities was probably due in part to poor recording of deaths, and to the very small proportion of women, infants, and children in the early population. Even as late as 1906 the death rate in Deadwood was estimated at about eleven per year per thousand, a healthy condition attributed to the mile-high altitude, the dryness of the climate, and the proximity of the pine trees with their "invigorating tonic."[44]

Deadwood people probably do not really live that much longer than anybody else, but two interesting incidents at least give some flavor of support to this widely held supposition. In 1925, one spry old lady, riding in a float on the Days of '76 parade, injured herself while dismounting from the vehicle and died—at the age of 106. And I, in 1976, had the privilege of shaking hands, one hundred years after the Deadwood gold rush, with an actual participant in it, Mrs. Horace Clark, who had come to the Black Hills at the age of 2, and although blind was otherwise in full possession of all her faculties, a glorious reminder of a glorious and healthy past.

SEVEN

A Sociable People

"Reverend Smith held first church service in Hills. Congregation composed of thirty men and five women. I attended.
George Ayres's diary, 7 May 1876

" . . . to perpetuate the memory of those whose sagacity, energy, and enterprise induced them to settle in the wilderness and become the founders of a new state."
Constitution and By-Laws of the Society of Black Hills Pioneers

Questioner: Do you believe in clubs for women?
Reformer: Only when persuasion fails.

ONE OF THE enduring characteristics of the frontier was that the people liked to get together, for whatever purpose, simply to enjoy each other's company. The need for such organizations, common anywhere, was augmented by the transitory nature of life in a new or mobile community, where almost everybody was either a new-comer or knew what it was like to be one, and consequently did his best to further the instant sociability of assorted organizations. Each organization of course served its own purposes and had its own goals, but underlying all of them was the overpowering need of individuals to become, as quickly as possible, parts of their new community. One of the most diligent of these organizations which provided community unity in Deadwood was the church, which in several of its various manifestations joined strangers together and made them friends and colleagues, in addition to whatever services it may have performed for their immortal souls.

The first church services in Deadwood were informal street gatherings conducted from the top of a packing crate by the lay Methodist preacher Henry (or Hiram) Weston Smith. During the week Smith worked at odd jobs in a sawmill or on the Pioneer ditch. His audiences were never large, but he was treated with much respect in his diligent efforts, certainly apposite, to "recall the wandering sinner home." It is claimed that Calamity Jane, hearing him preaching, came up, took his hat in her hand and circulated among the congregation, saying, "You sinners, dig down in your pokes now; this old fellow looks as though he were broke and I want to collect about two hundred dollars for him. So limber up, boys." When Smith, instead of at once accepting the money, went on with his sermon, she forced the collection upon him saying, "You d—— old fool, take the money first, then proceed with your preaching." If this story isn't true, it ought to be.[1]

On August 1876, while Smith was on his way to Crook City to preach, he was killed by Indians a few miles north of Deadwood, a martyr of the frontier. The notes for his sermon have survived, and the sermon itself is often given in the Hills, and one of Smith's poems, written during a late spring blizzard, gives an indication of his sensitivity and literary power:

> This evening is the first of June,
>   And snow is falling fast.
> The tall pines sigh, howl, and moan,
>   Responsive to the blast.
> The shades of night are gathered 'round;
>   The fire is burning low,
> I sit and watch the dying coals,
>   And think of long ago.

The first Episcopal service in Deadwood was conducted by Seth Bullock, who sadly read the burial service from the Book of Common Prayer over the grave of Preacher Smith.[2]

It is customary, nowadays, to blame every murder committed by Indians on roving white bandits instead, though why a bandit would expect a preacher like Smith to be worth either killing or robbing is hard to explain, and the proverbial respect for men of the cloth which prevailed on the frontier makes this notion unlikely. The story is told of the well-dressed and mannerly businessman on the Deadwood stagecoach who was offered in succession a smoke, a chaw of tobacco, and a drink, all of which he courteously refused. Arriving at the stage stop, his companions insisted on paying for his meal, saying, "We don't have much religion out this way, but we want you to understand that when a gospel sharp come along we know how to treat him right!"[3]

The sermon topics announced in the *Black Hills Pioneer* for early-day church services to be held "at the usual time and place" show a singular appropriateness to the mining frontier. On 10 February 1877 the text was Exod. 20:7, "Thou shalt not take the name of the Lord in vain," and on 7 April, 2 Cor. 4:7, "We have this treasure in earthen vessels," both texts which a miner might well find applicable to his personal experience.

A famous early-day sermon was preached in a bar by the Reverend W. L. Rumney, who had been an officer of a Georgia regiment in the War between the States. The service was held in the Melodeon (McClintock says the Bella Union, Bill Nuttall's dancehall) where the gaming tables were pushed aside and the representative of the church militant was established on the little platform, or stage, where bawdy vaudeville performances were usually given. The service was carried forward with strict decorum although many of the members of its audience had probably never taken part in a religious exercise before in their lives. A collection was taken, and when the stalwart preacher departed, Nutshell Bill, a gambler, bawled out to the assembled congregation, "Come on, come on! The old gentleman has been telling you how to save your souls; now I'm going to show you how to win some money!"[4]

It has been claimed that the Deadwood churches always outnumbered the Deadwood saloons, a census which must have been conducted by a man who visited the saloons first, for a glance at any of the city directories will show that the saloons came out considerably ahead, although the organized churches certainly put up a struggle. The Congregational church, as a result of the efforts of the American Home Mission Society, began its work late in the fall of 1876, led by the Reverend L. P. Norcross who conducted services wherever he could find a place: at the International Hotel, with five persons present, though the audience increased as he spoke; in a borrowed butcher shop; in the dining room of the Centennial Hotel; in Jack Langrishe's theater, although that frame and canvas building was too cold to offer the congregation much except spiritual comfort; and in a carpenter shop in South Deadwood, opposite Boughton and Berry's sawmill, where the congregation met for several months. Formal church organization was completed in January 1877, and a church building was erected in June 1877, and its melodious parlor organ was soon providing spiritual comfort to the whole community.

Saint Ambrose Catholic Church was begun by Father John Lonergan, who first said mass in Weber's carpenter shop on 23 May 1877, and went on to build first a frame and later a brick church and school. There seem to have been more than one Catholic church in the Deadwood area, perhaps to accommodate any foreign groups which were each accustomed to their own language and traditions.

The Episcopalians held their first service—other than Preacher Smith's burial—in Langrishe's theater, as did other congregations, where a Mrs. Dennee, an actress, worked vigorously to make sure that everything went decently and in order, while a lay reader read the service. One hundred men were present, but Mrs. Dennee and her two young daughters were the only ladies in the congregation.

The Baptists came late to Deadwood, organizing in 1888. They were most notable for Miss Ida Sherman's missionary work among the Chinese, for whom she conducted a missionary school, and ended up converting eleven of them to the faith, and a good many more of them to at least a passing acquaintance with the English language.

The Methodists, beginning with Preacher Smith's free-lance street sermons, set up their church organization in 1878 and continued through many tribulations. Their church was washed away in the flood of 1883, but they continued until the present to claim themselves the Mother Church of the Black Hills. Their Young Men's Rescue Band established a reading room, and their congregation was lighted to its evening prayers by the beams from an illuminated lantern advertising the Overland Sample Rooms, obtained from a defunct saloon, a most un-methodistical ornament and one which aroused considerable adverse comment. Dr. Clough, one of the pastors, set aside the three back pews in the church for strangers, and these seats were almost always filled with silent worshippers from the badlands who departed immediately after the benediction, the rest of the congregation allowing them to leave without further afflicting their afflictions with offers of sympathy or benevolence.[5]

The prosperity of the churches did not come from their collection plates, for in 1880 the editor of the *Times* made it known that he would like to see "more small coin in Deadwood, so when we drop a twenty in the contribution box on Sundays we may get a little change back," and again, a few weeks later, he pointed out that Stebbins and Post's bank had now got in sixty dollars worth of nickels, a great boon to those churchgoers "who heretofore, owing to the scarcity of nickels, have been obliged to drop dimes into the contribution box." One does not hear, strangely enough, of nuggets or pinches of gold finding their way into the collection plates; perhaps the churches would have considered this a little too worldly, but it is odd that no prospector is reported to have made such a gesture, for raw gold circulated in every other establishment, and the clunk of a two-ounce nugget dropping into the collection plate would probably have been heard clear up in heaven.[6]

Not all religious activities were confined to the church, for justices of the peace often took upon themselves the civil if not the religious aspects of uniting fervid couples in legal, if not in holy, matrimony. One such justice, carried away with the verbiage of his trade, concluded his ceremony:

> Know all men by these presents that I, being in good health and in sound mind and disposition, in consideration of a dollar and fifty cents, to me in hand duly paid and a receipt of which is hereby acknowledged, do, and by these presents have declared you man and wife, during your good behavior or until otherwise ordered by this court.

Other justices were said to conclude with the words, "I now pronounce you man and wife, *the sentences to run concurrently*," but as concurrent sentences seem more modern than gold rush Deadwood, such phraseology is probably apocryphal.[7]

> Sound the hewgag!
> Shake the tonquang!
> Let the loud hozannas ring!

With this quotation reminiscent of the "Clampers" (the lively fraternal Society of E Clampus Vitus of the California gold rush) the *Times* welcomed in the multifarious celebrations of the Fourth of July of 1878 with the ritualistic hurraw of the secret society and the lodge hall, institutions dear to the heart of the frontier American, for the hope of being a member, of what it mattered not, was endemic in every new and mobile community of strangers.[8]

The Ancient, Free, and Accepted Masons received their charter to work in Deadwood on 14 June 1877, and by the next year numbered twenty-eight brethren, including several recently taken into the organization, their membership roll constituting almost a roster of eminent men in the community. By 1881 Masonic societies included the Knights Templar, Royal Arch Masons, the four groups composing the Scottish Rite, the Order of the Eastern Star for both men and women, and the Nobles of the Mystic Shrine. The various parades of this last order were of hilarious solemnity, with the candidates for initiation clad in white robes and hoods (photographs of the festivities are often mistaken for a Konklave of the Ku Klux Klan) hauled along by a long rope to "the horrible fate which awaited them." Such neophytes, it was said, were "thrown down deep wells and over mighty precipices, impaled on spear points and hacked to pieces with sabres and enveloped in the blinding dust storms of the desert," so they were not unnaturally hesitant in their progress. A grand Shriners' banquet, however, followed the secret ceremonies, so the mysteries involved apparently did not totally incapacitate the new initiates. Similarly bizarre but perhaps less well publicized were the rites and rigors of the other fraternal orders, for death and resurrection seem to be a common theme in the rituals of most of them.[9]

By 1881 the Black Hills Encampment of the Independent Order of Odd Fellows, and its attendant female society, the Alta Rebekah Degree Lodge, were active. Marco Bozzaris Lodge of the Knights of Pythias and two accompanying companies of the URKP prospered. Markos Bozzaris, a Greek patriot who had died fighting against the Turks in 1823, was commemorated by Fitz-Greene Halleck's stirring verses, which were frequently memorized by school children—

> Strike—for the last armed foe expires;
> Strike—for your altars and your fires;
> Strike—for the green graves of your sires;
>   God—and your native land!

—which accounts for the selection of his name for this Deadwood Lodge. Lakota Tribe No. 1 of the Improved Order of Redmen, and Tecumseh Company No. 1 of Uniformed Red Men powwowed diligently, presided over by a sachem, a sagamore, and a prophet. The Ancient Order of United Workmen had its Deadwood Lodge and Esther Lodge No. 1, Degree of Honor. The Modern Woodmen of America had Camp No. 1186, and its female counterpart, Royal Neighbors of America, Star Camp No. 443. The Ancient Order of Hibernians was governed by M. J. Donovan, Deadwood's chief of police, and the Woodmen of the World had their Deadwood Camp No. 4. The Order of Yeomen, the Grand Army of the Republic, the Benevolent and Protective Order of Elks, and the Black Hills Aerie of the Fraternal Order of Eagles all came later, prospering on the almost universal desire of families to somehow get daddy out of the house at least one or two nights a week before the entire family went crazy.[10]

Deadwood ladies not only enjoyed their memberships in various branches of secret societies but formed their own women's clubs for purposes at once benevolent and sociable. As early as 1877 the ladies established Ladies Relief Society to set up a hospital for "the poor unfortunates in our midst who will be taken sick in the coming fall and winter," and to provide relief for the "destitute sick and despairing men" of the community.

A local lecturing association was set up in the fall of 1879, its members hoping "that they will get through it more originality of thought and a higher order of reason and eloquence than is secured through the Eastern Humbug bureau system" of lyceums and circuit speakers. Certainly the number of times the various halls, churches, and theaters of Deadwood were used for speakers on entertaining and uplifting topics shows that lecture groups enjoyed considerable success, although the prevalence of temperance lectures undoubtedly cut down a good deal on attendance.

A Deadwood Library Association, with the Reverend Mr. Peton its temporary chairman, was set up in 1882 to establish a library and reading room for the city, and the next year Keimer Hall was the scene of a "musical and dramatic entertainment" for the library's benefit. Admission was fifty cents, and the show consisted of an overture by the Deadwood Orchestra, recitations, and the farce *A Thumping Legacy*. In the days before television brought mediocrity right into the home, it was thought to be more sociable to enjoy it in the company of friends by participating in such an uplifting and useful occasion, and in doing so people, who tended to see what others had seen, had much to talk about afterwards. The work of the Library Association was later taken over by the Deadwood Ladies Round Table and the Deadwood Woman's Club, who with the assistance of Andrew Carnegie and Phoebe Hearst, wife of George Hearst of the Homestake, opened the Deadwood Library in 1905 with 4,353 volumes, a library which still serves the community, and which has done much to salvage and preserve the history of the city.

Other women's groups included the Home Forum Benefit Order, apparently a group composed of both men and women, though one suspects that the former attended more or less under duress; a Women's Relief Corps; Saint Anne's Court of the Women's Catholic

Order of Foresters, with Mrs. P. J. Winter its Chief Ranger; and the Women's Christian Temperance Union, which in Deadwood certainly had its work cut out for it. The Roundtable Club was set up in 1887, then the Thursday Club, the Culture Club, the Woman's Club, and the Twentieth Century Club—in later years it was claimed that this last was dedicated principally to the repeal of that century, a canard amply refuted by the progressive activities of its members—and various church Ladies' Aid societies, all more or less gathered together into a Black Hills Federation of Women's Clubs, which in 1897 united them into a loose confederation.[11]

Miscellaneous social groups included the Deadwood Pioneer Hook and Ladder Company No. 1, which in addition to its fire-fighting duties, in which it was aided by several other similar fire companies, paid much attention to properly celebrating the death and burial of departed fire laddies with proper obituaries, condolences, flowers, and funerals. Some of the fire companies appear to have been more in the category of sporting clubs, set up only to compete in the frequent races between companies which were so popular at the time. The Chinese fire company, for example, seems to have been established solely for that purpose—but the Deadwood Hook and Ladder was serious about its fire-fighting duties and functioned professionally up to at least 1936.[12]

Various ethnic and national groups also had their occasional clubs and outings. The Clan Stewart and the Germania Club seem to have been transient, depending on the vigor of a few individuals rather than the numbers or the unity of the group for their prosperity. It was in nearby Lead that the ethnic and national societies grew and prospered and set a social tone of ethnic diversity for the city; Deadwood, on the other hand, seems to have been a town relatively without distinctions, its social organizations tending to be open to almost everyone.

The purely social club, a party-giving loose association of people united only by mutually shared tastes in what constituted a good time, was of course a common feature of the era. The Pleasant Hours Club "closed the season with a dance at the Welch House" in the spring of 1879. The Deadwood Athletic Club began in 1882 to assist sedentary clerks and businessmen to achieve that "hardness of frame and development of physique so much admired," but it does not seem to have prospered; perhaps there was enough physical activity involved in climbing Deadwood's many stairs to preserve the physique of almost anybody. A Plug Hat Society was organized in 1883, its regalia consisting of a plug hat "of the von Moltke type, glossy in appearance and sublime in expression." Its officers consisted of "a master of ceremonies, a worthy past finding out, a chorister, shortstop, timekeeper, and sampler of liquids," so it may be assumed that it was an all-male organization and not entirely devoted to the extension of temperance. A similar group of young people of both sexes was formed in 1905 and called the Mumm Club either in an attempt at secrecy, "Mum's the word," or more likely in honor of the famous brand of champagne, although the list of its activities and entertainments sounds far from bibulous or abandoned.[13]

"When one is shown the Business Men's Club, with its 250 members," wrote the *Belt Cities Directory* of 1908, "and then the Olympic Club with its 200 members of the best young men in the city," one could not but feel that "none of the business or social advantages offered in the larger cities have been neglected in Deadwood." The Deadwood Business Club, begun in 1892, was formed to create a downtown men's club, shares one hundred dollars each, in which a respectable man of affairs could relax, have a meal or snack or soothing beverage, play cards or billiards, discuss business, and in general have a home away from home. Gambling, tipping, and "loud or boisterous noise" were strictly prohibited; all glass or crockery broken was to be paid for promptly, and all other bills were to be paid monthly. Seth Bullock and Judge Granville Bennett, at least, did not always observe this last requirement for membership, and the club directors secured not only their promises for prompter payment later but their notes for past debts as well before allowing them to continue as dwellers within the sacred precincts. A. O. Egbert was expelled for criticizing the officers of the Hidden Fortune mine, a crime apparently considered far worse than not paying bills, and in general the club acted not only as a social but also as a business organization, a Chamber of Commerce with clubrooms. Its charter members included William R. Steele, president; William Selbie, the banker, vice president; William Remer, a mining man, secretary; B. P. Dague, treasurer; and notable Deadwood men as follows: Seth Bullock, the businessman; Ben Baer, liquor; D. A. McPherson, banker; John R. Wilson, mining; R. H. Driscoll, banking; Henry Frawley, law; Harris Franklin, of the Golden Reward; Jake Goldberg, grocer; Max Fischel, merchant; T. J. Grier of the

Homestake; William Lardner; Sol Star, for twenty-two years mayor of the town; John Treber, brewer; and Porter Warner, newspaper-man—a group of community leaders who would lend tone to any organization.[14]

The Olympic Club, organized two years later, with over two hundred members in 1898, made its home on the third floor of Mar-tin and Mason's block, where a floor space fifty by one hundred feet was divided into a library–reading room for "those of its members who do not care for the strenuous life," billiard room, bathroom, and a large hall for social gatherings, evidently the club's principal activity and purpose, although some mention is made of "equipment for athletic training," which apparently went on between balls and parties. During a hiatus in the Deadwood Businessmen's Club's ac-tivities in 1899 the Olympic Club briefly took over the duties of both that organization and the Deadwood Board of Trade in pro-moting Deadwood's business interests, for all of these men's social clubs appear to have had as one of their stated or unstated purposes the advertising and advancement of Deadwood as a business town.

The Society of Black Hills Pioneers, which still meets, although not with its original roster of members, was begun in 1889, with Thomas H. Russell, a pioneer who came to the Hills in 1874 with the Gordon party, its presiding officer. Membership was confined to those who had come—or, later, whose ancestor had come—to the Black Hills before 1877. A second similar organization, the Black Hills Pioneer Society, with Judge Granville Bennett its president, was begun in January 1895, and admitted those who had come to the Hills before 1878; one senses some sort of internal rivalry and schismatic tendencies at work amongst the pioneer population, but the chasm has been healed, and apparently both organizations now have merged into the Society of Black Hills Pioneers. In its early days the group devoted much effort to the succor and relief of, as one old-timer put it, "indignant members," voting one hundred dol-lars in 1891 to convey one Alexander Miller to the state insane asy-lum at Yankton. They were also active in assuaging the grief of the relatives of departed members, for the minutes show the purchase of twenty dollars worth of funeral badges, and frequent resolutions glorifying departed Pioneers. This was in its early days, when fu-nerals were a major part of the group's activities, for as an old-timer put it, "People died a lot more, them days, than they do now." An entire funeral ritual was devised to provide a send-off for those who had embarked "on that vast and silent journey to the undiscovered country from which no traveler returns," and the wearing of funeral badges and white gloves was mandatory on such occasions, when the members might well remark:

> We saw not the lift of the curtain,
>   Nor heard the invisible door,
> As they passed where life's problems uncertain
>   Will follow and vex them no more.

Not all of the Pioneers' activities were funerary, for the society later furnished a pioneer room in the Adams Museum, and has done much steady work toward collecting and preserving the history of the Black Hills. Public support for the society has been whole-hearted—four thousand attended their first annual outing—and now that the descendants of the pioneers are admitted, the society continues to prosper and to uphold in true frontier fashion the traditions of those whose creed was staunchly summarized by Richard B. Hughes on a stone in a pioneer cabin in Halley Park in Rapid City:

> I was built in the olden, golden, days
>   When this was an unknown land;
> My timbers were hewn by a pioneer,
>   With a rifle near at hand.
>
> I stand as a relic of 'seventy-six,
>   Our nation's centennial year;
> That all may see as they enter the Hills
>   The home of a pioneer.[15]

Deadwood was, from its earliest days, liberally endowed with theaters, although the word *theater* in this case could and did cover a multitude of sins, extending from the legitimate drama to burlesque houses, hurdy-gurdies, and bars with a modest platform for immodest performances stuck up at one end, clear on down to outright houses of ill fame whose "actresses" were more provocative than decorative. Up to the big fire of 1879 at least, Deadwood claimed to have more places of entertainment—as liberally defined above—than any other town of its size in the country, and the anecdotes involving its stage—both legitimate and illegitimate—were legion.

William, more commonly called Billy, Nuttal (a name variously spelt) was one of the vast multitude who were tending the bar when Wild Bill was shot. He listed himself in Collins's 1878 *Directory* as "tragedian, lower Main." He and Banjo Dick Brown in December 1876 announced that they would conduct a "Temple of Music" with Fannie Brown (née Garrettson); Miss Luella Clarkson, "the Fascinating Danseuse"; Miss Winnetta May, "in her Lightning Changes, and a host of others" to provide the entertainment, and they stressed that "no *common* liquors will be kept, as our stock is from the well known house of Masten & Co., Cheyenne." Admission was free, but participation was probably expensive. Such an operation, on the border between a saloon, burlesque, and bawdyhouse, was fairly representative of Deadwood's theatrical activities.[16]

The legitimate stage was of course also well represented in Deadwood, but newspaper criticism of it could be vitriolic. Fanny Price, in *Camille*, "ain't good at dying, because she generally dies too hard," said the *Times*. "Her positions are not good in her passion scenes; when she should swell out like a mountain she sinks in like a gulch. That ain't right in this country—Camille is not her forte." It was enough to discourage anybody except a frontier tragedienne.[17]

Early in 1877 Mr. Miller, manager of the Deadwood Theater, advertised that he intended to "give a first-class entertainment for ladies and gentlemen, once a week." What the entertainment was like the rest of the week is veiled in the mists of an appropriate obscurity, but his decent weekly show was to consist of minstrel shows, ballads, bone and banjo solos, songs, dances, clogs, Negro acts, farces, and pantomimes, in all of which "nothing [would be] said or done to offend." Later that spring the Gem Variety Theater, Brown and Nuttal's establishment, advertised a complimentary benefit for Fanny Garretson Brown, a performance which "ladies can attend without fear of seeing or hearing anything that might offend," thus giving the respectable ladies of Deadwood an opportunity "of seeing this beautiful temple of amusement," which, during other performances, was probably off limits to anyone other than the inhabitants and patrons of the badlands.[18]

During General Crook's visit to Deadwood in the summer of 1876 Crook and his men were entertained at the "Deadwood Theater and Academy of Music" (when the word *academy* appears in Deadwood in those days, it generally meant a spot where young women were available rather than a strictly educational institution) by a vocalization by Miss Viola de Montmorency, the Queen of Song, just before her departure to sing before the other crowned heads of Europe who apparently had not received warning in time to get out an injunction. Her voice, said a reporter who had come along with the general, was all right but might have had several stitches taken in it and been none the worse: "If she never comes back from the other side of the Atlantic until I send for her she will be considerably older than she was the night" when a half-drunk miner called out that "she was old enough to have another set of teeth." [19]

Even the early theater had those folks in the audience who came to be seen rather than to see the performance. Such a one was Mrs. R. O. Adams, wife of the Deadwood postmaster, who affected an opera glass in Jack Langrishe's theater, an aid which she needed about as much as a waffle needed extra riffles, for the theater was so small and compact that a blind man could have seen from one end of it to the other. An old prospector, annoyed at Mrs. Adams' affectation, the next performance brought in a two-foot piece of one-by-six with two beer bottles stuck through holes in it, and peered through this device at the performance. Langrishe, who had never before looked at the bottom of a bottle *from the outside*, was convulsed, up on the stage, and even Mrs. Adams was amused.

In the coarser dens of iniquity—the Gem, the Bella Union, the Green Front, and many others—the girls were brought to Deadwood by the proprietors, who held out to them the prospect of respectable employment as waitresses and performers; actually they were expected to "rustle the boxes" and sell liquor, and anything else they had available, to the customers. Inez Sexton was one such innocent girl, and when she saw the vile situation she had got herself into, she announced to Al Swearengen, who by that time owned the Gem, that although her voice was for sale nothing else was, and she stalked out of his low dive in high dudgeon. Colonel Cornell, a spectator, loaned her money to put up at a respectable hotel, and a benefit was arranged by the good ladies of the town to provide the escaped songbird with stage fare back home again.

At least two marriages were performed on the stage, well advertised in advance, and were presumed to encourage attendance. Charley Ross and Mabel Fenton were married by Justice Hall, at 4:00 A.M. one morning in the Gem—probably one of the few respectable stage shows they ever put on—and during the summer of 1876 George Morgan and Mrs. L. McKelvey were similarly joined in holy matrimony, with "Judge" Kuykendall talked into conducting the ceremony against his better judgment.[20]

Undoubtedly the most dramatic performance on the Deadwood stage was the killing of Ed Shaughnessy, although unfortunately for profitable publicity it seems to have been unpremeditated. Shaughnessy was enamored of Fannie Garrettson, who had been his mistress, and he had come to Deadwood from Cheyenne to try to win her back from Handsome Banjo Dick Brown, with whom she had decamped. Appearing in the theater—reliable sources give it severally as the Melodeon, the Bella Union, or the Gem—Shaughnessy seized an axe and threw it toward Brown, who was strumming on the stage. Brown rose, drew his revolver, and fired five or six shots into Shaughnessy, killing him at once. Brown was acquitted on the reasonable grounds of self-defense, and Fannie Garrettson Brown wrote to the papers explaining that although she was a notorious woman and had lived with Shaughnessy, she had never married him so there was nothing immoral in her having run away to the Black Hills with Brown. Brown, a notable performer, continued singing his best-loved song of the California rush a generation earlier, "The Days of Forty-Nine," upon the stage:

> You're looking now on old Tom Moore, a relic of former days,
> And though they call me a bummer sure, I care not for their praise;
> For my heart is filled with the days of yore, and oft I do repine
> For the days of old, the days of gold, the days of forty-nine.

It was a rare performance that Brown was not called upon to offer this well-worn tear-jerker to the assembled multitude, and the song is still sung in Deadwood nowadays.[21]

The list of Deadwood theaters of all sorts includes the Gem, the Bella Union, the Melodeon, the Green Front (all of ill repute), Wertheimer Hall, Stone's Opera House, Nye's Theater, the Park Theater, Keimer Hall, the Deadwood Opera House, and most respectable and notable of all, Jack Langrishe's theater. Langrishe built it during the summer of 1876, a skeleton framework walled and roofed with canvas with a sawdust floor and seats made of stakes driven into the ground with round chunks tacked to the top of each one. During the first performance a violent storm tore loose much of the roof and drenched the audience with rain, but the performance continued, and everybody went away wet but happy. Mrs.

Langrishe too "loved the stars above the mountains better than any on the boards, and the western sunshine more than bright white lights," and was as thorough a westerner as her husband. Langrishe, although not the only, was certainly the principal representative of the legitimate theater in Deadwood, and he was highly regarded in his profession. The versatility of his presentations was illustrated at the beginning of 1877 when the miners had grown tired of seeing the cancan, and Langrishe brought in "a sentimental female vocalist" who sang "Sweet Spirit, Hear My Prayer" and "I Know That My Redeemer Liveth." The pilgrims all went crazy over her, but it didn't last, and they tired of her in about a week. Still, it was a noble effort and thoroughly in line with Langrishe's many efforts to haul profitable culture, by the scruff of the neck if necessary, into Deadwood.[22]

Western historians have made much of a 130-day run of Gilbert and Sullivan's *Mikado* in Deadwood, and have now and then spoken of it as clear evidence of the lust for culture which prevailed among the roughest of miners. The *Mikado*, of course, was written in 1885, and by that time Deadwood had pretty much gotten over being a raw gold rush camp of hairy prospectors and had been transformed into a businesslike little city which happened to be in the center of a mining industry. The first American performance of the *Mikado* was said to be in Deadwood, on 20 December 1886, at the New Opera House, but the long run that is so much talked about took place in the "dear, delightful, cosy" Gem Theater and bordello in 1887, and it was billed as "an elegant burlesque on GILBERT & SULLIVAN's Famous Japanese Comic Opera . . . especially localized and adapted by Henry Montague." Some of the characters were Chewing Gum, Ting-Ting, and Peek-a-boo, who certainly would have been unwelcome novelties to W. S. Gilbert, the irascible librettist. Costumes were by Nee-Ban of Chicago and were kept in a matchbox between performances. If the theater had been anywhere near full during the 130-day run, everybody in the Black Hills would have seen the *Mikado* about four times, but they probably didn't. It did do better, though, than an amateur revival at the turn of the century, in which "Nanki-poo can sing a very little but has no conception of acting" and "Ko-ko can neither sing nor act," which, combined with a severe cold in the head, made his efforts "positively painful to the audience." At least it was more respectable, though not as well or as frequently received, as the long run at the Gem.[23]

Further extravaganzas of entertainment included Professor Reno "the well-known magician," and his performing dogs, admission twenty-five and thirty-five cents. The Gentry Brothers Famous Show, held out of doors, presumably at the fair grounds, included two hundred trained horses and dogs and five hundred performing monkeys, plus three distinct herds of performing elephants, the Norman family with their juggling and Indian clubs, and the Yo-shamite Japanese troupe, "the highest salaried troupe of Japs in the country." A little later the Beatty Brothers group, including "the whole Dam Family," who were variously named to take advantage of their patronymic, appear to have been popular, for they appeared in more than one Black Hills community. In 1909 *On the Frontier*, billed as "a beautiful story of the west, in four acts, with special scenery and electrical effects," could be patronized, and in 1916 a final burst of cultural enthusiasm resulted in the presentation of *Cavalleria Rusticana* and *Il Trovatore* on the same day. Alas, times change, and usually for the worse: as early as 1905 the International Bioscope Company began to introduce "moving pictures without flicker or variation." It was the beginning of the end of the Dead-wood theater, which in 1927 was reduced to showing the film *Rough Riders*, whose cry going up San Juan Hill in Cuba was alleged to have been "Rough! Tough! Never get enough! Whoopee-e-e-e!" Even Noah Beery and Mary Astor could not save that scenario, and it was necessary to augment the bill with a two-reeler on Lind-bergh's flight from New York to Paris. Deadwood's theater, by 1927, seems to have pretty much lost its frontier flavor.[24]

The drama was not all that appeared upon the stages of Dead-wood. Contemporary theatrical successes and old favorites could not fill the insatiable thirst of Deadwood for culture and entertain-ment. "Grand Vocal and Instrumental Concerts" of both amateur and professional status were performed, often as a benefit, like that for Inez Sexton, to help one of a score of charitable endeavors. Trav-eling road shows passed through, with varying successes: Billy Casad's "Refined Minstrels" would have been better received said the *Times* "if less vulgarity had proceeded from the stage. People of Deadwood may be eccentric, but. . . ." The Olympic Club Min-strels assured their audiences that "they were forced into it" and that the town "will never again be afflicted" by similar performances, and it was perhaps just as well, for minstrels did tend to get a rep-utation for low and vulgar performances, and Irene Cushman primly wrote once in her diary that she wouldn't have gone to a show if she had known that it was going to be minstrels. Duncan Clark's Lady Minstrels arrived in Lead in the spring of 1899, and departed with the "reputation of being the rankest, most obscene and depraved company of people that ever appeared before the public," and the show, well advertised by its having been raided by the police in O'Neill, Nebraska, drew a satisfactory audience, which participated in "the rankest kind of a sell," an "outrage upon all sense of decency and propriety." The performances at the Gem were said to be chaste in comparison, except that none of Clark's performers was attractive enough to make even a box rustler at the Gem. The strictly masculine audience hooted many of the performers off the stage, and a projected second performance was stopped by the law.[25]

The Fourth of July was always a major celebration in Deadwood, and as the gold rush days of 1876 were also the nation's centennial year, the mining camps were even more demonstrative in their patriotism, although, like all good patriots, they asked something of their country in return, sending off a memorial written by Gen. A. R. Z. Dawson, the collector of U.S. Revenue, asking that the Sioux Indians' title to the Black Hills be speedily extinguished. In nearby Elizabethtown, lawyer A. B. Chapline delivered an oration, and Dr. Overman had read the Declaration of Independence, and in Montana City, later a part of Deadwood, Judge H. N. Maguire "stirred his hearers to a high degree of patriotic enthusiasm." The miners erected a huge flag pole and from it flew a flag made out of garments of "mystical sublimity, neither russet, silk, nor dimity" which was noisily saluted by one hundred anvil salutes (made by stacking two anvils face to face with gunpowder in the facing hardy holes—the upper anvil usually rose twenty or thirty feet in the air and with any kind of luck came down and injured one of the spectators), and a happy, noisy, drunken time was had by all.[26]

Similar celebrations, although not again distinguished by a centennial until 1976, were held year after year: a Firemens and Citizens Jubilee ball, admission two dollars, was held in 1879. "A sort of one-horse celebration, gotten up on the cheap but in the end about as good as could have been expected" was put on in 1880 and ran for three days, at the end of which it seemed to the *Times* that "the average citizen can get in all the enthuse that is necessary." In 1883 the celebration included a military band which "played different airs, which should be national, but which are difficult to distinguish, each performer being too deeply penetrated with the principles of independence." The order of march for the parade shows the scope of the program:

1 – General Dawson, The Marshal, and his aids
2 – The Deadwood City Band
3 – Carriages containing celebration and city officials
4 – The Fire Companies, in their order
5 – Car of state
6 – Secret Societies
7 – Citizens on foot and on horseback

Races followed, and the day concluded with a display of fireworks and a grand ball at Kiemer Hall, and potential participants were advised in advance that "the gentlemen who have hold of the anniversary celebration are old hands at the business, and know no such word as 'fail,'" giving at least some indication that earlier celebrations had perhaps been undistinguished for their success.[27]

It was in the realm of purely social events, the balls, dances, masquerades, and parties, that the nimble whirligig of Deadwood's high and low society spun with its greatest gaiety and abandon. It is hard to distinguish at times between respectable events and those abandoned orgies and excesses which seem to have been a part of the underworld's promotional activities, but the people at the time, of course, well knew the difference, although at a distance of a hundred years it is now sometimes difficult to tell one kind of event from the other. Respectable employers like Mr. Mund the banker might threaten that "anybody that goes will be fired," but how was he to know which of his employees attended unless he went himself?

The first dance in town is said to have been held at the Grand Central Hotel, where Aunt Lou Marchbanks presided over the kitchen and doubtless joined the festivities. Nine women were present, the floor was greased with candle shavings (every man who worked in a pit or a tunnel had lots of candles), and the fiddler played and called for two quadrille sets. Another, similar, dancing club was got up about the same time by the young bachelors and married men of the gulch who wanted a respectable party and arranged for what they hoped would be one. All went well until one prostitute came bawling into the festivities complaining that if her man was good enough to attend she was too, and when she was refused admission, she began to shoot up the house until she was disarmed. Her boyfriend resigned at once, presumably under some pressure from the rest of the group, and the dance club resumed its activities in a somewhat chastened mood. By the first of June 1876 three "dance halls," two "variety shows," and one legitimate theater—Jack Langrishe's—were prospering in Deadwood, but the theater was the only place a respectable woman would set foot in. One of the Deadwood doctors out walking with his wife nodded to a young woman he had met at some low entertainment, and explained cheerfully, "It's just a girl I know professionally." His wife acridly inquired, "Your profession, or hers?"[28]

Any excuse was sufficient to hold "a grand masquerade ball." The Bella Union, for example, celebrated Christmas Eve of 1876 with one. Judging from the few existing photographs of the loose ladies of the city, masks and costumes were just what they needed to enhance their popularity, most of them having been designed a good deal more for comfort than for speed. The General Custer House reopened after a temporary closing with a grand ball, and planned another for New Year's night, and not long after, the "Coterie Ball" at the same hotel was said to be "a most *rech ercher* [*sic*] affair," and it probably was. A grand ball to celebrate the coming of the telegraph was held at the Grand Central Hotel, with the ladies' dresses described in overblown detail: "Miss Ulrick—a beautiful vesture of deep mazzarine blue, bull train and flounces; scarlet necktie, coiffure 'pompadour sans poudre,' gold ornaments." In contrast the gentlemen in attendance were listed by name alone. In the spring of 1879 the Welsh House was the scene of a meeting of the Pleasant Hours Club, which held "a grand masked ball" with characters representing Pocahontas, Topsy, George Washington on roller skates, a Chinaman, an Irishman, an old lady, and so forth. These masked balls were probably a device by which wicked people could attain, at least briefly, a chance to associate on equal terms with the upper crust of town, and a chance, also, for the upper crust to meet the happily wicked, but one can almost hear the outraged snorting of the respectable matrons commenting, "Damned hussies! If they're honest women why do they hide their faces?" Masked balls continued popular, but by 1905 their reputations were such that announcements had to proclaim that "no improper characters will be admitted," in order to distinguish a proper from an improper affair.[29]

The lodges of the city—the Odd Fellows, the Masons, and the

Knights of Pythias—gave an 1880 Thanksgiving ball, with the customary "music by Gandolfo's String Band," a group of musicians which must have been kept pretty busy. On New Year's Day the Deadwood ladies with any social pretensions at all kept open house, treating any respectable man who came to the door with foods and beverages suitable to the season; it was a sort of contest to see if they could sozzle a youth into insensibility before he could go on to his next port of call. The newspapers published lists of the callers at each home, and presumably the hostess who achieved the longest list was held to be thereby distinguished from lesser competitors in the field of entertainment and popularity.

In the 1880s roller skating became a craze, and of course the roller skating rinks, being in the nature of large, level and commodious halls, could be used for other purposes as well. The story was told of the young lady who said, "I'd just got on my skates and made a start when I came down on my —" at which point in her story her parents gasped at the prospective impropriety. "My legs just scooted out from under me," she continued, "and I came right down on my . . . "—gasps again interrupted the story—" . . . on my partner, who had me by the hand, and liked to have smashed him flatter than one of George Stokes's [a competing reporter] funny stories." One young married woman spent $80 a month on roller skating, "morning, noon and night. . . . She was a familiar figure on the rink, always to be seen gliding over the floor and seldom alone," but, reading between the lines, it appears that she retired from her position as Queen of the Roller Rink to preside over a small but growing family.[30]

And there were bands! The Eighth Cavalry Band from Fort Meade performed in town repeatedly, almost always including a Sousa march or two in their popular presentations. They were followed by the Seventh Cavalry Band, when that regiment returned to the Black Hills and was stationed at Fort Meade. Once when it was performing in the Deadwood Opera House the wind that they generated (that is what the *Times* claimed, but it probably was a miniature tornado) blew the whole front off of the building, but nobody was injured. The Deadwood Band, conducted by Joe Ollerenshaw, got new instruments and new music in 1880—apparently the old had worn out quickly—and was full of pep. In 1889 it reappeared as the Deadwood Metropolitan Band, performing for a ball in which, as was the custom at respectable balls, a dance program of twenty dances was issued to each girl's partner long before the conflict began, it being his duty to fill every dance for her with a new partner, reserving only the first and the last dances for himself. A girl who was a wallflower under those circumstances could always blame her partner, and a young man who had to dance all evening with the girl he came with had only himself to blame. In 1899, ten years later, yet another New Deadwood Band under the guidance of Professor George Mullen got underway in the melodious basement of the steam laundry and with twenty-two members worked at not only good music but at precision marching as well.[31]

Churches, in addition to caring for the spiritual wants of their people, provided entertainments designed to uplift, acquaint, enlighten, and, above all, confine their members, who might otherwise have ventured into the fleshpots of the badlands. The basic notion of the so-called muscular Christianity then prevalent seems to have been, "An exhausted Christian is a virtuous Christian," and the ladies did their best to see that no church member had either the time or the strength to seek more lavish entertainment elsewhere. In 1880 the Episcopal church put on a party—as one example of hundreds—in Nye's Hall, with piano selections by Professor Hirschfield and vocal music by Mrs. Seth Bullock, after which Gandolfo's orchestra and string band provided music for dancing. The innocuous nature of the entertainment was testified to by the fact that children under twelve could be admitted to this "wholesome and unalloyed pleasure" for half price. The Congregational ladies the same year put on a social, with lemonade, ice cream, raspberries and a multitude of cakes, apparently its staple refreshments, and the award of a handsome walking cane (men carried canes more in those days, a custom which came from England as a defense against "garroters," as muggers were then termed) to the group's most popular candidate for territorial representative in congress. The Methodists put on a "Necktie Party," and although that kind of entertainment *was* popular in the Hills, *their* party consisted of a contest to see who could make the most attractive necktie. Unlike the more common type of necktie party, the winner was not given a suspended sentence, but was condemned to wear his creation for the balance of the evening.

"I'm tired of ham, veal loaf, bread, Saratoga chips, olives, almonds and ice cream," wrote young Irene Cushman as the winter social season of 1890 began. Deadwood's social life for a young woman, or for a married one, for that matter, who could afford it was not just a recreation; it was a career: Trips to Rapid City to stay at the Harney Hotel. Trips to Hot Springs to bathe in the Evans Plunge and attend the Chautauqua lectures. A constant stream of church-oriented meetings, and now and then a lecture: on 5 November Miss Cushman heard Susan B. Anthony, "a tiresome old lady," and Anna Shaw on women's rights, but did not much enjoy it. Dances, after which she was always weary, and no wonder, considering the hours these lasted. Musicals ("Mrs. Bullock sang horridly"). Crushes on Miss Hamill her elocution instructor. A frightening lecture on Stevenson's *The Strange Case of Dr. Jekyl and Mr. Hyde*, with subsequent "awful dreams all night;" Minstrels if they were not coarse; And mocking attendance on the Odd Fellows banquet, "the countriest crowd you could imagine." This was the life of a young lady of fashion when Deadwood was the center of Black Hills trade and mining, a diligent pursuit of happiness and marriage relatively untrammeled and, except for the sorrows naturally inherent in late adolescence, happy and carefree. Boys and girls walked out into the mountains together, picnicked together, came home late, and no one complained, for nothing morally questionable was ever suspected. This was the happy life of Deadwood's gilded youth, for gold and commerce supplied a gilding which only major cities, elsewhere, could afford to duplicate. [32]

From its earliest days the Deadwood community has been addicted to gaudy and extravagant fairs and similar outdoor activities. The Second Annual Black Hills Fair, held in 1881 at the park association's grounds, promised to award five thousand dollars in prizes, which gives some idea of the liberal scope of the proposed activities. If a fair was not held in Deadwood, both railroads, after 1890, would provide a reduced rate so that fair-lovers could go to one somewhere else. This passion for such festivities eventually culminated in Deadwood's famous Days of '76, which annually erupts in town during the early days of August, with three days of parades, rodeos, and both open and covert hoopla and shenanigans designed to attract the tourists, entertain the citizens, and enrich the merchants of the town. This gaudy event is immediately followed by an infestation of motorcyclists coming in from their convention at Sturgis, a few miles away, and the antics of their varied groups provide considerable amusement to those of Deadwood's citizens that can observe them from a safe upstairs window without having to participate along with them in the gutters, but even the most repellent cyclists are welcomed as long as they behave themselves, for even today no one can claim that Deadwood's people are not fair-minded.

Sports were common. Children and young people slid down streets all winter, and slings and crutches were as common then as blue jeans are today; only the soft, heavy Deadwood snow saved the sliders from worse damages and maims. Prizefighting was popular. Johnny Marr, "the Belfast Chicken," and George "Cook the Kid" Latimer fought to a draw in 1877 at Al Swearengen's Cricket Saloon, a considerable feat in those days of bare knuckles and limitless rounds, and similar pugilistic contests continued to be promoted as long as Deadwood remained the entertainment center for the northern Hills. Horse racing was enormously popular, and 1880 saw a large race meeting at the track maintained by the Deadwood Driving Park Association. A purse of one thousand dollars a side was put up (presumably that meant that each participant had to put up one thousand dollars to enter, winner to take all), and the thoughtful veterinarian Nelson Armstrong was in attendance with his trotting horse Gold Dust, who "was as open as the smile of an alligator, and as active as a flock of scared bats." Gold Dust, alas, was not allowed to compete in the contest, for fear that the notorious Armstrong might use some devious device to ensure an unmerited victory.[33]

The Black Hills Sportsmen's Club, begun in 1883, based its constitution and bylaws upon those of the Saint Joseph, Missouri, club, and devoted itself largely to wing shooting and to the preservation and increase of such birds as might be conveniently and profitably shot at. Fancy shooting was a popular sport for participants and spectators alike. Sometimes live birds were released from cages, but more often in later days stones or bottles were tossed in the air to test the skill of the shotgunners. Target rifle shooting scores ran from 16 to 119 out of a possible score of 125, indicating that at least some but not much of the old frontier aptitude prevailed as late as 1905. The Olympic Club put on various field days, with banks closing at 10:00 A.M. so that their clerks could participate in the bicycle races, foot races, and other contests and feats of strength and agility.

Hunting, of course, was a common sport—early in the 1900s Seth Bullock escorted Kermit Roosevelt, Paul Martin (son of the congressman), and others northward from Belle Fourche in pursuit of game, and the party returned with three wildcats and a bear cub. When they reached Medora, North Dakota, young Roosevelt persuaded Martin to assume the Rooseveltian name and honors to give him a rest, and young Martin as a result was mobbed by the young women of the community, all of them giggling and screaming.[34] Camping too became an important recreation, and the Black Hills streams and mountains made it, in those days when open camp fires were less restricted than they are today, a happy and flexible way to fish, relax, and get away from Deadwood's modest urban pressures. Dining out, taking an excursion train to resorts at Pactola and Hisega (a resort in Rapid Canyon named for the initials of six young ladies), and a drive to Sylvan Lake were common, though hardly sporting, recreation, and by the turn of the century polo was introduced also, to give a social turn to horsemanship, and provide activity for the cavalry officers at Fort Meade and the horse breeders who supplied their mounts.

All of these social activities—the lodges, churches, clubs, even the theaters to a large extent, and certainly the many balls and entertainments—fulfilled not only their stated purposes, but even more importantly, they brought people together in a new land, provided instant fellowship, immediate acquaintances, and a reasonably structured social life on a mining and later, on a business, frontier. Entertainment was not merely amusement but companionship; the people gathered together to *be* together, and in a new community with a mobile population the need for this kind of togetherness, for an artful artificial social unity in which each could participate as much or as little as he wanted, was extensive, and it produced, as has been indicated, the variety of social activities which made Deadwood seem to many of its citizens "the biggest little city in the country," a town in which it was fun to live, and, if the funerary gyrations of the Pioneers are any indication, a town in which it might even have been fun to die. There were available, however, other, equally social, activities of considerably less respectability.

EIGHT

Fêtes Worse than Death

"We saw very little if any drinking, and the general tone of the place was one of good order and law, to which vice and immorality must bow."

John G. Bourke, 1876

"Never take your hat off, and never sign your name!" (Advice on visiting a whorehouse)

An eminent physician

"Age don't tell on a woman's beauty out here in the Hills; the longer they live here the younger they look."

Black Hills Times, 20 February 1800

ENTERTAINMENTS may have shaded imperceptibly from the respectable to the abandoned, but the badlands themselves, the raucous, flashy, shabby home of Deadwood's life of sin, made no pretense of being anything but what they were, the stews, saloons, and gambling hells that catered to the basest lusts of those who had money and passions and wanted to get rid of both. There was nothing of an "underworld" nature to these wild-eyed enterprises; they were open and above board, and a visitor had to be blind, deaf, and stricken with olfactory paralysis not to identify the dens and dives by merely walking by them. All was visible and apparent, and nobody except a fool or a stranger was ever seduced into such places unaware.

The saloon was beyond a doubt the most common and the most popular institution of both socialization and dissipation. Whiskey in the 1870s could be bought in the states for $1.65 a gallon, and sold by the ounce at $0.50 a drink so that a gallon of whiskey produced $64.00, a margin of profitability that was certain to attract the enterprising to the saloon business. The liquor trade on an Indian reservation like the Black Hills was of course illegal, but to compensate for the risk of federal arrest the Deadwood Board of Health kept the liquor license fees low, and the prevalence of saloons is a strong indication that there was little loss in the business. The first saloon in town, built by Ike Brown and Craven Lee, was a rough log house about fourteen by twenty feet, on the corner of Main and Gold streets. The liquor served, not only here but in the numerous "ranches" that sprang up in and around town, was not highly regarded by the connoisseurs, who during the Indian War of '76 claimed it was more dangerous than the Indians, and that "as a rule it would be better for the traveler to have some Indian lead in his carcase than a glass of ranch rot-gut in his stomach." These noxious beverages were potent enough "to kill an ordinary alderman," while their effects on the uninitiated lasted up to a week and tended to incapacitate the victim for any useful activity whatever. General Crook was twice forced to move his command, during the turbulent summer of 1876, to new locations where his men could not find easy access to these debilitating excesses.[1]

On 1 July 1877 there were seventy-five saloons in town, including the Bella Union, Eureka Hall, Gem, Grand Central, Hazen House, Health Office, Little Bonanza, Paul and Wall's Office, the Custer House, the Red Bird, the Headquarters, the Walsh House, and the Old Crow. Many of these were mere makeshift bars, two barrels with a board nailed across them, in a tent or a dugout, but some saloons were already grandiose establishments, with rich carpets, tony (later described as classy) bartenders, carved back bars, plate glass mirrors, and real or at least mechanical music. By 1880 the number of saloons had declined to sixty-three, served by seven wholesale liquor dealers, five brewers, and thirty-eight bartenders; for apparently many of the saloons were so small that their proprietors tended bar for themselves without assistance. Even so, about 3 percent of the town's population was identifiably concerned in the liquor business, and probably two or three times that many were to some degree involved.

Inebriation was of course common—a reporter for the *Times* counted fourteen drunks in the streets on 22 May 1877; a typical news item ran, "An intoxicated man wanted to be monarch of the whole affair, but was borne off to his chamber in the embrace of the law." Nobody worried much about drunkenness as long as it was confined to the badlands area and the drunks did not annoy respectable citizens. "Perhaps you saw them," said the newspaper article. "She was small, fairhaired and neat. He was tall and awkward, and could scarcely stagger under the burden of too frequent imbibing." During the afternoon the husband had "fallen from grace with a dull thud," but she pursued him "like an avenging angel" and hauled him out of the saloon, he wearing a "leer that changed to an imbecile smile at her determination." She loaded him onto the train and gave a "sigh of relief, for . . . they were out of sight, and tomorrow would again see him in his right senses." It was such scenes, repeated over and over again, which eventually led to the prohibition movement.[2]

Nobody liked the bouncer, that robust and earnest official who kept order in a saloon. One bouncer, who had the habit of throwing out irate customers so they lit upon their heads, attempted this feat on a little Irishman, who, instead of submitting tamely drew his knife, and starting at the bouncer's neck made a series of artistic slashings and incisions clear down to his ankles. It took old Doc Howe two hundred stitches to sew the bouncer back together, and the experience so unsettled the patient that he went totally insane and had to be hauled off to the laughing academy at Yankton. At another bar, across from the Bella Union, a big ruffian from Missouri, pretty well tanked up, waved his gun and announced to the assembled multitude, "I'm a wolf, and it's my turn to howl!" A little fellow, probably employed by the saloon, came up with a determinedly pointed pistol and remarked, "You howl once more and it will be your last howl this side of hell," and the Missourian went out the door a good deal more like a lamb than a wolf. Another mountain man, filled to the ears, entered a bar and announced, "I give fair warning for no one to disturb me. If they do I'll crimson the streets of Deadwood with the blood of all the men you see. I am full of the concentrated ginger of holy horror, and when I get mad empires totter and kings abdicate—Beware!" He seems to have got away with it, at least for a little while, but a thoughtful bartender who saw his trade being driven away by the rantings of such a ruffian frequently offered the bully "one on the house" that had been liberally laced with chloral hydrate, the celebrated Mickey Finn of the saloon business, in which the alcohol and the hypnotic combined synergistically to lay the victim out colder than a wedge, to awake the next morning with a stomach feeling as if he had swallowed, but not yet properly digested, a hive of bees.[3]

Turnover in the liquor business was high; the 1898 *Directory* lists only twenty-two saloons, although there probably were more, but includes only the Gem and the Health Office from 1878. Other names were the Bodega (still in operation nowadays at the same site), the Green Front, the First Ward Saloon, Hob Jim's Place, the Last Chance, Pabst's Headquarters, Pete's Exchange, the Silver Star, the American, the Court, the Derby, and the Lobby, which last advertised, "The Lobby—It Leads, Others Follow—Best Brands of Goods, Fine Music, *and an Orderly House*." It was, apparently, something which they felt they ought to mention, as a distinction from other, more disorderly, establishments.[4]

One of the most potent sources of disorder was gambling. Scores if not hundreds of professional gamblers came to Deadwood to work the free-milling pocket deposits of gold dust to be found on the honest prospector looking for entertainment and relaxation. The desire of the recreation-bound for excitement rather than for winnings made him an easy mark for "oily-tongued individuals whose oratorical attainments and attractive personalities well fitted them for driving a profitable trade" at the gambling tables, which were as much a fixture as the bar in each saloon. Jim Persate's Wide West Saloon, on the corner of Main and Gold streets, operated one of the earliest faro banks, presided over by a short, pudgy, and unattractive French woman called Madame Mustache. Faro, which seems to have but little percentage for the house if honestly played, was probably crooked in most saloons in order that the proprietors might profit from the enterprise. Across from the Wide West was Eureka Hall, a den with a bar, a stage, and a keno layout, in which a large wheel was spun, and the number at which it stopped would pay, the holder of the lucky number bawling out "Keno!" while all the other punters muttered "Oh, hell!" Other games which were popular were three-card monte, which was a variation of the old shell game, roulette, craps, chuck-a-luck, and of course poker, with the house taking a percentage of each pot. The Bodega's books as late as 1904, just before Deadwood gambling was ostensibly closed down, mention blackjack, poker, faro, roulette, and policy (a refinement of keno). The Bodega's roulette wheel had but a single zero, in European style, as opposed to the more profitable double zero common in American, so the presumption is that it was now and then given some trifling assistance by its operator to make up for the lesser profitability embodied in the more liberal mechanism. The Bodega's faro layout on the other hand seems to have been operated honestly—or to have had a dishonest dealer—for the Bodega's account book shows that the game lost money steadily.[5]

Many unfortunate suckers, finding themselves losers, even in an honest game, became obstreperous, and the services of the bouncer, or even of a resident gunhand, might be required to pacify them, after which the complainant would be hauled to the crowbar hotel to recover enough of his equanimity to appear peacefully before a justice of the peace the following morning on a well-founded charge of disturbing the peace. Everybody profited from the arrangement: the gamblers had the money, the officer and the courts the fines, and the unfortunate player at least got the excitement that he came for and could return to his companions with the smell of the prison yet upon his garments to testify that he had been successful in his search for entertainment.

By 1881, when Deadwood became an incorporated city, the act of incorporation granted the city fathers authority "to restrain, prohibit and suppress tippling shops, billiard tables, ten-pin alleys, ball alleys, houses of prostitution, and other disorderly houses and practices, games and gambling houses, desecration of the Sabbath, commonly called Sunday, and all kinds of indecencies." These extensive responsibilities, undoubtedly copied without much thought from the charter of some sober city farther east, seem to have been too much for the civic authorities, and with admirable evenhandedness they refused to enforce any one of these restrictions any more than they enforced another, with the result that none of them were enforced at all, although Sheriff Bullock in at least one instance did receive an information and complaint of the "crime of persuading another to visit a gambling house." In general, however, gambling, as a concomitant of saloon-keeping and recreation generally, proceeded undisturbed except by the quickly stifled cries of outrage from its occasionally swindled customers.[6]

Respectable women, of course, did not go into a saloon, except by accident or to retrieve an erring husband. One earnest churchworker, Miss Neill, her head full of an item for a Deadwood newspaper, did wander into the adjoining bar, but, not finding the expected editorial offices, smiled, bowed to the assembled souses, and withdrew. Another housewife, married to a compulsive and congenitally unlucky gambling man, did come into Bedrock Tom's on purpose late one evening. Wearing an expression like a meat ax and a large and sturdy apron over her dress, she swept up to the table where her husband was playing poker with several others, a huge pot of gold, silver, and bills heaped up in the center of the table. With one sweep of her arm she scooped the pot into her capacious apron, and marched out of the saloon without anyone raising a hand to stop her. The general opinion among the gambling men of Deadwood was that she had done the right thing, but they never played cards with her husband afterwards, for fear that she might do it again. It is one of the few instances known in which a wife has been able to effect the reform of a gambling husband. Old Poker Alice Tubbs with her dead cigar, her steely eyes, and sleepy demeanor was another exception, always welcome at any gaming table, but even she made it a fixed policy not to play cards with strangers, in case they might be dishonest, and stir her up into some sort of argument.[7]

Not every bar had prostitutes, but every house of prostitution had a bar. Nuttall and Brown's Temple of Music advertised, on 2 December 1876, that they had the "Best Entertainment in the City," with the patrons "served by pretty waiter girls with the best Wines, Liquors and Cigars," while the notorious Fannie Garrettson and Banjo Dick Brown her paramour, Winetta May, Charles Clifton, and William Wallace provided musical amusement. The waiter girls often made their money by cadging drinks—you could tell, in the morning, how well they had done by the number of empty bottles in the street in front of each establishment—but they also had more to offer, and theirs was not considered a respectable employment. The cancan was a favorite dance, and the variety show and the jokes were "slung . . . as low as possible." The Gem, the Bella Union, the Melodeon, and the Cricket were all in business by the fall of 1877, and a pretty sordid business it was. Helm's (or Heim's) Union Park Brewery and Beer Gardens, in South Deadwood, had a "spacious dancing pavillion" and a brass and a string band, and was a place where people could dance and meet—such spots can be respectable, and maybe this one was, but the likelihood is that this one wasn't, for few respectable women would participate.[8]

The blending of entertainment and dissipation was well illustrated in many of the so-called theaters. Tom Miller's Bella Union, as early as September 1876 "seemed to be drawing a liberal share of the patronage," although of course "the show is of a vaudeville type, and in addition is a little naughty," although Pete Reed's songs and Miller's own solo on the bones were said to be worth the price of admission in themselves. "Ribald song and smutty jest," however, seem to have constituted the bulk of the "variety" performance.[9]

Troy L. Parker, a visitor from Dartmouth College in the summer of 1909, was staying with the Trasks, a staid lumber family with a liberal supply of comely and virtuous young daughters. His first day in Deadwood young Parker went out to look over the town, and having heard, as far away as Chicago, of the Green Front as a place of entertainment, he devoted his youthful but unsuccessful energies to trying to find that recreational establishment. At dinner that evening, when Mrs. Trask hospitably inquired what he had done all afternoon, he guilelessly replied that he had "been looking for the Green Front," and at that a pause, indeed a coldness, fell upon the conversation as Mrs. Trask wondered how she could hope to protect her innocent daughters from this open and admitted viper who confessed willingly that he had spent his first day in Deadwood searching for the town's most famous whorehouse.[10]

The Green Front was an unquestionably low dive, "the toughest place in town," run by Eugene Ecker, who was usually referred to contemptuously as "that Eyetalian." He had been run out of Sioux Falls, and in Deadwood ran a place nobody could ever mistake for a legitimate theater. After the turn of the century the Green Front brought the pugilist John L. Sullivan for a one-week exhibition at a cost of over one thousand dollars in advertising alone, which indicates the scale of his operations. This "home of burlesque, vaudeville and drama," self-proclaimed as "Deadwood's most Popular Place of Amusement" took as its slogan

From Erin's Golden Harp Resounds the Silvery Strain,
Come Back to the Green Front, and You'll find your're Home Again.[11]

Of all the low spots the longest-lived and the most continuously notorious was "the dissolute and degraded" Al Swearengen's Gem Theater. It had begun so brightly in the spring of 1877: "Al Swearengen's New Gem Variety Theater will open tonight . . . as neat and tastefully arranged as any place of its kind in the west," said the *Pioneer*, but it did not stay that way for long. The two-story building, thirty by one hundred feet long, quickly became "an infamous den of prostitution under the guise of being a dance hall," or "hurdy-gurdy house." This "notorious den of iniquity," it was claimed, drew its support from many "so-called leading citizens" and so prospered financially and was let alone by the city authorities, an "everlasting shame of Deadwood," a "vicious institution," a "defiler of youth, a destroyer of home ties, and a veritable abomination." Swearengen's first installment of girls was "a motley crew, of ungainly features and uncertain ages." Swearengen's own wife habitually wore at least one black eye, and his girls managed by his "box herder," Johnny Burns, were treated worse than she was. His ordinary night's take was five thousand dollars, yet he died broke, killed by a train while trying to hitch a ride in the Denver railroad yards.[12]

Along with its saloons, gambling hells, and hurdy-gurdy houses, Deadwood had its crimes and its criminals. Crime was not organized—that would have been like trying to organize a barn full of boiled hoot owls—but it got along well enough without organization. A good many of the early gold rushers had come to town for the fun of it, and were both unskilled and unwilling to work at mining, and when their grubstakes ran out, they were ready for anything in the way of profitable activity. Other more determinedly dissolute characters came to the new rush with criminal activities in mind from the start. Miners, attempts at a census showed, constituted but a fifth of the total population, and many ostensible miners did little work on their claims, fearful that too much development might expose the worthlessness of what, undeveloped, they might have a chance of selling. In such an atmosphere of idleness, speculation, and chicanery it was a short step to gambling, confidence schemes, and outright criminality. One old prospector, with a sack apparently full of nuggets which he ostentatiously displayed, was invited into saloon after saloon, where he was plied with drinks, food, and small change in the hope that he would inadvertently disclose the source of his wealth, and when he staggered groggily to his hotel room with promises that he would head for his claim early next morning, the local sharpers congratulated themselves and resolved to rise early and follow him to the new diggings he had found. Alas, he was an older hand and held his liquor better than they thought, and he departed in the night, to cadge his drinks in yet another mining camp, a prime example of the ease with which prospecting for gold could descend to prospecting for suckers.

By the end of the placer season in the fall of 1879 the sharpers and confidence men and drifting opportunists had pretty well moved out of the community. "Deadwood is as orderly as any Eastern city of its size" said the *New York Times*, but they were mistaken, for a considerable residue of guile stayed on to keep the city lively. Nutshell Bill worked a thimblerig scheme, the old shell game, in which he placed a pea beneath one of three shells and took bets as to which shell, as they were adroitly shifted, held the pea. He was particularly clever at fumbling drunkenly with the shells so as to expose the pea, and even more adroit at surreptitiously moving it from its exposed position once the bets were down. The supply of suckers seemed to be infinite. Indeed, the hypnotic spell woven by a professional sharper has to be experienced personally in order to properly appreciate how anybody else could be so stupid as to fall victim to it. In my own experience two young men—now both eminent men of science—were taken in to the extent of several hundred dollars in just such a swindle during the Days of '76. Soapy Taylor, "a rough visaged individual with a big mouth and brazen lungs," was another such shyster. He peddled cubes of wrapped soap, a few of which were also wrapped up in one-, five-, or even ten-dollar bills. The cubes sold for $0.50 each, and a confederate or two invariably bought and found wealth as well as cleanliness inside the wrappings, but nobody else ever did. Lurline Monti Verdi, representing the female of the species, sang and dealt blackjack, and ran with highwaymen, but Boone May, one of the shotgun messengers, was her undoing, for he became her favorite and obtained enough information from her about her friends to bring several road agents to justice.[13]

Nowadays the people of Deadwood like to claim that it was not the wild characters, the Wild Bills and Calamity Janes, that gave the town its fame and character, but the zeal with which the wild lives are remembered and the obscurity with which history cloaks the respectable is a pretty good indication that Deadwood liked its people with the hair on. Swill Barrel Jimmy, Johnny-Behind-the-Deuce, and the Grasshopper, who walked the streets bawling out obscenities, were the remembered part of Deadwood, and Deadwood took them to its heart. Pancake Bill, Mysterious Jimmy, Bedrock Tom, Happy George, Johnny the Oyster, Club Foot Frank, Cheating Sheely, Laughing Sam, Bloody Dick, and the Bottle Fiend were the kind of people that Deadwood liked to talk about, and the respectable merchants, the Bullocks, Stars, Ayreses, Adamses, Fischels, and Hunters went about their constructive business unsung and usually unremembered.

Cheating Sheely, for example, was one of the dozens of badlands hangers-on, and was a notorious coward. One day when he had won three hundred dollars in gold dust, he fell asleep in Carl Mann's saloon. Mann piled furniture over him, exchanged his poke of gold for one full of brass filings (a common item in the commerce of early

Deadwood and stocked by merchants for just this purpose) and with other even less valuable material, then fired a pistol beside his ear. Sheely arose in a panic and carried on so over his loss that after two days of suffering Mann gave him his gold back again.

Pink Bedford was a talented poker player, and a gifted souse. Carl Mann, sorry to see so much talent wasted, extracted a promise that he would not take a single drink of whiskey for six months, supposing that by the end of that time he would be cured. Pink took the oath, and kept it: he drank pink gin, instead, and thereafter took his name from that soothing beverage, compounded from gin and Angostura bitters.

Mann had a bench outside his saloon, a practice still kept up by many Deadwood businesses, and at one end of it a needle was arranged to come up through a hole in the seat, to stab whatever victim the jokester could get to sit there. This humorous arrangement sent Johnny the Oyster into fits of laughter every time he worked it on somebody, and he could hardly leave it alone. One day, alas, Mann changed the bench end for end, and Johnny sat upon the end with the needle, but he didn't sit there long, and rose about three feet in the air and came down vowing to assassinate everybody in the saloon, and it took some time to calm him down.[14]

Deadwood never seemed to exhaust its supply of characters. When some died or otherwise departed, new ones were elevated to the throne of eccentricity, and their antics enjoyed for yet a while longer. English George, or the English Kid, Stevens made a hobby of committing suicide, but does not seem to have been a particularly adept practitioner. Madame Erb, of the Bulldog Ranch, weighed an eighth of a ton, and set a good table for passing freighters, but she was notoriously quarrelsome. Her ranch's name came from the time she kept a stage stop south of Sturgis where the Black Hills National Cemetery is now, and kept bulldogs to keep the passing freighters from lassoing her chickens with their bullwhips. She apparently took the name along with her to her later location north of Rochford, and a considerable temper along with it. Arguing over the distribution of the family property when her husband left her, she shot at several people, more or less indiscriminately in a fit of pique, and was put under five hundred dollars bond to keep the peace. She didn't keep it, and when Gale Hill went to arrest her for bigamy, she ran him off with a "three-foot six shooter," and Hill, "not wishing to force a lady, much less the madame, to accompany him against her will" departed for reinforcements. Deputies Noah Siever and Tom Faught, two days later, found her in a more mellow mood and were able to bring her to the bar of justice.[15]

Poker Alice Tubbs, already mentioned in connection with her banking and gambling business, ran an establishment in Sturgis, but often came to Deadwood to deal a few hands of poker, smoke a few cigars, and garner a little additional notoriety. She died in 1930, greatly lamented, for Deadwood knew that it would be hard to find a genuine replacement for her combination of good sense, good humor, and consistently good cards.[16]

Of all the characters that ornament the pages of Deadwood's gaudy history, none are more frequently recalled, or more variously remembered, than James Butler "Wild Bill" Hickok and Martha "Calamity Jane" Cannary. These two, between them, typify Deadwood's gold rush days the way folks for a hundred years have wanted to remember it.

Wild Bill was one of those western gunmen who traded on his ability to kill without hesitation and without regret, an attribute which, when coupled with natural and cultivated dexterity, made him formidable in any kind of a battle, for when the chips were down no conscience slowed his adept hand. He was quick with his gun, he never hesitated, and he never looked back. His philosophy was to shoot a man first and talk about it afterward, if at all; he fought without fear and buried the dead without remorse. He was an excellent shot, capable in his youth (he was thirty-nine when he came to Deadwood) of hitting an astonishing variety of targets with every shot, but he was not above sneaking out in the early morning, perforating a promising nearby target on the sly, and later in the day betting that he could hit it from an impossible distance. His distant eyesight was going, possibly as a result of ophthalmic gonorrhea, by the time he reached Deadwood, and although he could still shoot brilliantly up to about twenty-five yards, beyond that things had pretty much begun to blur. Recently married to Agnes Lake, a circus performer, he drifted into Deadwood in the summer of 1876, along with Colorado Charley Utter, Calamity Jane, and a few other dissolute characters who had been asked to leave Cheyenne. Once in town he gambled a little, told tall stories, cadged drinks from the tenderfeet, and waited for something to turn up, possibly hoping for an offer of a marshal's job to keep Deadwood's disorderly elements in line, a task for which his reputation ideally suited him.[17]

He had a number of cautious habits. He always poured his drinks with his left hand, to leave his right free for action, and he always sat with his back to the wall so nobody could sneak up and get the drop on him from behind, for he had killed a good many men whose friends might well welcome an opportunity to take revenge upon him. His old flair for law enforcement had not departed from him, even though his sight was failing, for when he was told that six Montana men were "talking against" him in the Montana saloon, he coolly walked up to the miscreants and told him to shut up or "there will shortly be a number of cheap funerals in Deadwood." Possibly the rest of the criminal element in town, fearing that Wild Bill would similarly put the kibosh on their activities, conspired to have him murdered, but if they did, no real evidence of it seems to have emerged. At any rate, on 2 August 1876 Wild Bill was playing poker in Nuttall and Mann's saloon, and for the first time in his career had to take a seat with his back to the door. While so seated at the poker table he was shot through the back of his head by one Jack McCall, a shifty drifter of no other distinction whatsoever.

A trial, held in a miners' court presided over by "Judge" W. L. Kuykendall, acquitted McCall because of his claim that Wild Bill had killed his brother, and the acquitted murderer rode rapidly out of town. At least one member of the jury was later killed while attempting to rob a stage, and it may well be that the "jury" was packed by those criminals who may have conspired to have Bill killed. Bragging about his killing of Wild Bill led to McCall's arrest in more civilized parts of the country, and he was taken to the territorial capital at Yankton, tried, convicted, and hanged. Colorado Charley provided a headboard for Wild Bill's grave which proclaimed, "Pard, we will meet again in the happy hunting ground to part no more," and the grave was subsequently moved to Mount Moriah Cemetery, where it is a noted tourist shrine. As late as the summer of 1979 a young couple were married in a "Wild Bill Wedding," dressed in costumes suitably antiquated in Bill's honor, at a performance of Deadwood's cheery summer tourist show, *The Trial of Jack McCall*. It would make Wild Bill happy to know that in death as in life he is an object of veneration by the visiting tenderfeet.[18]

"The Black Hills boosters would publicize Typhoid Mary as Florence Nightingale if it would help the tourist trade," wrote an indignant editor in the *Huronite and Daily Plainsman*, in connection with South Dakota's Governor Sigurd Anderson's refusal to endorse a movie about Calamity Jane, and Deadwood's hundred-year attempt to beatify this boozy old bawd bears out the allegation. Her association with Wild Bill is purely accidental, and attempts to show that the two were even friendly, let alone lovers or married, seem not to have come to much. Calamity Jane first came to the Black Hills disguised as a soldier along with Colonel Dodge and the Jenney expedition during the summer of 1875, and looked "as rough and burly as her messmates." In and out of the Hills more than once, in April 1876 she was said by Jesse Brown to be "about the roughest looking human being I ever saw" when he noticed her in a Custer saloon "where she was soon made blind as a bat from looking through the bottom of a glass." Another observer coldly remarked that "she was real tall and built like a busted bale of hay." Her name, Calamity, perhaps came from the various venereal calamities which may have afflicted those who patronized her charms. Her story is further complicated by the presence of other putative "Calamity Janes" throughout the West, each one vying with the others to achieve the greatest notoriety.[19]

On the other hand, everybody gives Calamity credit for being brave, kind, generous, and above all, active. She nursed the smallpox-stricken miners in the Deadwood pesthouse. She robbed a customer in a whorehouse—all the girls did that—but she told the judge, only to get the money to pay the hospital bills of one of the girls who was "sick, very sick and broke." At a benefit given for her at the Green Front somewhere around the turn of the century, she took the money that was raised by her friends and bought drinks for the crowd to such an extent that there was none left over to put her little daughter in a convent as her benefactors had planned. A Mrs. Drowley, of Glendive, Montana, records that when as a child she broke a finger, Calamity Jane had cuddled and comforted her, singing "There'll Be a Hot Time in the Old Town Tonight" in a whiskey tenor until her mother returned. In and out of Deadwood, Jane was a common sight in the bars, and as she drank she howled, and was booted out to the next bar down the street, where she would cadge drinks until she howled again, a peace-disturbing process which she kept up until some kindly soul took her home and bedded her down with a bottle to keep her quiet for the night. She briefly traded on her full-blown reputation at the Columbian World's Fair in Chicago in 1893, when "she was about 50 but she looked 100." When a member of the audience doubted that she was the pure-quill Calamity, she shot at his feet, hollering "I'm a howling coyote from Bitter Creek, the further up you go the bitterer it gets, and I'm from the head end. Now apologize before I shoot the toes off your feet." He did so.[20]

She ran up a bill at Jake Goldberg's grocery, and anywhere else that would give her credit, and most places did give her credit, for she became a sort of public charity and in addition was a nuisance when she was crossed or hindered. She sold patent bachelor buttons, which could be attached without sewing, and with an adroit snip of a large pair of shears made sure that every man she talked to needed one or two of them. She died in nearby Terry on 1 August 1903, just a day short of the anniversary of Wild Bill's death, and she was buried beside him in Mount Moriah Cemetery, he not being alive, at the time, to file a protest. The Black Hills have since had a good many contenders for what might be thought of as the Calamity Jane Badge, but none have worn it with the distinction of its originator.[21]

A grand masquerade ball was planned for 23 January 1880: "The girls will be there in force. A large number of new costumes to select from will be on hand." The underworld too had its parties. As soon as Deadwood had begun to boom in 1876, "a round dozen frail daughters of sin" had left Cheyenne for the new mines, "mounted on horseback with a foot in either stirrup" (an enormity equivalent to walking downtown stark naked, nowadays) as they rode off for bagnios of the Hills. These early-comers, "painted, padded, and leering," were "too hideous to hope for a livelihood in any village less remote from civilization" than Deadwood. They lined up at the bars, cavorted on the sidewalks, and cried out from second-story windows, a notable "crowd of brazen and bedizened harlots." Eventually things got a little quieter, and houses "in which canary birds, lap-dogs and yellow-covered novels [all evidently considered emblems of luxurious dissipation] are prominent features" soon provided opportunities for more sedate dalliance for those who could afford it.[22]

Deadwood, of all the Black Hills mining camps, achieved the most lurid reputation for its houses of ill repute. It was the oldest active camp in the Hills as well as the commercial center of the area, and vice and crime were present in such large quantities that their practitioners, made bold by numbers, tended to flaunt rather than conceal their nefarious activities. Nine out of ten bartenders were said by McClintock, a crochety critic of the passing scene, to live "openly and apparently shamelessly with a low class of prostitutes," and the practice, although typical of bartenders, was by no means confined to them, for "many of the leading business and professional men were equally guilty" and led continuing lives of complacent vice with prostitutes of a somewhat higher and more retiring type. For the average man, however, an excursion into the badlands district was likely to be disastrous for few emerged, at least from the lower-class houses, with much left except their clothing and often not much of that.[23]

Times were always lively in the badlands. Two girls at one of the dens put on a "jigging match" which lasted for an hour, and as the girls grew heated with their exertions, they shed their surplus clothing until one had on about as much as a boy would if he was dressed in a pair of suspenders, and the other was "barefoot to her ears." Prostitution was never an amiable trade, for as a reporter said at the time, "If black eyes made beauties then Deadwood contains more pretty women than any other town," provided, of course, that a man "doesn't object to the shade of one eye being darker than the other." The various "female seminaries" and "immoral factories" were constantly in the news. One Annie Carr was arrested for indecent exposure, when she danced on the front porch of The 400 "with not enough clothing on to wad a shotgun." She was said to be drunk at the time. Another prostitute, a Frenchwoman (such girls often claimed that nationality, and those from New Orleans, at least, were sometimes able to maintain their pretense) was hauled into court by Marshal Hank Beaman and charged with disturbing the peace, but the court, being at that time under the influence of the underworld, released her; reformers claimed that it was hardly possible to get a conviction in Deadwood's early days.

"A well known character of the female gender has been on the hurrah. . . . She is an all night girl when she turns loose and never thinks of going home until carried there by some chance friends at peep of day," wrote the *Times*, possibly of Calamity Jane. Deadwood smiled tolerantly, with now and then a chuckle at the kind of man who, keeping a woman in Ingleside, was caught by his wife, who "tore the clothing all off of him" and then departed from him leaving him a wiser and a colder man, and as naked as a jay bird. Deadwood's respectable people were so respectable that the high jinks of the disreputable could be laughed at and ignored. [24]

In 1878 the *Deadwood Times* urged that a tax on individual prostitutes would not only fill the city treasury but also drive "women of the street out of town or into the house of a responsible madame." The life of a madam, responsible or otherwise, was not an easy one. The great flood of 1883 flushed away a good many of the academies, and the male friends of the girls, in response to plaintive calls of "Where is my man?" and "My trunk, oh, my trunk!" swarmed in to be of assistance, carrying luggage, pianos, and miscellaneous equipment through waist-deep water to higher ground. [25]

Mme Smith, "a boisterous female domiciled on Sherman Street," caused considerable annoyance to respectable people by "her unseemly conduct and language." *She* probably was not one of the responsible ones. Mrs. (you always called them Mrs., it was a common courtesy) Katie Smith, who ran the Hidden Treasure No. 2, expired from an overdose of morphine and laudanum, mixed; it was a common way for prostitutes to go. Hattie Bell, who ran the Castle on Fink's Flat, called on Judge Granville Bennett and the Reverend Alexander McConnell of the Congregational church, who in his side whiskers, frock coat, and high silk hat looked, it was said, like God Almighty, to sit the night beside her while she died, to make sure that the combined human agencies of the law and religion pointed her in the right direction. Ray (a female) Taylor was a "notorious" madam who was run out of nearby Sturgis, but Chief of Police Diltz would not even let her start a house in Deadwood—she was not responsible either, most likely. [26]

The newspapers did not carry identifiable ads for houses of prostitution, although their news items certainly gave all the information the curious might desire, and the city directories also tended toward modest obscurity. Nevertheless, when three or four Misses this, that, or t'other gave their addresses as "at Miss B. ———'s", or at a well-known bar, there seems little doubt about what the directory was advertising. Later the custom of respectable single women listing their occupations in the directories seems to have become common, but it does not necessarily mean that females named without an occupation after them were necessarily immoral. In Collins's 1878 *Directory* about thirty names can be identified as possibly disreputable, but it's hard to be entirely sure, and with so transient a group as prostitutes no directory would be likely to list more than a small part of the total number of girls available.

Prostitution was a highly temporary and transient business. The girls made money for a while, but most of it went for clothing, drugs, and liquor, while violence, suicide, drink, drugs, and disease rapidly thinned their ranks. The average prostitute lasted two or three years: the path, "although apparently strewn with flowers, leads down to infamy, unloved, unwept and unsung." It seemed to old Doc F. S. Howe, who always went out on badlands calls with his stomach pump, that he had doctored poisonings from every poison known to man: potassium cyanide, carbolic acid, strychnine, corrosive sublimate, iodine, morphine, lysol and chloroform," for "it seems to be a regular occurrence with these girls that every time they had a fight with their sweetheart they ended up by taking poison." He also treated many gunshot and knife wounds, and patched and poulticed broken limbs and various contusions beyond counting, for the primrose path, in practice, seems to have been a lumpy one.[27]

By 1900 the badlands occupied an entire block of two-story brick buildings on the west side of Main Street from the Mansion House on Wall Street to the northern end of the block. A Deadwood druggist's son who used to deliver (which says something about drugs and diseases there) could enter at the Mansion House and walk the length of the district on the second floor, a veritable smorgasbord of sin.

The attitude toward the upstairs girls, as they were called, was one of amused toleration. Doc Howe never spoke to them on the street—it wasn't expected of him—but Judge Bennett bowed courteously when he saw a face familiar to him from the court, for he was sufficiently dignified that he could afford to acknowledge their existence, and Mrs. Bennett now and then did her best to be of assistance to some of them. When the Deadwood ladies met the upstairs girls downtown, there was often a guarded though nodding recognition, for in Deadwood nobody was really an outsider.

Deadwood prostitution continues to the present: there is no city ordinance against, nor is there much civic opposition to it. Pillars of the church and government often own the buildings housing the remaining "upstairs rooms," and the girls, at least, pay their rent with punctuality. Four houses still flourish, with perhaps twenty to thirty girls, and the police interfere only in case of a disturbance. The girls are inspected weekly by the Lawrence County health officers, who are paid to prevent disease rather than misbehavior, but it probably doesn't do much good. When the Days of '76 and the motorcyclists' convention erupt in August, the houses all demurely close down, not wanting any trouble, and knowing that Deadwood's modest police force will probably be too busy elsewhere to come to their assistance.[28]

There is a remarkable variance of opinion regarding the general law-abiding or law-breaking tendencies of Deadwood's citizens. Some visitors referred to gold rush Deadwood as a "remarkably quiet, orderly, law-abiding town," in which honest prospectors watched out for each other's interests and lived a life of honorable probity. Others described the town, as did Nathan Butler in 1877, as "full of crooks of all kinds—gamblers, confidence men, pickpockets, thieves, highwaymen and murderers." He never came to town, he wrote, without two or three bunco steerers accosting him, and he finally inquired of one of them "what he saw about me that looked like an easy mark," and after that the sharpers let him alone. A newspaper correspondent reported that "there is not much law or order in Deadwood" in 1877, and another visitor the same year remarked that he didn't "know what they were doin' about law, but there sure wasn't much order." Others who were on the spot believed that "at no time in its history could Deadwood ever be classed as a 'gross town'" and that it had always been "singularly free from the bad elements" that made other mining towns notorious. In 1883 the *Deadwood Times* wrote that Deadwood was "one of the most moral and best behaved mining towns in the west" and proved their assertion by pointing out how little police news there was in their paper. The *New York Times*, on the other hand, said crime was so common in Deadwood that it had "given the town a national infamy."

All in all, the probable situation was this: there was, at least during the placer rush, a tradition of considerable honesty because men were few, knew each other, and were armed and on the spot. Later, when Deadwood shifted to a mining rather than a placer town, there was about as much petty crime as anywhere else, and perhaps a bit more. In the badlands there was a great deal of crime, but it rarely touched those citizens who kept to the respectable areas of town, and even the ordinary visitor to an ordinary saloon or gambling hall was probably pretty safe as long as he stayed sober and behaved himself, although it was said pretty generally that when such a man "took his roll from his pocket he almost invariably lost sight of it." The opinion is generally held that by 1879 the worst of the rough characters had departed for more verdant fields, and by the 1880s the town had passed through and survived the "maladies incidental to its growth," and had settled down to sedate and genteel dissipation.[29]

A brief survey of a few petty crimes will give an indication of their nature. High on the list was "indiscriminate discharge of firearms," for "idiots, boys and men" often fired thoughtlessly toward the downtown area. Not only was this dangerous and annoying, but the constant shooting tended to dull the quickness of response needed in case of an Indian attack. Throughout Deadwood's first generation, however, the ebullient cowboy or pot-valiant miner would now and then let off a few shots, but if anybody got hurt by it, it was put down to the high spirits of all involved. When Troy Parker came to Custer and took a room over the local bar, as late as 1909, he found a sheet of boiler plate under his bed to protect its occupant from those drunks who might give vent to their enthusiasms of the moment by shooting through the ceiling of the saloon below, and social life in Deadwood bars was probably conducted on similar principles, the prevalent notion being that "a little dignified shootin', stompin' and hollerin' never hurt anybody."[30]

Counterfeiting, both the substitution of brass filings for gold dust and the more ambitious passing of fake fifty-dollar bills, was fairly common, and the newspapers frequently complained about it. The postmaster, R. O. Adams, absconded with the post office funds. Fights and brawls were common—one burly miner bit off the lips and ear of another, and the school fund received the fine for his disorderly conduct. Miscellaneous petty crimes included selling oleomargarine, impersonating a U.S. revenue officer, passing bad checks, hauling explosives through the public streets, and frequent cases of indecent exposure, a clodpoll's misdemeanor which is as old as ancient Athens and which is still common nowadays. Many a minor crime was doubtless punished by a rap on the head with a policeman's nightstick or a boot in the britches by a burly bouncer and never got onto the police blotter at all, while much that would today be recorded as juvenile delinquency was remanded to parental correctional facilities consisting of a woodshed, a razor strop, and a few choice expletives. [31]

Thieves and robbers were common, although not very bright, for it is hard to see how they could either dispose of stolen property in so small a community, or easily escape with it over populous trails to a larger one. Seth Bullock broke up one major gang of thieves in early 1877; and thefts of chickens and watermelons were common enough, but not many serious-minded criminals risked being the chief attraction at a volunteer "tight rope performance" by taking part in more felonious activities.

The literature of stage robberies along the Deadwood trails is voluminous. As soon as the roving bands of hostile Indians were suppressed in the late 1870s, the outlying districts of the Hills along the stage trails became habitable to the bandits, and it was a rare traveler who escaped their attentions. Hardly an early issue of the Deadwood newspapers is without its news of "midnight assaults of a band of coach-robbing ruffians." The bulk of the bandits' activities took place in the southern end of the Hills, for too many well-armed and ill-tempered miners worked and roamed around Deadwood for a highwayman in that area to feel secure in his profession. It was in the empty end of the Hills that the bandits habitually stopped the stages. The Northwestern Stage Transportation Company required its passengers to exchange their money and gold dust for bank drafts or money orders, payable at the conclusion of the trip, before embarking on their perilous adventures. The terminal cities served by each stagecoach line assiduously invented terrifying tales about bandits along the trails that served other communities, in the hope of encouraging traffic to come their way instead of some other, so perhaps there are more tales than actual robberies, but the robberies were enough. Cornelius "Lame Johnny" Donahue operated on the Sidney route, along the eastern edge of the Hills, and when he was finally captured, a group of vigilantes intercepted the coach on which he was being hauled to Deadwood for trial, and he was incontinently hanged near Buffalo Gap. A headboard erected over his grave bore several legends, including threats of revenge from Johnny's friends, but the most memorable inscription read:

> Pilgrim, pause.
> You're standing on the mouldering bones of Limping John.
> Tread lightly, stranger, upon this sod,
> For if you make a move, you're robbed, by God! [32]

The most famous stage holdup of all, the robbery of a Home-stake gold shipment in September 1878, took place at Canyon Springs station, three miles east of Four Corners, Wyoming. The bandits had seized the station and its tender, and opened fire on the stage and its guards when they arrived. Several of the robbers were killed or wounded in the battle, and almost all of the stolen gold bars were eventually recovered, although local gaffers still now and then claim to know just where one or two of them are hidden and to be willing to reveal the site for a small fee. Even the one last bar presumed to remain missing was probably found by Old Man Grif-fith, who was out plowing his fields near Cold Springs one day, and was seen to stoop, lift up something heavy, put it in a bag, and take off for parts unknown, never again to be heard of by his wife and family, which, given such a character, was probably something of a biessing to the wife and family. [33]

An odd problem in Deadwood was the prevalence of what were called roughs, or, later, hoboes. In January 1878 it was reported nationwide that 150 men, "mostly roughs from the outside camps," had taken possession of the town, and that this mob was "yelling and shooting through out the town" and that the honest citizens were arming and organizing to protect their lives and property. Lo-cal newspapers did not seem to be aware of the invasion. Later, with the coming of two railroads, there actually were several invasions of hoboes, tramps, and idle laborers, who got so unruly that the police had to chase them into a corner in Wall Street and hose them down with a fire hose to get them under control. Foreign newspapers, unaccustomed to American nomenclature, reported that the Dakota Territory was "having considerable difficulty with the Hobo Indi-ans." This kind of roaming ruffian really was a constant nuisance, for unlike Deadwood's settled criminal element, they roamed all over town begging, stealing, and insulting girls and women until the police got them rounded up and shipped away again. Deadwood was not unique in having this affliction, but it came to Deadwood as a special shock, for the town had long been accustomed to un-locked doors, unguarded property, and the sanctity of respectable women.

It was in the crimes of violence, in assaults and murders, that Deadwood really showed what it could do in the line of criminality. Murders, during the gold rush days of the 1870s, ran about eight times higher than the present-day national average: thirty-four murders in the gold rush years 1876 to 1879, and ninety-seven violent deaths if those due to Indian depredations are included. Deadwood sporting life was seriously alleged to "kill off a man or two every night," but this seems to have been an exaggeration. During the 1890s murders ran even higher, nine times the national average, although of course when dealing with small figures such comparisons do tend to fluctuate wildly. Assaults in the 1890s, when they began to be properly recorded, were also eight times higher than the national average, and it is impossible to avoid the conclusion that Deadwood was a violent town. One old gentleman, who delivered morning newspapers in the badlands early in the 1900s, alleged that he rarely made his rounds without finding a bleeding corpse along the way; an old lady, who had lived on Forest Hill right above the badlands where all this was supposed to take place, alleged that she had never heard a shot fired in all her life. Both seem to have been exaggerating, but there is little doubt that when it came to crimes of violence, Deadwood did much to pad out the national averages, or that the Deadwood badlands were the main contributors. [34]

In 1878, to give an example from a single gold rush year, there were sixteen murders in Lawrence County, which of course included Lead, Sturgis, Spearfish, and many other mining camps as well as Deadwood. "The peaceable and law abiding," however, were assured in the various commercial club reports that they were "as secure here as they would be in any part of the East." It was only among the criminal classes and their patrons that the death rate from murder was excessive, and among them it seems to have been terrific. The Cheyenne newspapers suggested that the name of the Gulch be changed from *Deadwood* to *Deadman*, and Ambrose Bierce, the professional cynic, wrote a story based upon Deadwood's violence at the time. Rougher elements (Deadwood always was strict in making this distinction) "insured early additions to our cemetery," but, like the Kilkenny cats which ate each other up, they tended to fight mainly among themselves, and with similarly beneficial effects upon their population. [35]

A visitor from Manitowoc, Wisconsin, reported, with perhaps a touch of exaggeration,

> Every man in Deadwood carries about fourteen pounds of firearms hitched to his belt, and they never pass any words. The fellow that gets his gun out first is best man, and they lug off the other fellow's body. Our graveyard is a big institution, and a growing one. Sometimes, how-

ever, the place is right quiet. I've know[n] times when a man wasn't
killed for twenty-four hours. Then, again, perhaps, they'll lay out five
or six a day. When a man gets too handy with his shootin' irons, and
kills five or six, they think he isn't safe, and somebody pops him over to
rid the place of him. They don't kill him for what he has done, but for
what he's liable to do. I suppose that the average deaths amount to about
one hundred a month.

Such a death rate would have thinned out Deadwood's population
to a noticeable degree, and had it really ever existed, it would have
attracted the attention of both the Deadwood newspapers, the local
authorities, and the cemetery reports, none of which seem to have
been aware of it.[36]

These murderous carryings-on were of course entirely illegal,
and in direct contravention of the laws promulgated by the city's
board of health in October 1876 to assure the peace, rule, and dignity of the city, laws which in part provided that

> no person shall fire or discharge any cannon or gun, fowling piece, pis-
> tol, or fire-arm of any description, or fire, explode, or set off any squib,
> cracker or other thing containing powder or other combustible or explo-
> sive material [mining interests here excluded] . . . without permission
> of the mayor.

There is something delightful in the spectacle herein envisioned of
some doughty western desperado roaming the streets of Deadwood
thoroughly armed not only with a cannon but with the mayor's express permission to shoot it off as the occasion might require. Probably the law had in mind a direct prohibition of firearms, and the use
of explosives only with mayoral permission, but whatever the law
meant, it seems to have been entirely ignored, and Deadwood's
population, like that of the West in general, roamed the streets
armed to the teeth and fully prepared to either inflict or resist the
resulting mayhem and slaughter.[37]

Although the *firing* of guns may have been illegal, the *carrying* of
them was of course taken for granted in a country where hunting,
badmen, Indians, and general disorder all frequently threatened the
ordinary citizen. As the pioneer merchant George Stokes put it, "I
have known localities where the blue barrel of a pistol would catch
the eye of people taking chances with the rights and property of
others in a way that the law would not," for "in a new camp, a 'six
gun' takes the place of courts, judges, and jury." It was a commonly

held attitude, and in 1880 the *Times* urged its readers to "invest in a first class gun of some character" in order to ward off the almost nightly holdups taking place on the city streets. The firm belief that crime was prevented when "everyone went armed, and each carrier of a gun was supposed to be able and willing to use it" seems to have ruled supreme, and as late as the 1900s it was said by Charles W. Merrill that the citizens of the area "would as soon appear on the streets without their pants as [without] their six-shooters." The effect of all this armament was of course what the statistics show it to be: a great many murders, but most of them probably committed by one violent citizen upon another, and the death rate from this cause among ordinary citizens probably not much higher than it was in the more peaceable areas of the nation. Indeed, it might be claimed that a well-armed criminal population served a sort of eugenic purpose, the ruffians tending to kill each other off at a good deal faster rate than they killed honest people. It would have warmed the heart of the eugenicist David Starr Jordan, who was then advancing similar theories in regard to both poverty and disease.[38]

There were of course lynchings, although whether these were statistically included among "murders" or among "executions" is not at all clear from the records. In 1875 the *Cheyenne Daily Leader* pointed out that the Black Hills mining excitement was bringing in a good many rough characters and that "a little hemp could be used to good advantage." Used it was, and every now and then a horse-thief or similar malefactor was taken out into the wood, where he could grow up at his leisure with the trees. Occasionally some negligent ornithologist climbed up a sturdy cottonwood, presumably to rob birds' nests, and became entangled in his equipment, and every once in a while a criminal, tied up too short by his captors, did not survive his captivity long enough to stand a trial. The suicide rate, usually by hanging, was notoriously high among the criminal classes, and particularly so amongst those who dealt most heavily in their neighbors' cattle, although the newspapers did now and then express some curiosity as to whether those who had thus "received a suspended sentence" from a local cottonwood had actually "got up there by their own selves." No lynch gang was perfect, and now and then the wrong man was elected, for lynchings tended to take place in the dusk of evening or the dark of night, and mistakes were as inevitable as they were unfortunate. In such cases the vigilance committee usually expressed "sincere regrets" but also a certain satisfaction that even though they had hanged the wrong man, his death would still serve as a lesson to scare off the truly guilty. The first *legal* hanging in the Hills, that of Jimmy Gilmore, did not take place until 1882. Gilmore was a "good hearted and handsome young man," but his "high temper" had led him to be too quick with his gun, and he had murdered Vincente Ortiz and was quickly hanged.[39]

One of the most dramatic murders went unpunished. Slippery Sam had been run out of the Bella Union by the bartender, Harry Young, and told that if he returned he would be shot. Sam, anxious to get this nonsense over with, loaned his gaudy and distinctive overcoat to poor Bummer Dan Baum and sent him into the Bella Union, where Young shot him at once, but was acquitted by a miners' court on the excuse that "the defendant did not kill the man he set out to kill, and did not mean to kill the man he did kill." Slippery Sam left town for San Francisco, and later Young joined him there in a bunco-steering game, renting hacks to drunks at extortionate prices, so the supposition may well be maintained that the murder was some sort of put-up job designed for some reason to get rid of poor Bummer Dan.[40]

Jim Coburn, shot by Billy Woolsey, died at the Sisters' Hospital in 1880, but Marshal Hank Beaman was there to inquire, presumably of the bystanders rather than the sisters, "Would you d——d pilgrims stand around here and see a man die with his boots on?" and not getting any response, pulled off the boots himself so that Coburn might not die a coarse and unbecoming gunman's death. Mrs. Murphy, who rented out lodgings in "lover" (the typographical error in the report is suggestive) Main Street was shot by one Moll Solace in a quarrel over the rent; Moll apparently was not providing enough solace to the community to enable her to pay. Martin Couk murdered the school teacher Mrs. John Callison, and was hanged for it, a case that occupied the front pages of the local papers for weeks. One boy, disappointed in love, shot his competitor, then in sorrow and remorse put his .45 pistol under his chin and blew his own brains out. Old Doc Howe had to have the corpse hauled out through the window near which it lay—evidently on a first story—because the room was such a mess of blood and brains that he couldn't get anybody to go in through the door to help him remove the body. Such stories are typical of Deadwood's turbulent badlands

The Homestake Mine's shaft houses and mills on the northern edge of Lead, with the huge open cut beside them. The picture was taken from the present-day location of most of the Homestake's works. *Centennial Collection—Deadwood Public Library*

Young men about Deadwood in 1887. *Centennial Collection—Deadwood Public Library*

Estelline Bennett, representing the Deadwood Central Railroad, and Irene Cushman, covered with money to represent the Merchants National Bank, in the 1890 Deadwood Merchant's Carnival. *Adams Memorial Museum.*

Judge Granville Bennett's little house with its stylish mansard roof, on Williams Street, in the fashionable Forest Hill district that looked down upon the badlands with toleration and amusement. *W. Parker photo*

The Lee Street stairs still lead from the posh Forest Hill residential area directly into Deadwood's business district. *W. Parker photo*

Ruins of the Belle Eldridge Mill in Spruce Gulch. *W. Parker photo*

Dredging on Whitewood Creek below Deadwood during the 1970s. *W. Parker photo*

Dignitaries and old-timers ride in the Days of '76 parade each August in and upon the Deadwood stage. *Centennial Collection—Deadwood Public Library*

The Franklin Hotel has been a social center in Deadwood since it opened in 1903. *W. Parker photo*

One of Wild Bill Hickok's several gravestones. The likeness is as apocryphal as the sentiment. *Centennial Collection—Deadwood Public Library*

and typical too of the toleration of the town for the violence which accompanied one of its major industries.[41]

Toleration, however, could go only so far, and throughout Deadwood's history many sincere efforts at reform have intruded upon both social and political life, for as the Reverend C. B. Clark said as late as 1904, "The line of demarcation between good and evil is strongly drawn in the Hills," and a "spirit of intense worldliness" at times seemed likely to take over the community and needed to be battled constantly. Temperance and the prohibition of the sale of spirituous beverages was naturally one of the principal reforms pushed forward by those who wished to

> Compound for sins they are inclin'd to
> By damning those they have no mind to.

As early as 1879 the Reverend Father Mackin founded a society of Murphyites sworn to total abstinence, and this was followed by a Red Ribbon Club of those who had been "reduced mentally, financially and physically by too much fire water." In 1880 Sheriff John Manning proclaimed to the attention of the community that the statute forbade the sale of intoxicants on election day, but the violence accompanying many of Deadwood's elections indicates that this prohibition was not taken very seriously. A survey of the use made of the Deadwood theaters, when not offering dramatic performances, indicates a large number of temperance lectures, and the indomitable WCTU (Women's Christian Temperance Union) did its best, with lectures, exhortations, and banjo and pianola presentations to woo the weak from the Demon Rum. One notable effort towards prohibition arose out of local political controversy. Sol Star, many times mayor of Deadwood, found his election disputed by Romeo Dwyer, and in retaliation Star closed down Dwyer and Jack O'Dell's saloon and gambling house, but it was the only such establishment that he did close, and not content with that, Star also raided Hattie Bell's "castle" because Mrs. Bell was Dwyer's mother. This kind of selective law enforcement did not meet with wide approval, and public opinion forced Star to back off a little on it.[42]

The reformers did receive sporadic support from the South Dakota legislature, which in 1889 enacted a prohibition law which seems to have been distinguished for the degree to which it was ineffective, for most of the state's judges could neither understand or enforce it. In 1909 Deadwood still had sixteen saloons—one for every 250 inhabitants—and in 1911 a statewide local-option law only made Deadwood's bars more prosperous as other Black Hills communities closed down theirs. It was not until national prohibition in 1917 that Deadwood's saloons closed down, and even then they seem to have reopened surreptitiously as bootlegging became a major Black Hills industry during the prohibition era. Prohibition, plus the vigorous suppression of gambling, was a deathblow to Deadwood's badlands, and when the oil fields of nearby Salt Creek, Wyoming, attracted the last of the professional sinners, that part of Deadwood's industry and business devoted to wild life departed westward, leaving a spectacular gap in the population. The census of 1910 shows about 3,600 persons; that of 1920 about 2,400, although the reduction of mining activity due to higher costs during and after World War I doubtless accounts for some of the decline.

Gambling too was suppressed with vigor. Always regarded as an honest, if unproductive, business, it seemed so closely allied to drinking and prostitution that it partook of the scandal associated with those businesses, and in 1905 it was suppressed by a city law, and eight or ten gambling houses closed. Restaurant trade was somewhat reduced, drugstore business, oddly, lessened, and some fifteen thousand dollars in yearly gamblers' wages (there being from seventy to eighty such men employed) was of course eliminated from Deadwood's economy, but those merchants who gave credit found it much easier to collect what was owed them, and Judge Eckhardt reported that there had been "no arrests to speak of for the last three weeks, and there is no doubt that it can be attributed to the shut down of gambling." Like the closing of the saloons, the suppression of wide-open gambling seems to have been only a temporary reform, but never again did gambling rise to the heights which it had achieved before its prohibition, when Deadwood was the fun and sin city of the Hills.[43]

Prostitution never has been completely eliminated from Deadwood, but the limits placed on gambling and drinking severely reduced it, for as one madam remarked after prohibition, "You can't run a sporting house on crick water." The 1881 act of incorporation empowered the city fathers to "restrain . . . houses of prostitution, and other disorderly houses and practices," but the restraint employed seems to have been mild and benevolent. In 1889 a "vigilance committee" of irate harridans was formed to tar and feather whores, and to reveal the names of erring husbands patronizing them to the wives concerned. This probably would not have done much to slow down single men, and in any case the committee does not appear to have been very active. Temporary closings of individual houses, usually when they became too noisy, violent, or disorderly, were common, and now and then a citizen's petition to close a "blackening, sickening, nauseating, filthy and dastardly hole" (in this case the so-called Family Liquor Store) was presented to the public authorities, but rarely with much result. In 1910 Edward E. Senn, editor of the *Deadwood Telegraph*, crusaded against all forms of vice, but inasmuch as a third of Deadwood's population in one way or another drew some of their living from some form of dissipation, Senn did not make much progress. Every now and then in modern times a raid picks up a few of the upstairs girls, and temporarily inconveniences business. Deadwood to this day still has no ordinance against prostitution, and as the state of South Dakota does not often think it worth while to prosecute it where it has been tolerated so long, nothing much is done about it, and tolerant Deadwood continues happily in at least some of her wicked ways.[44]

It is not easy to properly assess the place of the bad men and the badlands in Deadwood's history and psychology. Undoubtedly the respectable inhabitants outnumbered the disreputable, and as they in time gained the upper hand and to all intents and purposes cleaned up the town—with the few exceptions already noted—it may be supposed that virtue rather than vice set the overriding tone of the community. On the other hand, fifty years of wild life did not go on in Deadwood without a considerable amount of public approbation and support, or without leaving behind it sins the people still like to talk about, so it must be assumed that even the town's most solid citizens may have had some degree of ambivalence about closing down the wild life for good. The constant clash between those who, on the one hand, wanted to advertise and profit from civic respectability, virtue, and decorum, and those who, on the other hand, hoped to profit from Deadwood's well-deserved reputation as whoopee town in which every dissipation could be bought, and likely bought at a lower price than anywhere else, was constant, and as their story shows, the victory of the righteous is not yet completely decisive. Deadwood enjoyed being respectable, but viewed respectability, as Mark Twain reputedly viewed chastity, as all right only if it wasn't carried too far. To see that neither vice nor virtue got carried too far for civic comfort was the care and duty of the various governments which necessity and progress imposed upon the city.

NINE

The Voice of the People

"Every once in a while the boys call a mass meeting, draw up resolutions, etc., and decide to incorporate the town, and have a board of aldermen, but at the end of the week nobody knows what in h——l has become of the resolutions or the aldermen."

Quoted by Spring

"Education? Hell yes! We got four female academies in town already, and more girls coming in all the time!"

An old-timer

"Rapid City? It's like Purgatory: you have to suffer there before you get up into the Black Hills!"

An old-timer

THE NEED TO preserve health and order, to protect the populace from crime and dissipation, to ward off Indian attacks, to fight the fires which were inevitable in a wooden city, and to raise enough money to pay for these many public services led to the creation of governments, quasi-governmental associations, and various permutations thereof at several levels in the Deadwood community. The county government of Lawrence County, named for its first treasurer, was organized at Crook City, a few miles below Deadwood on Whitewood Creek, during April 1877, with a county board composed of the following worthies:

Fred T. Evans, Commissioner
John Wollsmuth [or Wolzmuth], Commissioner
Captain W. A. Lavender, Commissioner
C. E. Hanrehan, Probate Judge
Colonel John Lawrence, Treasurer
W. J. James, Assessor
Seth Bullock, Sheriff
A. J. Flanner [or Flannery], Attorney
Dr. ——— Babcock, Coroner
Captain C. H. McKinnis, School Superintendent

The election of these officials was apparently disputed, for in December 1877 it was necessary for the Supreme Court of Dakota Territory to certify that they had been lawfully elected. This county board, noting the decline in the prosperity and prospects of Crook City, and the increasing importance of the placer mines at the forks of the Whitewood, quickly moved to Deadwood, which has ever since held the seat of Lawrence County and jealously guarded this valuable community commercial asset.[1]

Deadwood's own city government had already begun late in April 1876, when the town of Deadwood was platted, or at least laid out, with the aid of a compass and a lariat used as a substitute for a surveyor's chain. This sort of prissiness about formally organizing a town on a wild mining frontier was the result, not of a fussy addiction to civilized formalities, but of the hope of gaining federal recognition and a federal grant of the land beneath the townsite so that town lots could be sold. It was the regular way of doing things, and done correctly, it resulted in profit as well as convenience for the town's founders. The founders at once organized a provisional (for they recognized that they were illegally in the territory) city government, and elected E. B. Farnum, a local merchant, as mayor and justice of the peace, an office which doubtless helped his business. After he had dispensed justice from the judicial seat on a sack of flour or a box of bacon, the participants in the trial as well as its audience stayed on to do their shopping. Indeed, it may well be that the degree to which the litigants had earlier patronized the judge's business had some trifling influence on his decisions.

Deadwood Gulch's first city council consisted of Keller Kurtz, Sol Star, Frank Philbrook, Joseph Miller, and James McCauley, with John A. Swift the city clerk and Con Stapleton the city marshal. Later in the summer of 1876 this rough-and-ready government of the general area embracing Deadwood and Whitewood gulches was narrowed down to a government for the camp of Deadwood itself, with five commisioners, who also acted as fire wardens, elected as follows: C. R. Clark, Seth Bullock, Thomas Short, James Van Daniker, and Henry Feuerstein, with J. W. Matkin their secretary. It was this organization which was referred to, from its original duties, as the Board of Health and Street Commissioners. By 1880 most of the mining camps of Deadwood and Whitewood gulches, including Montana City, Fountain City, Elizabethtown, Chinatown, Ingleside, Forest Hill, Cleveland, City Creek, South Deadwood, and Whoop Up, were incorporated under a long and formal charter into a single city of Deadwood, with Judge Daniel McLaughlin the first mayor of the at last throughly established town.[2]

Deadwood, in its early days, was of course an illegal settlement on land set aside a few years earlier for an Indian reservation, but the federal government, acting upon the Emperor Vespasian's comfortable maxim that money smells sweet whatever its source, quickly appointed Gen. A. R. Z. Dawson, brother-in-law of Judge Granville Bennett, as the local collector of federal revenues. It is a tribute to the general's amiability that he was widely liked, was asked to speak at all sorts of public festivities, and was commonly viewed not as an interloping publican but as a visible symbol of federal acceptance of the gold rush in the northern Hills, for the miners were quick to seize upon the notion that the federal government would not have appointed a collector of its revenues unless the production of those revenues was itself legitimate. Aside from General Dawson, the government at Washington allowed the Deadwood community to fend for itself without federal assistance, and the laws which the infant city created on its own were fearful and wonderful to behold.

The first duty which each of the early Deadwood city governments took upon itself was that of raising money to support its other activities. A licensing scheme for every business was soon settled upon by the earliest board as providing the most easily collectible revenues: assayers paid five dollars a quarter, brewers fifteen dollars, billiard tables five dollars each, Chinese laundries ten dollars, and dance houses, which were probably responsible for much of the disturbance and a considerable quantity of the disease which the city fathers wanted to control, twenty dollars each. Hawkers and peddlers, on the principle that they were likely to be outsiders, were charged twenty-five dollars a quarter, which, for itinerant peddlers amounted to a ferocious fee for merely entering the town, and doubtless served to keep out most of them, retaining the business which they might have had in the hands of the local merchants.[3]

Other ordinances set up a system of fire wardens, a system for reporting contagious diseases, a hospital to care for the sick, and laws for the disposal of refuse and for the sanitation of the city. Considerable attention was given to the abatement of what were then referred to as "nuisances," a word of spacious capacity, but in those days generally referring to unsanitary or indecent conditions.

Removal of the carcasses of dead animals within twenty-four hours was required, the use of firearms prohibited (although this prohibition was, as has been noted, entirely ignored), and in general, city ordinances were established which, had they been obeyed, would have transformed Deadwood from a rough frontier mining camp into a model city. They were not obeyed.

The city ordinances of 1881 were similarly visionary in their zeal; the city fathers were by these ordinances authorized to suppress "tippling shops, billiard tables, ten-pin alleys [what low conduct must have gone on in these, today, innocent establishments!], and ball alleys," as well as houses of prostitution and other disorderly establishments. Persons who disturbed the peace, a segment of the population which must have been extensive, "by clamor and noise" or by "intoxication, drunkenness, fighting, using obscene or profane language" or otherwise annoyed the good citizens of the city, or who came to the attention of the authorities because of their "indecent and disorderly conduct, or by lewd and lascivious behaviour," as well as vagrants, beggars, pickpockets, prostitutes, gamblers, theives, confidence men, and any other "habitual disturbers of the peace" were all to be properly punished. To set some limit on their number, the license for selling liquor was set at what was hoped to be a discouraging $150 a year. Deadwood, however, with that legal insouciance which is still a hallmark of the town, continued in her riotous ways and even today winks at many of the peccadilloes which her early ordinances so stringently condemned.

Of all the officers who served the city, none is better known than Seth Bullock, whose brief official tenure in the office of sheriff during 1877 carried forward his earlier and less official activities as a local law enforcement officer. Bullock set the tone of ability and dignity for those who followed him in public office, showing his successors what could be accomplished by strength of character and quiet perseverance. He never actually found it necessary to kill anybody in the performance of his varied duties, but he was "well prepared to use the requisite amount of force even if it involved blowing off the top of the skull" of some recalcitrant malefactor. In general, however, Bullock's forceful demeanor—"He could outstare a mad cobra or a rogue elephant," observers claimed—enabled him to carry out his duties with a minimum of violence, for a single glance into his steely eyes convinced most criminals that this was not a man with whom they could much prank around. As his grandson Ken

Kellar put it, when "he went out into the streets of Deadwood in the blazing sun of high noon, he was looking for his lunch, not looking for some one to shoot." He was the kind of law officer that Deadwood liked.[4]

Sheriff John Manning, Bullock's successor, was equally determined but less restrained. Ordered by the county commissioners to take forcible possession of county treasurer George E. Brigham's account, safe, and records, Sheriff Manning made his way to the city offices, where he found the defaulting treasurer attempting to open his safe in order to decamp with both the city funds and the evidence. Manning shoved his knee into the safe door, and Brigham slammed it upon him, then struck him violently in the face. Manning, at last provoked to violence, drew his revolver, an old and unreliable cap-and-ball model, aimed and pulled the trigger within a foot of Brigham's head, but the decrepit weapon failed to fire, and Brigham was saved from a second shot by the arrival of various deputies who escorted him to jail while Sheriff Manning took possession of the incriminating records. Six weeks later Manning was presented with a magnificent badge of office, a silver sheriff's star set in a golden circle, the work of D. M. Gillette of Deadwood, in recognition of his successes in his office.[5]

In general, however, the city ran along more smoothly than its tumultuous population would have suggested; the force of the law was evident, but the eye of the law was often lenient or dim. This judicious combination of force and judgment has always run the town with less conflict and excitement than the dime novelists have portrayed. Sol Star was elected mayor ten times, which indicates the degree of political stability in town, and when he was succeeded by Edward "Mac the Saddler" McDonald, the new incumbent could boast that "there is only one policeman on duty in Deadwood at any one time, and he has very little to do." The policeman probably could not have done it very well, anyhow, for the uniforms of Police Chief M. J. Donovan and his three officers, Henry Donovan (the chief's brother), John McInerny, and Walter Simpson, at the turn of the century consisted of navy blue Prince Albert frock coats buttoned to the collar with brass buttons, and the regulation chamber-pot helmet. It was a uniform which upheld the dignity while restricting the activity of the law, which was probably about what the city fathers had in mind.[6]

Local government, with its personnel and its processes, was not the only concern of politically oriented Deadwood citizens, for early in Deadwood's history a movement to set up a new territory which would embody the Black Hills, northeastern Wyoming, and the southeastern corner of present-day Montana was widely boosted among the mining camps. A bill "to establish the Territory of the Black Hills" was introduced in congress in December 1876, and early the next January Dr. C. W. Meyer went to Washington to urge a similar territory, to be named El Dorado in honor of its golden possibilities. The boosters, however, obviously all good Republicans, finally settled upon Lincoln as the title for their proposed new territory, and by June 1877 it was said that "one can hardly walk down Main street or fall into that good natured but interminable line at the Post Office without being 'button-holed' by an ex-delegate from Colorado or Montana who is in search of a grindstone for his political axe." A bill supporting the new territory was introduced by Sen. Alvin Saunders of Nebraska in the senate in February 1877, and received much support from Sen. J. B. Chaffee of Colorado, who quoted extensively from the 1875 reports of Professor W. P. Jenney. In subsequent debates he pointed out that the region was "rapidly becoming the permanent home of a prosperous and enterprizing people who will not be dependent upon the production of precious metals alone" but who would, presumably, soon be seeking government subsidies to assist them in settling the Black Hills in a less flamboyant manner.

Eastern newspapers could not believe that the proposal for a Territory of Lincoln was a serious one, and surmised that "since mining is unprofitable, and real estate transactions consist chiefly in burying ground lots, a knot of uneasy spirits propose to introduce the game of politics to enliven the dullness of classic Deadwood," and noted that "there is more politics than pay dirt coming out of Deadwood just now." Nevertheless the committee set up to draft the legislation to establish the new territory of Lincoln busily plundered the organic acts of Colorado, Wyoming, and Montana in order to work up a presentable proposal. The committee was notably Republican in orientation, and the whole proposal became embroiled in party politics, but by the spring of 1878 interest in the project had died down. The bill was again brought up in the spring of 1879, at which time it died from congressional neglect. The proposed new territory was not heard of again until 1935, when similarly depressed times in the Hills generated a scheme for the creation of a Black Hills state of Absaroka, the name of the original Crow Indian inhabitants of the region. If it had been difficult for the Black Hills to secede from three adjoining territories in the 1870s, it was impossible for them to secede from three existing states in the 1930s, and the movement again was dropped into oblivion after having provided a modicum of excitement and entertainment for its participants.[7]

Deadwood's early excesses of frenzied political activity were doubtless due in part to the presence of about fifty unemployed lawyers in town. All of them attended, in a bunch, the unsuccessful prosecution of Laughing Sam for the murder of poor Bummer Dan Baum, and each one felt free to frequently advise or correct "Judge" W. R. Keithly, who was presiding. Keithly was not a man well learned in legal technicalities, and indeed the Deadwood bar habitually referred to him as Old Necessity from the proverbial supposition that "necessity knows no law," but the plethora of legal talent displayed annoyed even the jury, and their foreman felt obliged to point out to the court that if Deadwood's lawyers felt that they really had to advertise themselves, the pages of the *Pioneer* were a better place for it than the proceedings of a court conducting a murder trial.[8]

The seats of justice in Deadwood have always been a subject of jest and witticism. Justice Gooding presided over his minor court from an ample chair of office, which was made from a large barrel. When he was succeeded by Justice Charles E. Barker, a slender man, it was claimed that Barker looked like "a single toothpick in a tumbler," a remark that did little to enhance the dignity of the bench. In June 1877 a formal court to admit to the Deadwood bar some fifty aspirants for legal distinction was convened in the weak and flimsy upper story of the Deadwood post office. The floor, overstrained by the weight of so much legal talent, began to collapse, and as one reporter well versed in legal terminology is reputed to have put it, "On motion of the Court the session was adjourned." The opening of the courts in general, however, did "favorably influence the social and moral condition of the six or seven thousand people in the place," who all seemed to take pleasure in slyly admonishing their neighbors that thereafter *they* would have to behave themselves.[9]

The first judge of the Black Hills District Court was the notable Granville G. Bennett, whose fame has been continued by his daughter Estelline's charming memoirs. He was appointed by President Hayes to take office in April 1877, and he retired from the bench, although not from his title of Judge, to win election as territorial delegate to congress in September of the following year. Bennett presided over his court from a crude homemade chair labeled "made for Judge Bennett's first term of court in Deadwood, October 1877," but the judge did not find it either comfortable or becoming, and it was soon replaced by another, the gift of some of the officers of the court, who, "having tried undue influence upon the head of His Honor and failed, now applied thier efforts to the very seat of justice." Judge Bennett was meticulous in avoiding investments or gifts which might in any way in the future seem to influence his decisions; this self-imposed curb upon his financial success in the community may explain why he chose to serve so brief a term upon the judicial bench. He was careful in cases of child custody to assume that "the Lord knows where he sends children," and he did not often tamper with these heaven-sent "decrees of the Almighty" by removing children from even the most careless parental supervision. Road agents and stage robbers studiously avoided any stage on which Bennett might be traveling, fearful of annoying a judge before whom they might one day appear, for although Bennett from religious scruples would rarely sentence even a murderer to death, he had no reservations at all about condemning a robber to life imprisonment. Apparently some charges of misconduct were filed against Bennett during his service on the Deadwood bench, for the U.S. solicitor general and the attorney general were forced to report that they, at least, saw no cause for his removal. His service as territorial delegate to congress was uneventful, and in his later years he seems to have involved himself mainly in the practice of law with a few excursions into various mining promotions which were not uniformly profitable to all of those who invested in them.[10]

The courts, however rough-and-ready, seem to have upheld about as much law and order as the community desired. A justice in Gayville, hearing profane language, declared that "unless such god-damned profanity was stopped" he would fine the defendant for contempt of court. The court in its dignity might swear, but those before it did not have that privilege. One could forgive a judge for swearing when faced with a complaint alleging battery which was worded (as many of them were) "that John Varnes with a certain pistol revolver then and there loaded with gunpowder and diverse lead and bullets, did shoot and wound him, the said Joseph Ludwig, with intent then and there feloniously and maliciously to kill, against the peace and dignity of the United States." The attempt to touch all legal bases does appear to give a degree of redundancy to such complaints. Robert Jackson and John Gordon similarly complained of an "assault" in which "one or more of the above named parties or other, by and with a deadly weapon known as a revolver, loaded with powder and ball, which said loaded revolver being then and there in the hands of one John Riley, unlawfully, wrongly, and feloniously and with malice aforethought then and there discharged said revolver and killed a valuable Newfoundland dog, and then swore he would kill any son-of-a-bitch who would take the part of the dog." Riley was arrested, and of course such profuse legal jargon was familiar to all involved, a relic of the days when scriveners were paid by the word.[11]

"Why no school yet?" asked the *Black Hills Pioneer* in late October 1876. One taught privately by William Commode, that fall, had collapsed, and the sixty children in town were running wild, but by January 1877 Mrs. John Collison (who was later murdered, although that was not, as would nowadays be surmised, in connection with her teaching) offered to teach school for the ensuing three months at a tuition of one dollar per week per scholar. The next fall a two-story frame building near the corner of Pine and Water streets provided better educational facilities, and in it the pupils taught by Professor (any learned man was called "professor" in those days, including the musician who played piano in a whorehouse) Dolph Edwards, assisted by Miss Eva Deffenbacher. Schools were lively places, apparently. A Mrs. Brennan, annoyed that her son had been expelled from school for drawing a knife on another pupil, came roaring into the school house with a pistol in one hand and a whip in the other, and the principal disarmed her only after a considerable struggle. By 1880 it was being suggested that the school fund could be enhanced if the town's copious supply of drunks could be arrested and the fines given, as then provided by law, to the schools. This plan does not seem to have been widely carried forward, for drunks continued common and common schools poor.

By the fall of 1880 Professor A. T. Lewis and three female teachers were on hand to generate wisdom among the youth of the city, with Lewis handling the entire school end of the business. The teachers, two of them unmarried, were evidently well thought of: one young man about town called his pedagogue–girl friend Experience because she was "a dear teacher." The newspaper reported that "he still lives" but had some doubt that he would long continue to do so. The smallness of the high school system, compared to the size of the Deadwood population, is of course an indication that not many children were yet in town; by the turn of the century twenty-three teachers were teaching 1,473 children, although two or three teachers still sufficed to handle all of the high school instruction. It was claimed that only Massachusetts exceeded South Dakota in literacy, so the school systems must have worked reasonably well. In 1968 the Deadwood schools merged with those of nearby Lead into a single school district, and from 1971 onward they functioned as a unit, but not without resentment on the part of the Deadwoodians who had long prided themselves on their supposed superiority and cultivation.[12]

One of the functions of any government seems to be the erection or encouragement of not only schools but of all sorts of public buildings. These structures, monumental in every sense of the word, act as visible symbols of the community and of the dignity of its laws. The long struggle of Deadwood's citizens to obtain for the city a federal building commensurate with the supposed status of the Black Hills community placed many plaintive appeals upon the pages of the *Congressional Record*, but it was not until the turn of the century that the activities of the Deadwood Business Club resulted in real progress with the appropriation by Congress of some $175,000. Ex-congressman Freeman Knowles sourly complained that the appropriation was deviously delayed by political opponents in order to deprive him of the credit for having obtained so fine a building for his city. This edifice, an ageless Grecian temple of civil and postal services, still stands in the center of town, a monument to Deadwood's once central position in the governmental affairs of the Black Hills.

Similarly, the Lawrence County courthouse with its handsome dome and tower attests to Deadwood's continuing importance as a county seat. An earlier structure, condemned "by the court, by the county commissioners, and by numerous grand juries" as unhealthy, unsafe, and a danger to the county's records, was replaced in 1908 when the Deadwood contractors Mullen and Munn finished work on the present noble structure, which was completed at a cost of $125,000. Various alterations and additions to the building have kept it up to date, and it continues to serve not only as a place for the county's business but as a central landmark dominating Deadwood's downtown skyline.[13]

Fire prevention was one of the earliest duties imposed by necessity upon the city's governing bodies. The town, at first composed of tents, log cabins, and jerry-built frame business buildings, all jammed cheek by jowl together along three miles of a narrow canyon swept from end to end by violent Black Hills winds, needed only a spark to touch off a major disaster, and the citizens from the beginning recognized the need to combat this never-ending menace. In December 1876 a committee headed by Capt. C. V. Gardner, Sol Star, and E. B. Farnum, "feeling the necessity of some immediate action to prevent a conflagration to which we are at all times liable," called a mass meeting in order "that everything possible may be done to secure our city from so terrible a visitation." The *Pioneer* urged that a standing committee be appointed to inspect every chimney in town, provide ladders adequate to reach the tops of even the tallest stores, and require a barrel of water and two fire buckets in every building. Fire companies, which as has already been pointed out, were sporting, convivial, and social clubs as well as civic organizations, were encouraged, and the Deadwood Pioneer Hook and Ladder Company No. 1, was organized on 20 June 1877, and followed shortly by other similar groups, doubtless assisted and encouraged by Cairns and Brother, "Manufacturers of Firemen's Equipment," who happily furnished the fire laddies with a handsomely bound minute book in which to record their multifarious activities. In October 1877 a fire watch tower was built on a mountain west of the city, to keep an eye on both the city and the surrounding forests. It is evident from the amount of activity that early Deadwood took its fire prevention seriously.[14]

Serious or not, these prudent responses to the threat of a major fire were not long-lived, for the *Times* complained in 1880, while the memory of the town's disastrous fire of 1879 was still fresh upon the memories of its citizens, that the city still had only two fire companies, "one for actual service [the South Deadwood Hose Company] and the other [the Homestake Hose Company] for dress parade." Arson, then called incendiarism, seemed endemic, and seven fires appeared to have been started by arsonists during September, October, and November of 1880. The fire companies, thus upbraided and encouraged, continued to improve in both quality and quantity. In 1883 the Hook and Ladder Company moved into its newly built "truck house" on Lee Street, and there its members preened themselves on having at last "quarters as good as those of the other companies." By 1898 there was a Deadwood City Fire Department with

James Frawley its chief, and five additional volunteer fire companies
as follows:

> Deadwood Pioneer Hook and Ladder Company,
> W. H. Moore, foreman; 40 members

> South Deadwood Hose Company,
> W. B. Tyler, foreman; 38 members

> Deadwood Hose Company,
> Ed. Curley, foreman; 35 members

> Fountain City Hose Company,
> W. B. Anderson, foreman; 40 members

> Homestake Hose Company, of Deadwood,
> Frank Peck, foreman; 35 members

There was plenty for them to do, for the threat of fire in Deadwood
was never-ending.[15]

Gayville, a couple of miles up Whitewood Creek, burned to the
ground in August 1877, with about two hundred houses being destroyed, and only two or three saved from the flames. None of the
buildings seem to have been insured, and careless storage of gunpowder in various stores and buildings not only made the firemen
timorous about actively fighting the fire, but, when these explosives
blew up, the explosions scattered the flaming embers all over town
and spread the fire. It was a portent of even worse to come.

During the dry December of 1878 a destructive prairie fire broke
out below Crook City and burned many ranches, and the entire hay
supply for the army's military post at Bear Butte; Sturgis was saved
from destruction only by the fortunate arrival of a rainstorm. A few
weeks later a fire, followed by violent winds, swept toward Deadwood from the north, but by good luck only the winds got as far as
the city limits, and the fire burned itself out. On 25 September
1879, what was to become the great Deadwood fire broke out in
Mrs. Ellsner's Empire Bakery (others said it was in the Star Bakery),
quickly spread to Jensen and Bliss's Hardware Store, and when
eight kegs of gunpowder stored there blew up, the fire was at once
spread all over town. Three hundred buildings were destroyed in
an area measuring about one-half by one-quarter of a mile, two
thousand persons were left homeless, and the total loss of property
was estimated at $3 million. Troops from Fort Meade were sum-
moned to prevent looting and disorder, and the townspeople at once

began to rebuild. Bank vaults, when they cooled enough to open, were found to have preserved their contents intact, so the town had at least a legal and a financial base to build on. The *Pioneer* did not miss an issue, but their first edition after the fire was admittedly a small one. Everybody pitched in to rebuild, and there was little gouging and profiteering by those who had supplies or property left to sell. Prospectors panned the ashes of their ruined equipment, and generally got enough dust to get back into business, and one enterprising group of enthusiasts got two thousand ounces of gold by working the ashes of several stores that had burned down. Jack Langrishe, the impressario, looking over the ruins of his famous theater, turned to Jimmy Martin, one of his actors, and remarked, "I guess we'll have to put out the 'standing room only' sign, Jimmy, there isn't a seat left to sit on in the house."[16]

Deadwood rebuilt in brick and stone; she could afford to. Inside of six months a new town had risen up on the ashes of the old, and in its Victorian elegance set the architectural tone for the Deadwood of today. Other fires continued to threaten. In 1880 a forest fire raged around Terraville and flung flaming brands into the Deadwood streets. In 1889 a "sea of fire" swept over Boulder Park to the northeast, and it took the efforts of hundreds of citizens to contain its fury. In 1894 two business blocks in downtown Deadwood were destroyed, and in 1952 the city hall with all of its invaluable records was burned to the ground, the last of a series of fires which one after another removed many of the town's historic downtown buildings.

On 8 September 1959 the temperature at Deadwood reached ninety-six degrees, the humidity was a low 10 percent, and a gusty twenty-five-mile-an-hour wind came in from the southwest. At an old peoples' home between Central City and Deadwood sparks from a trash burner got out of control around noon, and by mid-afternoon produced a forest fire which was soon out of control despite the efforts of thirty-five hundred men from all over the Hills who quickly came to fight it. Evacuation of Deadwood then began, as the mile-wide fire besieged the city from the northwest. About 3:30 P.M. a violent meteorological cold front passed through the Hills, reversing the winds and bringing the fire directly down onto the city. Powerlines, lumber companies, motels, and homes on the outskirts were burned as the fire swooped down upon the town from three directions cutting off one after another—but fortunately not all of them at the same time—all of the roads by which the people could escape. It took seven days of fire fighting to at last control the flames. Deadwood was badly singed on every side, and the forests on the valley slopes all around the town were totally denuded of their vegetation. Nearly one million dollars in damage was done to the outlying portions of the city, and five hundred thousand dollars to forty-five hundred acres of forest surrounding the city limits, but the town itself was saved. Once again Deadwood was ringed by the dead and fallen timber which in 1875 had given the gulch its name.

The internal affairs and safety of the city were one aspect of the responsibilities of Deadwood's local governments; Deadwood's commercial success and prosperity and its dependence upon the outside world for both was the other. Throughout the city's existence a pressing need of the Deadwood community, on which government, business, and individuals were in complete agreement and accord was the necessity for thorough, widespread, diligent, and effective publicity for the Black Hills in general and for Deadwood in particular. The succession of booms—the gold rush of 1876, the hardrock boom of the 1890s, the cyanide boom of the early 1900s—and the subsequent depressions, particularly that following the closing of both the mines and saloons with all their raucous accompaniments in the 1920s, all united the community in a continuing effort to somehow advertise the city to bring in newcomers, new businesses, and new money. The early Deadwood publicity of course centered on bringing in investors, the "capitalists and speculators" so dear to the hearts of mineral promoters. Later on bringing in tourists, particularly when the widespread use of the automobile made tourism increasingly possible and popular, was the main goal of the Black Hills' boosterism. The need for such publicity is apparent in the fluctuation of Deadwood's population figures here taken from the federal, state, and territorial censuses:

    1875: a few hundred prospectors
    1876: a few thousand prospectors
    1880: 3,777
    1885: 1,768 (seems very low)
    1890: 2,366
    1895: 4,204 (hardrock boom)
    1900: 3,498
    1905: 4,364 (the cyanide boom)
    1910: 3,653
    1915: 3,113

1920: 2,403 (mines closing; prohibition)
1925: 2,432
1930: 2,559
1935: 3,662 (mining boom on increased price of gold)
1940: 4,100
1945: 3,413 (mining closed because of World War II)

The censuses, of course, do not coincide exactly with the peaks and hollows of the actual population movements, but they are sufficient to show that in the fluctuation of Deadwood's fortunes and population lay the genesis of its fascinated interest in and heavy dependence upon advertising, publicity, and promotion.

It was presumptuous, perhaps, for so small a city to be so ambitious, and yet there was a considerable justification for at least some of Deadwood's aspirations. Deadwood was undoubtedly the focal point of the Black Hills gold rush and of the subsequent hard-rock mining booms. It was for generations the legal, mercantile, entertainment, railroad, and financial center of an immense area of the West, an area which was noted for its wealth and its property. Lead, three miles to the southwest, although twice the size of Deadwood, did hardly a tenth of Deadwood's business, and was regarded by Deadwood's boosters as little more than an industrial company town. Sturgis, to the northeast, was seen as an appendage of Fort Meade, and even its sins, let alone its society, seemed to lack the gentility to which Deadwood's pretended. Belle Fourche, on the plains to the north, was thought of as an overgrown cow camp, as was Rapid City to the southeast. Hot Springs, at the southern end of the Hills, despite its pretentions to social prestige and the prosperity bestowed upon it by two veterans' hospitals, was, in Deadwood's eyes, nothing but a hot water spa and a divorce mill which had only temporarily boomed to profit from South Dakota's lenient views regarding holy wedlock.

Psychologically, in Deadwood's corporate mind at least, Deadwood was the only Black Hills town that really mattered, and whenever their lofty position of wealth, dignity, and importance was threatened, the citizens of Deadwood acted vigorously to restore themselves to the status to which their past successes and present virtues alike entitled them. It was more than a mere attitude of commercial greed; Deadwood sincerely believed that she deserved to be the principal city in the Hills. For Deadwood, the boom times were meant to last forever, but Deadwood's citizens fully understood that boom times also needed all the assistance and encouragement that they could get.

The earliest publicity for the Black Hills did not, of course, originate in the area, but among those in the surrounding towns which wished to promote a profitable movement to the Hills. George W. Kingsbury's 1865 *Circular of the Black Hills Exploring and Mining Association*, published in Yankton, laid the groundwork for later, more successful movements to the area, as did Charles Collins's Sioux City pamphlet published in 1873. The year the gold rush began, 1875, brought a rash of Black Hills guide books, including W. W. Brookings's typically titled *Southern Dakota, the Black Hills, Big Horn, and Yellowstone Countries: The Richest Mineral Regions in America*, published in Chicago. D. K. Allen's map of the Hills, which a reviewer remarked "would answer just as well as one of Boston Harbor. . . . To say that it is incorrect will convey only a slight idea of its utter absurdity," was followed by J. B. Minick's map which was more reliable, and the next year W. M. Masi's map was said to be "a marvel in neatness and execution." Frank Wixson's *Black Hills Gold Mines* was a complete guide to outfitting, travel, and prospecting in the Hills, as was E. H. Saltiel's *Black Hills Guide*. Early in 1876 Colonel Richard Irving Dodge's widely circulated description, *The Black Hills*, praised not only the minerals but the agricultural possibilities of the land which he had explored while guarding the Jenney expedition during the summer of 1875. In July 1876 enterprising speculators bought the right to run off from 150,000 to 200,000 stereographed facsimile copies of each edition of *The Black Hills Pioneer*, which were sold throughout the nation on the railroads and by newsstands. J. H. Trigg's *History of Cheyenne and Northern Wyoming*, Edwin Curley's *Guide to the Black Hills*, and Robert E. Strahorn's *Handbook of Wyoming and Guide to the Black Hills* (1877), among many others, continued the rush to gather literary gold from the placers of the Hills.

Judge H. N. Maguire's *Black Hills of Dakota* in 1879, and Maguire's many other writings, brought to a close what may be thought of as the promotional literature of the gold rush days of the 1870s, but by no means ended the steady stream of Black Hills promotional books. It is safe to say that, even excluding those works devoted entirely to scientific subjects, there has hardly been a year since the gold rush that has not produced a good many periodical articles and at least a book or two on some aspect of the virtues or the history of the Hills. Brought to the Black Hills by such wild-eyed literature, and raised up on it thereafter, it was natural for Deadwood's citizens to turn to still further literary efforts to woo newcomers and new money into the Hills.

Doubtless the presence of large numbers of Deadwood businessmen, men accustomed to act to produce the results that they wanted, and with some access to the money with which to back their aspirations, did much to create the many organizations which, with the enthusiastic approval of Deadwood citizens in general, strove valiantly to promote the Hills. In the spring of 1877 Messrs. Wooley and Wilson set up a Black Hills Mining Bureau in Stebbins's Bank to disseminate information about the mines of the area, and to transact business connected with mining properties—in short, a sort of mineralogical real estate office—but its activities showed what could be done by a larger organization more fully devoted to publicity. In 1881 the Deadwood Board of Trade was organized, with most of the important merchants of Deadwood among its members, and its twenty-five-page pamphlet, *The Black Hills of Dakota*, painted a glowing picture of Deadwood's commercial and recreational possibilities. This organization, temporarily falling into desuetude, was revived under the same name in 1891, and worked diligently toward the building—by somebody else—of a new hotel in Deadwood. In the mid-1890s much enthusiasm for a Twin Cities–Black Hills railway was generated at a well-attended promotional meeting in Minneapolis. William Selbie, the Deadwood financier, on 9 November 1895 wrote to the promoters of this new railroad scheme extolling the virtues of the nearby town of Whitewood as the principal terminus for their project. He maintained that his advice was offered solely in a spirit of public service and for the good of the Black Hills as a whole, but the cornerstone of his Selbie Block of buildings in Whitewood bears the date of 5 September 1895, which tends to cast some doubt upon the complete disinterestedness of his protestations. The next year a local Black Hills Improvement Association encompassing the mayors and other representatives of all the towns in the Hills did its best to advertise for new capital and to present the Black Hills to the American public as a summer resort as well as an area of economic opportunity.[17]

In the early 1900s the Deadwood Club, composed as usual of the financial and mercantile leaders of the town, vigorously promoted investments of all kinds in the Deadwood area, issuing pamphlets and sending out embassage and displays to encourage both immigration and investment in the Hills. This club seems to have shifted, during its existence, from a social to a commercial organization, later becoming the Businessman's Club, and in 1929 reorganizing into the Deadwood Chamber of Commerce, which, under the skillful and dedicated management of Nell Perrigoue for many years, reflected much credit upon the whole community.

In 1901 the Black Hills Mining Men's Association was begun with fifty members, "every individual being a mine owner or interested in the development of mining property," although the association's roster shows a good many bankers, who if they were much interested in mining property probably got their interest through foreclosures. A complete change of officers in 1904, "all young men of proven ability," resulted in the publication of the splendidly detailed and embellished *Black Hills Illustrated* upon which Hills historians have leaned heavily ever since. The organization also maintained in the office of its secretary, W. S. Elder, "a record of all the mining operations in the Hills, the character of their ores, the formations in which they occur, and other particulars valuable to the mining man" in order to discourage fraud and "the foisting upon the investing public of worthless propositions," evils from which Black Hills mining promotions had not previously been entirely free. Through the efforts of the association twenty-five mining companies changed hands for a total of $5 million, and another $2 million-worth of capital was brought into the Hills to develop these mines. In addition, eleven new ore-processing plants, at an average cost of one-hundred thousand dollars each, were erected, and in all, the association claimed that it had been instrumental, coincidentally of course with the cyanide boom, in bringing over $8 million in new mining investment into the Hills. The association's ample efforts crowned and completed the lesser promotional endeavors of a host of private boosters who had been vigorously publicizing the Hills since the gold rush days.[18]

As early as December 1876 the *Pioneer* had ingeniously warned poor men who would have to depend on employment for a livelihood to stay away from the Hills until the placers reopened in the spring of 1877. On the other hand, the canny *Pioneer* encouraged "capitalists [to] come here now; let them examine the country; now is their time, if they would purchase mining property at anything like reasonable figures." A story, obviously planted by Black Hills interests in the *New York Times* in the spring of 1878, trumpeted, "Gold is here in great abundance, but it does not grow on trees nor rest upon the surface of the ground, but is secured only by the outlay of money and the hardest kind of toil." Many an eastern optimist who had the money came to the Hills but unwisely supposed that he could dispense with the toil and soon departed bitterly disappointed. An unidentified diarist from New England, wooed to the Hills by a florid mining prospectus and by the blandishments of Judge Granville Bennett, arrived in February 1882, and after acquainting himself with his investment and his colleagues in it, wrote, "Am most discouraged, cannot understand what they mean by such unnecessary delays. They seem to have no sense. Should I fail in this venture I do not know what I am to do." The next day, 3 March, he wrote, "Everything seems to be going wrong with me, and none of the plans succeed. The fates are against me and I am doomed to constant battle with penury and misfortune." There are no further entries, and the presence of this diary in the vaults of Deadwood's Adams Museum leads to the supposition, unsupported by any evidence in the records, that the poor man's financial sufferings were too much for him to bear.[19]

Among those works of fiction which did much to publicize the Black Hills and their opportunities must be included the prospectuses of potential mines. Unprotected by modern laws requiring either truth or candor in these literary efforts, the prospective investor could only rely upon his uninformed judgment to guide him through their exuberant mendacities. In 1903 the Echo Mining Company promoted itself as being practically the same mine as the Homestake, which as everybody knew was "an actual gold manufacturing business, where the price does not change and the United States Government is the purchaser." The Echo's favorable location, supposedly on the Homestake's Columbus vein and within half a mile of the famous Penobscot at Maitland, was touted as a sure thing, and the potential investor was informed that "stock bought now at the present selling price, 25 cents, will be worth several times this in a year from now. Whoever buys now, buys well." This prediction does not appear to have been distinguished for its accuracy.

Jesse Simmons, a mining promoter, spread far and wide the news that, contrary to most notions, the Black Hills were actually a "poor miner's country," for with custom mills and smelters readily available by the 1890s and processing ore at a cost of sixteen to twenty dollars a ton, even a small mine could operate without the extensive capital required to build a mill. Simmon's pamphlet *Gold Mines in the Black Hills*, published in 1904, listed many mines in which an optimistic capitalist might invest his money, and is a splendid example of the unrestrained publicity given to these opportunities for achieving poverty by the quickest possible route. Other mining brokers, including the Deadwood-Colorado Investment Company and Burt Rogers "Mining Broker" advertised that "if you want to make MONEY buy active stocks." There was in existence an active Deadwood stock market, at least during the early 1900s, in the shares of a good many Black Hills mining companies, although only the shares of the Homestake are still readily traded today.[20]

Cyanidation, which could efficiently remove up to 94 percent of the gold contained in many of the Hills' refractory ores, opened up new and thrilling prospects for the Black Hills mines and their promoters. The prospectus of the Deadwood Lead and Zinc Mine, published around 1910, pointed out with unconscious irony that a whole new class of mines had come into existence "where the company has bodies of ore definitely proved, where money is sought for the building of mills and other plants, where ores may be treated *and money earned for the owners*" if a sufficient number of stockholders could be recruited. Nominally, no doubt, the stockholders *were* the owners, but in ordinary Black Hills practice it was generally the promoters who ran the mine, made the money, and regarded themselves as the actual owners of a paying proposition.

The Golden Eagle pointed out, as had the Echo at the turn of the century, that because of the cyanide process, mining in the Hills "has become the same as any other *manufacturing business*," and that "no other section of the country affords the opportunity for so many *safe investments*." The company planned to sell no more than 1.2 million of its 2.5 million shares, "only enough stock to prosecute further development, and erect a cyanide mill," and pointed out that "there is every probability that those who invest now in the Gold Eagle Mining Company's stock will make a *great deal of money*." Because of the absorption of mines into each other it is hard to tell if these investors did make money, but the Golden Eagle seems not to have been heard of again, although the mining engineer and promoter A. J. Simmons (not the same man as Jesse) did his best to push it forward.

The Cheyenne Gold Mining Company, next to the Father De Smet, in an undated prospectus implied to potential stockholders that their mine was "a treasure house of precious minerals that has no equal on earth," and explained that the ore taken from its thirty-six-foot shaft was immensely rich, and that they were only selling a few shares in the enterprise in order to build an eighty-stamp mill and avoid the five dollar a ton cost of custom milling. With a shaft no deeper than thirty-six feet it is hard to believe that their milling costs had so far been excessive. Because of its location the Cheyenne was probably later incorporated into the Homestake's holdings, and investors in it, if honestly dealt with, may well have been rewarded for their speculation, for not everybody who invested in a Black Hills mine poured his money completely down a rat hole.

Mining, however, was not the only opportunity that the Black Hills had to offer to a prospective immigrant or investor. Agriculture, forestry, and grazing were also widely advertised, and in 1875 Robert Flormann, an inveterate promoter, wrote that "the Black Hills country is not only an Eldorado, but also a land where the hardy farmer, stock-raiser and lumberman will find his expectations realized." Robert Strahorn's *Handbook* similarly stressed the lasting attractions of these more prosaic commercial and agricultural opportunities, as opposed to the transient beckonings of the mines. Nor were governmental benefits neglected, for the Deadwood Board of Trade campaigned strenuously in the territorial legislature to have a fifty thousand dollar state insane asylum built in Deadwood, perhaps, as Yankton claimed, to care for those demented by mining disappointments, and the efforts of the Deadwood board to bring a major hotel to their city have already been recounted.

Deadwood's social eminence was much stressed, and the town's transition, over twenty-five years, from "Wickedest Camp on Earth" to "Richest 100 Square Miles on Earth" was frequently mentioned, as were the opportunities for the newcomer to dwell in this "live, up-to-date, wide-awake, progressive, manufacturing metropolis" of the Black Hills, a town possessing "many of the elements of metropolitanism usually found in a city of 100,000," a city which could with a modicum of justice lay claim to that much overworked title, "the biggest little city in the world." The need for a woolen mill to make use of the five-hundred thousand pounds of wool that left Butte County every year, a foundry for the mines' machinery, a canning plant for the produce of the foothills, a soap works and a packing plant, a wagon factory, and wholesale mercantile houses were all pointed out to potential citizens as golden opportunities for profitable investment, and by 1915 a "motion picture studio" had been added to the lists which were frequently published by the various commercial clubs. Considering the number of movies which have since been made in the Black Hills, this last notion at least would appear in retrospect to have contained a good deal of promise. Rapid City, alas, eventually supplanted Deadwood as the Black Hills' major commercial city, and today it has a population twenty times that of Deadwood, and an even greater disparity exists in their commercial activity, but well into the 1930s Deadwood continued to be a good place for business and investment.[21]

The beauty and salubrity of the Black Hills were another source of pride and self-congratulation which in most cases sooner or later found their way into the promotional literature of the area. The *Times* inquired in 1883, "What money can pay a man for having malaria, chills and fever or chronic rheumatism," the price that an incautious investor might have to pay for "taking chances, and making money in a bad and feverish climate?" The Hills, as opposed to such miasmic hellholes, was "the healthiest climate on the continent, where also chances for investment and unexampled profit lie around on every side." In those days when medicine frequently relied upon "a change of scene" for lack of anything better to cure a sufferer, such blandishments often fell upon receptive ears.[22]

"As a health resort the Hills and Deadwood in particular are unexcelled, and many invalids are coming here to recruit and almost always with the best results," said the board of trade in 1892, and pointed out that doctors, at least would do well to settle somewhere else, for the death rate for the past ten years had been lower than for any other city in the West, and "the air is so saturated with piney odors that it builds up an invalid in the most magical way," an effect that is still commented upon by newcomers in the Hills, although modern science nowadays likes to claim that the pollen and fumes of the ponderosa pine in the Hills are asthmatogenic, deleterious, and possibly carcinogenic. The cheerfully optimistic official report, already cited, of B. P. Smith, the Lawrence County coroner, pointed out that in 1882 only 105 persons had died in the county, a death rate of 6.56 per thousand, as compared to death rates several times higher in major cities of the world. These figures, of course, were based on a somewhat liberal population estimate for the county, and on an incomplete record of deaths, but nevertheless the prospective immigrant could reasonably get the impression from them that Black Hills people tended to pretty much live forever, and that the principal demographic abnormality in the area was likely to be overpopulation by those of ample years.[23]

The beauty of the Black Hills was also stressed in almost all of the promotional literature. The area around nearby Whitewood Falls below Deadwood was described as looking "as if Titans had been fighting with devils and had been throwing mountains at each other." The surrounding mountains were "not like the towering peaks of Colorado and the Rockies, which overwhelm the observer with the inapproachable vastness," but rather "in the Black Hills one feels in touch with every hill and mountain, and that he can reach out and grasp it." It is this intimacy, with even the Black Hills' largest mountains easily accessible to the ordinary tourist, that even today gives them much of their charm, for these magical mountains combine grandeur and coziness into an inimitable feeling of friendliness and hospitality. The climate too was frequently praised, for the mile-high altitude of most of the Hills made blankets a necessity every night, which was a major blessing before the days of air conditioning, and the brilliant sun warmed most of even winter days without overheating those of the mild summertime. In short, the Black Hills were an earthly paradise, with many opportunities for sound investment.[24]

Deadwood promotional organizations, in addition to issuing pamphlets and brochures, repeatedly sent out ambassadors bearing messages of wealth, health, and good fortune. Z. Swaringen, in 1875, carried fifteen ounces of placer gold to Washington, to support and assist him in his plea for relinquishment of federal restrictions on mining in the Hills. A "Colonel" C. C. Carpenter who organized parties to the Hills seems to have devoted himself largely to cadging transportation for himself and such followers as he could gather, and when he turned his devotion from Cheyenne to Sidney as a jumping-off place for the Hills, the *Cheyenne Daily Leader* soured on him, and referred to him as a "constitutional deadbeat" and "drunken braggart." Still, such men do gain publicity, perhaps more than would be gained by honest men, and their efforts are usually welcomed for a while in a new community. W. H. Wood, during gold rush days of 1876, traveled to Omaha with a carefully selected chunk of rock that assayed $4,516 in gold to the ton, with $10 worth of silver in addition: that kind of assay was invaluable to any mining promoter. A Dr. Nichols of Deadwood went to the 1876 Centennial Exhibition in Philadelphia with seventy boxes of placer gravel from Negro Gulch, and set up sluice boxes to show the easterners how easy it was to find gold in the Hills' gulches. Another group of miners, that same year, went to Chicago, taking a ton of assorted hardrock ores and Smokey Jones to grind the gold out of them with a mortar and pestle "to show the skeptical eyes of the East just what we've got." George Stokes hauled selected ore that ran $650 to the ton to a smelter in Denver, and there much impressed the population, including the famous mining engineers N. P. Hill and Henry Janin, with the richness of the new-found Black Hills mines.[25]

C. W. Meyer, on the other hand, toured the country publicizing the Black Hills but seems to have made more enemies than friends, at least in the opinion of the *Cheyenne Leader*. Judge H. N. Maguire, the Pactola and Rochford promoter and editor, published a *Black Hills Exposition Offering*, four pages of newsprint and an imaginative map of the gold fields, apparently for distribution at some sort of early fair in Denver. The Black Hills Mining Mens' Association later prepared a mineral exhibit for display at the Festival of Mountain and Plain at Denver in the fall of 1901, and the year after sent a large delegation to the American Mining Congress at Butte, Montana, where they campaigned so vigorously that they won the next year's convention for Deadwood. In 1905 the association sent S. W. Russell as South Dakota's commissioner to the World's Fair at Saint Louis, where at a cost of twenty-seven hundred dollars he set up a five-stamp mill, concentrating jigs, amalgamation tables, and cyanide vats, and processed five to ten tons of ore a day for the enlightenment of the spectators. An advertising railway car, crammed with products from the Black Hills, toured the nation during 1905, and a newspaper, *The Black Hills Headlight*, was printed and distributed en route. To Deadwood, advertising has always been something of a way of life; the modern notion that "if you've got it, flaunt it" came naturally to a little city which had so much to offer and so few customers to buy.

Everybody entered into the spirit of promotion. The various fairs and race meetings and civic festivities which have already been mentioned were advanced as not only beneficial and entertaining in themselves, but as likely to attract attention, settlers, and business to the city, and as early as 1885 the Black Hills Fair Association was

selling stock to finance itself with such promotional aspects of its
endeavors well in mind. In 1889 the whole city united to put on the
Congregational women's Merchants's Carnival. Each firm in town
paid a young and presumably handsome young lady to wear a cos-
tume representing its particular line of business. Estelline Bennett
wore a sort of dark blue conductor's uniform and cap, her skirt
fringed with an embroidered railroad track running around its hem,
to advertise the Deadwood Central. Irene Cushman, later Mrs.
A. D. Wilson, wore a money-covered dress to represent the Merchants National Bank. Emily Wringrose represented Deadwood's
gold mining industries and "looked like a walking jewelry store." In
all, forty intricately costumed young ladies paraded for the good of
church and business, for the promotion of Deadwood's economic
welfare was from the earliest days the concern of everyone in
town.[26]

By the dreary days of the 1920s Deadwood was forced by hard
times to cast its promotional net still wider in an effort to bring in
tourists who could replace the revenue that was lost as mines closed
down and bartenders and gamblers departed. To celebrate the
fiftieth anniversary of the towns of Lead and Deadwood in 1926 a
temporary Camp Jubilee was erected, with many false fronts of
cheap slab lumber, near Central City. This replica of an early mining camp was replete with dancehalls, gambling hells, scheduled
shoot-outs, and much frontier hurraw in general, but its saloons, in
those prohibitory days, served only near beer, a detoxified potion
which customarily required additional fortification in order to be
drunk with any degree of satisfaction. Even so, the two towns managed to make quite a celebration out of it.[27]

Two years earlier, however, had begun the much more famous
and long-lasting Days of '76 which continue to the present, a magnificent summer compound of festival, pageant, parade, rodeo, and
abandon, for Deadwood laws, never too strict to begin with, seem
to be even more relaxed during these two or three days of wild and
profitable festivity. In 1927, in honor of President Calvin Coolidge,
who was then vacationing in the Hills, an Historical Pageant, "not
a rodeo" but "entertaining and historical" was created for the occasion. A Miss Columbia introduced the proceedings, announcing
firmly that "with pride we recognize in Deadwood a picturesque
city, unique in history, whose citizens still manifest that same courage and optimism which half a century ago brought it into being."

She was followed by an extravaganza representing the Dawn of Creation, in which "ghostlike forms lifted their veils to reveal the birth of land, sky, flowers and water, shaped and moulded into a beautiful harmony of movement." Further episodes showed the Spirit of the Wilderness along with various powers of the Forest, Rivers, and Mist "dancing in the forest in merry play." Following this eruption of pageantry came the presentation of Miss Deadwood and her attendants, Father Time, Indian life in the Black Hills, the Gordon party, a holdup of the Deadwood stage, the arrival of freighters and prospectors, and in conclusion a "Masque of Nations" in which various allegorical and historical characters—Fever, Death, Famine, Jack McCall (the murderer of Wild Bill), various flowers, and the forty-eight states—were gaudily represented. As an old-timer remarked in happy recollection, "It was one hell of a spectacle!"[28]

In addition to the pageant, the 1927 festivities which accompanied the Days of '76 included the induction of President Coolidge into the Oglala Sioux Tribe. This traditional ceremony, which appears to have been a requirement of the office in those days, was conducted by Chauncey Yellow Robe, who was assisted by Rosebud Robe, "the most beautiful Indian maiden in the world." Yellow Robe bestowed upon the President a suitable Indian name, which Coolidge's detractors always claimed was "Big Chief Stone-in-the-Face" in honor of his notorious taciturnity. The program continued, somewhat anticlimactically, with an Indian attack on a wagon train, a "squaw's tepee race," and a reenactment of the defeat of General Custer and his command at the Battle of the Little Big Horn. Throughout these dramatic presentations were interspersed "bronc riding, trick and fancy roping, and clowning," and when the performances were concluded, the spectators retired to the Deadwood auditorium in which had been created "an early gambling den, saloon and dance hall, with demonstrations of the various gambling devices." President Coolidge went home early, but the dancing continued "until the wee, small hours." The Days of '76 celebration continues to the present, although somewhat shorn of its pageantry, and with the addition, in its place, of two magnificent parades through the narrow streets of Deadwood's downtown business district. Deadwood Dick Clark often marched in these parades, as did Poker Alice Tubbs, and later the last of the successful prospectors, Potato Creek Johnny Perrett, accompanied by innumerable citizens dressed up as Wild Bills, Calamity Janes, and assorted desperadoes.[29]

As early as 1877 the *Pioneer* had predicted that the Black Hills were destined to become famous as a summer resort, but it was not until the 1920s that tourists, who for years had in small numbers been "charmed and carried away with the variety and completeness of the beauty displayed," became a major business. Earlier, the railroads, both the Burlington and the North Western, had done their best to publicize tours into the Hills, but it was the freedom of motion conveyed upon the traveler by his automobile that made the spectacular trails and byways of the Black Hills a haven for the tourist. By 1915 Deadwood publicity claimed that "all roads lead to Deadwood, the center of good highways in the Black Hills," but the condition of the roads in bad weather was such that the prospective visitor was urged to "drive to the Black Hills in your auto *this summer*" (emphasis added) rather than at any other season. The "Black and Yellow Trail" from Chicago to Yellowstone Park passed through the Hills, where "Lawrence County has spent over a quarter of a million dollars in obtaining the best mountain roads in the west, and where a four-mile portion of the Deadwood-Spearfish highway cost $40,000 to complete." Suggested trips were limited to a maximum of eighty-five miles (a visit to the Belle Fourche irrigation dam), and most were considerably shorter. The Roosevelt Monument on top of Roosevelt Mountain, Roughlock Falls in Spearfish Canyon, and the fishing resorts on Wyoming's Sand Creek were all mentioned as pleasant drives which the tourist, basing himself in Deadwood, might enjoy, and the city some time after 1919 purchased "a beautiful, well-sanded and park-like tract situated between Whitewood Creek and the hillside . . . for use as a free camp ground," by those travelers who wanted to do their roughing it inside the city limits.[30]

More important than any publicity that Deadwood could generate for itself was the summer vacation in 1927 that President and Mrs. Calvin Coolidge took in the Black Hills at the Game Lodge in the Custer State Park, where the president fished for fish imported specially from a local hatchery, and Squaw Creek was renamed Grace Coolidge Creek in honor of Mrs. Coolidge. Gov. Sam McKelvie of Nebraska entertained the president and his party at a rustic summer cabin in the wilderness on Slate Creek, and on that one day the little Mystic telegraph station sent out twenty-five thousand words of publicity for the Black Hills. The local publicists claimed that the president had "selected this wonder spot as the most desirable place in the United States to spend his summer vacation," and implied that the tourist could do no better than to join him where "among the pine-clad peaks he takes respite from his arduous labors as the chief executive of the greatest nation of the world." In 1929, four-hundred thousand tourists followed Coolidge to the Hills to see the sights that he had seen, and gawk at the little church in Hermosa which he had attended, and where, it was claimed, the president, when queried about the minister's sermon concerning sin, had allowed that the youthful preacher "was against it."[31]

A still greater and much longer lasting advertisement for the Black Hills began in 1925 when the sculptor Gutzon Borglum chose Mount Rushmore, near Keystone in the central Hills, as the site for his monumental statues of Presidents Washington, Jefferson, Lincoln, and Theodore Roosevelt. Republicans have since claimed that the waste rock remaining at the bottom of these gigantic carvings commemorates the administrations of subsequent Democratic presidents, and many an old-timer now and then expresses the wish that the mountain had been left as God had made it, but the construction of this memorial, which went on for many years, and the continuing visits of hundreds of thousands of tourists to view it every year, transformed the Black Hills from a scenic and interesting mining backwater to the tourist mecca of the Midwest. Unfortunately for Deadwood, most of the tourists came to see Mount Rushmore from the east, and they came through Rapid City, so it was necessary for Deadwood to still further increase her efforts and her offerings in order to get even a part of this new flood of tourists to visit the northern Hills.

A *Trial of Jack McCall* for the killing of Wild Bill Hickok, with a jury empaneled from its tourist audience, was begun in 1928 as a part of the Days of '76 celebrations, and subsequently Nell Perrigoue of the Chamber of Commerce and Mrs. Pat Woods ran it as an ongoing private venture which continues to delight tourists to the present day. The Deadwood cemetery, on Mount Moriah, displays the graves of Wild Bill, Calamity Jane, and the martyred Preacher Smith, and advertises in addition a splendid view over "the historic city." W. E. Adams, Deadwood's leading merchant, endowed the Adams Memorial Museum, the crowded displays of which continue to attract, delight, and inform its many visitors. The Deadwood

Chamber of Commerce opened up and made safe the old Olaf Seim pyrite mine, which had produced many thousands of tons of flux for the Deadwood smelters, and advertising it as the Broken Boot Gold Mine (the flux did contain a small percentage of gold, so the title is not entirely misleading), conducts underground tours which are well worth the tourist's time and money. A Chinese Tunnel Museum Tour with reconstructed scenes of oriental dissipation has been established among the many passages created by the erection, years ago, of bulkheads to control the numerous floods occasioned by the rising of Whitewood Creek. The Bodega Bar continues its existence, and displays the gambling equipment and account books that it used during Deadwood's wilder days. A bus tour of the area advertises tours that last "approximately 30 minutes to 3 months, depending on bandits, Indians, flash floods, breakdowns, epidemics or other unforseeable incidents," which pretty well sets the tone of modern-day Deadwood's approach to its historic past.

The whole downtown area is irregularly maintained to resemble the roaring days of the gold rush of 1876. Weathered boards and antique lettering abound, and the old brick buildings, many of which are historic in their own right, give the town an air of antiquity which to some extent authenticates the spurious creations of modern commerce. Small gift shops cater to the tourists' desire for curios, and the famous "Black Hills Gold" jewelry with its grape leaf designs is still sold to those who can afford it. Those ornate pots, candles, and leather outrages produced nowadays by otherwise unemployed young people are readily available, and a delightful puppet theater and factory is gaining nationwide attention. The Homestake mine, now down to a depth of ten thousand feet, continues in operation at nearby Lead, and it provides a payroll which in part finds its way into the hands of Deadwood's businessmen, but even the rise in the price of gold has not by 1980 been able to reopen any of the other mines. The discovery that the winter snows lie deep on nearby Terry Peak and Deer Mountain has brought in skiers for the winter months, and these, along with the tourists of the summer, make it possible for Deadwood to prosper year around.[32]

The fortunes of present-day Deadwood are based more or less in equal part upon commerce, tourism, snow, and gold, and Deadwood loves them all. During the summer the Days of '76 bring in their thousands for a few days, and immediately afterward the mo-

torcycle races at Sturgis for a week or two flood Deadwood with the
same sort of coarse, bearded, jovial ruffians who used to arrive behind the ox teams a hundred years ago. In the main Deadwood is a
dignified little town, her primness something like that of an old lady
who has a lively past to be happily remembered but only occasionally relived. Her memories are to Deadwood pleasureable and profitable assets which are carefully cultivated and preserved. Young
people still come to town, as they did in the gold rush days, to seek
adventure and to match their youth and energy against the good
luck that lurks in the Black Hills, and although now, as in the past,
there are a good many bearded faces on the narrow streets, there are
laughing, youthful eyes behind the whiskers, eyes that look back
upon a past well worth remembering, and forward to a future built
in part upon that past, a future which, if fortune smiles, may yet be
better still.

Notes

CHAPTER ONE: HOPE IN THE MOUNTAINS

1. G. Hubert Smith, *The Explorations of the La Vérendryes in the Northern Plains, 1738–43*, ed. W. Raymond Wood (Lincoln: University of Nebraska Press, 1980); the Reverend Peter Rosen, *Pa-Ha-Sa-Pah; or, The Black Hills of Dakota* (Saint Louis, Mo.: Nixon-Jones Printing Company, 1895), p. 304. The extensive literature of Custer's 1874 expedition to the Black Hills is, as are other general references, discussed in the bibliography below.

2. *New York Times*, 11 June 1875.

3. Letter, ibid., 28 June 1875.

4. Richard Irving Dodge, *The Black Hills* (New York: James Miller, 1876), p. 150; Watson Parker, "The Report of Captain John Mix of a Scout to the Black Hills, March-April 1875," *South Dakota History* 7 (Fall 1977): 385–401.

5. *New York Times*, 16 August 1875.

6. Watson Parker, "The Majors and the Miners: The Role of the U.S. Army in the Black Hills Gold Rush," *Journal of the West* 11 (January 1972): 99–111, discusses the many efforts of the army to exclude the miners from the Hills.

7. *New York Times*, 20 March 1875.

8. *New York Times*, 4 February 1877.

9. *Yankton Press and Dakotaian*, 28 April 1875; Richard B. Hughes, *Pioneer Years in the Black Hills* ed. Agnes Wright Spring (Glendale, Calif.: Arthur H. Clark Co., 1957), p. 27 and passim.

10. Hughes, *Pioneer Years*, p. 323.

11. H. N. Maguire, *The Black Hills and American Wonderland*, The Lakeside Library, 4th set., no. 82 (Chicago: Donnelly, Loyd and Co., 1877), p. 289.

12. *Frank Leslie's Illustrated Magazine*, 8 September 1877, mentioned the logging chains and other alleged artifacts. John S. McClintock, *Pioneer Days in the Black Hills: Accurate History and Facts, Related by One of the Early Pioneers*, ed. Edward L. Senn (Deadwood: John S. McClintock, 1939), pp. 40–41, disputes that any such artifacts were ever actually discovered.

13. Annie Donna Fraser Tallent, *The Black Hills; or, The Last Hunting Grounds of the Dakotahs* (Saint Louis, Mo.: Nixon-Jones Printing Co., 1899), p. 175. I am much indebted to Robert M. Bryant, Sr., of Spearfish, and his son-in-law, Linfred Schuttler who have compiled an extensive history of the Bryant party, for some of the details of this Deadwood gold discovery.

14. George W. Kingsbury and George Martin Smith, *History of Dakota Territory* (Chicago: S. J. Clarke Publishing Co., 1915), 1:925. Kingsbury and Smith's volumes contain a wealth of primary material on the rush.

15. *Black Hills Daily Times*, 17 May 1883. Deadwood lawyers were always eager for an opportunity to advertise.

16. George W. Stokes and Howard R. Driggs, *Deadwood Gold: A Story of the Black Hills* (Chicago: World Book Co., 1926), p. 58.

17. The great flume from Spearfish is mentioned in Charles Collins's *Collins' History and Directory of the Black Hills* (Central City, privately published, 1878), p. 38, and progress at least was reported in the *Black Hills Daily Times* of 10 February 1880. The problems of the High Lode and Terra are in the *Times* of 16 May 1880. McClintock, *Pioneer Days*, p. 120, is contemptuous of the Boulder Ditch.

18. *Black Hills Pioneer*, 1 July 1876.

19. In Hughes, *Pioneer Years*, p. 338.

20. *Appleton's Encyclopedia* (1877), p. 246.

21. Hughes, *Pioneer Years*, p. 329; Jerry Bryan, *An Illinois Gold Hunter in the Black Hills*, introd. and notes by Clyde C. Walton, (Springfield: Illinois State Historical Society, 1960), pp. 28, 29; *New York Times*, 13 August 1877.

22. Jesse Brown and A. M. Willard, *The Black Hills Trails: A History of The Struggles of the Pioneers* (Rapid City: Rapid City Journal Co., 1924), pp. 546–47, and Rosen, *Pa-Ha-Sa-Pah*, pp. 380–81, give slightly differing versions of this song, written originally by Jack Langrishe, the Black Hills theatrical impressario.

23. "Gold Production of the Black Hills," *Black Hills Engineer* 18 (January 1930): 77.

24. Parkhurst's ad appeared in an early issue of the *Pioneer;* Coleman E. Bishop, "The Black Hills of Dakota," *The Chautauquan* 7 (June 1887): 540.

25. Glenn Chesney Quiett, *Pay Dirt: A Panorama of American Gold Rushes* (New York: D. Appleton-Century Co., 1936), p. 260.

CHAPTER TWO: UNGODLY MILLS

1. *U.S. Bureau of Mines Information Circulars*, 7688, 7707 (1954, 1955) prepared by Paul Gries of the South Dakota School of Mines and Technology, constitute the *Black Hills Mineral Atlas* and will be found to be invaluable in any study of their mines. Francis Church Lincoln et al., *The Mining Industry of South Dakota*, South Dakota School of Mines Bulletin no. 17 (February 1937), is also of great help, and both are excellent guides to many of the Black Hills' more esoteric minerals.

2. *New York Times*, 13 August 1877.

3. H. N. Maguire, *New Map and Guide to Dakota and the Black Hills* (Chi-

cago: Rand, McNally and Co., 1877), apparently prepared by George Henckel, U.S. deputy surveyor, lists these mining districts.

4. C. L. Fuller, *Pocket Map of the Northern Hills* (1887) lists the mines and their dividends.

5. Bryan, *An Illinois Gold Hunter*, pp. 12–13.

6. The Lawrence County Board's advertised offer of $250 appeared in the *Black Hills Daily Times* on 26 July 1877, and is reprinted in Bob Lee, ed., *Gold—Gals—Guns—Guts* (Deadwood: Deadwood-Lead Centennial, 1976), p. 92. Capt. James E. Smith, *A Famous Battery* (Washington: D.C., W. H. Lowdermilk and Co., 1892), is a little-known account of early days in the Hills, and on p. 222 contains one version of the tale of the man who brought in the Indian's head. A summary of the rewards offered and the sources giving them may be found in my "Majors and Miners," p. 111 n. 43.

7. Kingsbury and Smith, *History of Dakota Territory*, 1:930, quotes Goerham. The *Cheyenne Daily Leader* during the spring of 1876 is a good example of the vacillation of the newspapers on the Indian question.

8. The accuracy of the average soldier's shooting is discussed in Edwin A. Curley's *Guide to the Black Hills* (Chicago, 1877), p. 100.

9. Crook's campaign in the Hills is described by John G. Bourke, in *On the Border With Crook* (New York: Charles Scribner's Sons, 1892); Capt. Charles King, *Campaigning with Crook* (Norman: University of Oklahoma Press, 1964); and John E. Finerty, *War-Path and Bivouac: The Big Horn and Yellowstone Expedition*, ed. and introd. Milo Milton Quaife (Lincoln: University of Nebraska Press, 1966).

10. Finerty, *War-Path and Bivouac*.

11. The petition was printed in the *Black Hills Pioneer* on 16 September 1876; Rosen, *Pa-Ha-Sa-Pah*, p. 404, gives Crook's reply.

12. *Black Hills Daily Times*, August 1880, passim, and 3 August 1880.

13. The "Pansy" letter is in Brown and Willard, *Black Hills Trails*, pp. 116–18. Rex Alan Smith, *Moon of Popping Trees* (New York: Reader's Digest Press, 1975) is a considered analysis of the whole Wounded Knee tragedy.

14. This battle was described in a pamphlet by the husband of Sheriff Miller's daughter: Ernest M. Richardson, *The Battle of Lightning Creek* (Pacific Palisades, Calif.: privately published, 1956). Barton R. Voight, "The Lightning Creek Fight," *Annals of Wyoming* 49, no. 1 (Spring 1977): 5–21, is a recent account.

CHAPTER THREE: DUST IN THE BALANCE

1. Stokes and Driggs, *Deadwood Gold*, p. 82; Bourke, *On the Border with Crook*, p. 385; Bryan, *An Illinois Gold Hunter*, p. 28.

2. The *Cheyenne Daily Leader* during 1876 is an excellent source of early

Deadwood history; the lascivious pictures were seen by Maguire, who mentions them in his *Black Hills*, p. 292.

3. *New York Times*, 13 August 1877; *Frank Leslie's Illustrated Magazine*, 8 September, 6 October 1877.

4. The price list was published in the *Custer Black Hills Harald* [*sic*], 27 December 1876.

5. A. T. Andreas, *Andreas' Historical Atlas of Dakota* (Chicago: A. T. Andreas, 1884), p. 123. Other estimates may be found in the Deadwood Board of Trade's promotional pamphlet of 1881, *The Black Hills of Dakota* and the anonymous *The Black Hills: America's Land of Minerals* (Omaha, Nebr.: Herald Job Printing Room, 1889).

6. The statistical survey of the 1898 *Black Hills Residence and Business Directory* (Deadwood: Enterprise Printing Co.) prepared for my 1978 seminar by Eugene E. Detert provided many of my insights into the structure of Deadwood's business population.

7. Robert E. Driscoll, *Seventy Years of Banking in the Black Hills* (Rapid City: First National Bank of the Black Hills, 1948), p. 13.

8. *Collins' Directory*, p. 34; George P. Baldwin, comp., *The Black Hills Illustrated: A Terse Description of Conditions Past and Present of America's Greatest Mineral Belt* (n.p., Black Hills Mining Men's Association, 1904), p. 19, a truly excellent survey of Hills history up to that time, and recently reprinted by Deadwood Graphics; *Rapid City Journal*, 11 February 1978.

9. *Black Hills Pioneer*, 11 November 1876; *Manitowoc* (Wisconsin) *Pilot*, 23 August 1877; Quiett, *Pay Dirt*, p. 252.

10. The W. E. Adams papers in the Adams Memorial Museum are an as yet untapped resource of Deadwood history. The suit against Adams and his wife by his mother-in-law, Pamela Burnham, was considered by those who knew Adams to be baseless.

11. *Pioneer-Times*, 1 March 1899.

12. The story of the modern druggist came to me secondhand, from a noted South Dakota historian, but it seems to me somewhat of an exaggeration.

13. Stokes, *Deadwood Gold*, p. 105, and *Black Hills Daily Times*, 1880s. The corset ad appeared in the *Cheyenne Daily Leader*, 23 May 1876 and the *Black Hills Daily Times*, 22 March 1883. The experiments with this garment were performed in modern times, my father having bought up the entire corset supply of McEachron's General Store in Hill City when that ancient business closed for good.

14. Holzman's advertised heavily in the *Black Hills Daily Times*; the "Perished in the Storm" item can be found in the 3 January 1880 issue and elsewhere.

15. Both Star and Bullock are frequently mentioned in all histories of the Black Hills. See also Seth Bullock, "An Account of Deadwood and the Northern Black Hills in 1876," ed. Harry H. Anderson, South Dakota

State Historical Society, *Collections* 31 (1962): 287–364. Kenneth C. Kellar, *Seth Bullock: Frontier Marshal* (Aberdeen: North Plains Press, 1972), written by Bullock's grandson, is based upon the Bullock papers as well as family recollections.

16. The menu appears in the 20 July 1880 issue of the *Black Hills Daily Times*.

17. Detert, statistical survey; *Black Hills Illustrated*, pp. 93, 98; *Pioneer-Times*, 5 June 1903; W. E. Adams to the Otis Elevator Company in Omaha, 26 December 1933, in the Adams Museum, regarding the financial problems of the hotel.

18. *Black Hills Daily Times*, 28 April 1877, provides the doggerel.

19. Rosen, *Pa-Ha-Sa-Pah*, p. 364.

20. Bob Lee and Dick Williams, *Last Grass Frontier: The South Dakota Stock Grower Heritage* (Sturgis: Black Hills Publishers, 1964) is a detailed history of the South Dakota cattle industry.

CHAPTER FOUR: THE PROFESSIONAL MEN

1. *Frank Leslie's Illustrated Magazine*, 25 March 1876. The widely variable estimates of the number of lawyers perhaps arises from the disparity between those claiming legal training, and those actually engaged in legal work.

2. Kenneth C. Kellar, *Chambers Kellar: Distinguished Gentleman, Great Lawyer, Fiery Rebel* (Lead: Seaton Publishing Co., 1975), is a notable account of the life of this noted practitioner.

3. *Collins' Directory* of 1878 is full of peculiar listings. The other occupations can be discovered by skimming through the spring 1899 issues of the *Deadwood Pioneer-Times*.

4. Douglas Crawford McMurtrie, *Early Printing in Wyoming and the Black Hills* (Hattiesburg, Miss.: The Book Farm, 1943) is an excellent survey; the aurora is quoted from him. The *Manitowoc* (Wisconsin) *Pilot*, 8 March 1877, mentions the ballistic uses and irresponsibility of the Deadwood press, and does so again on 23 August.

5. *Black Hills Daily Times*, 24 July 1880, 13 February 1883. *The Checklist of South Dakota Newspapers in the South Dakota State Historical Society* (Pierre, 1976) will be of great use to any researcher.

6. The gaudy tale of the lively old banker came to me from a man who had it directly from the banker's grandson, who certainly must have known it was a lie, but like many Deadwood people, he much preferred a good story to the truth, for it was always to Deadwood's interest, as we shall see in Chapter 9, to appear to be a lively town. Driscoll's *Seventy Years of Banking* is the principal source of banking history. The party held at the opening of Brown and Thum's was reported in the 23 August 1877 *Manitowoc Pilot*.

Tallent, *Black Hills*, and *Andreas' Atlas* are useful, here and there, on banking.

7. The ingenious swindles practiced by those who handled gold dust are mentioned by Harry Young in *Hard Knocks: A Life Story of the Vanishing West* (Chicago: Laird and Lee, 1915), p. 197 and passim. The *Black Hills Weekly Times* for 29 April 1877 mentions the brass.

8. Interest rates of 5 percent a month are mentioned in the *New York Times*, 21 May 1878; Driscoll, *Seventy Years of Banking*, p. 21, speaks of 2 percent a month in the 1880s, and the *Black Hills Illustrated* praises the turn-of-the-century Deadwood merchants for being able to prosper on money borrowed at 12 percent a year.

9. Driscoll, *Seventy Years of Banking*, pp. 20, 54–55.

10. Ibid.

11. Mel Williams, "Tales of the Black Hills" in the Chicago Westerners' *Brand Book* 23 (June 1966): 26, tells the story of Poker Alice and her loan, but he tells me that he has since heard that the story was current centuries earlier, involving all sorts of solemn religious conclaves.

12. McClintock, *Pioneer Days*, pp. 209–10; the postmasters are castigated in the 1 June 1878 *Weekly Times*.

13. Cheyenne's mayor is quoted in Tallent, *Black Hills*, pp. 377–79; the irregularity of telegraphic service is discussed in the *Daily Times* of 21 July 1880.

14. Agnes Wright Spring, *Cheyenne and Black Hills Stage and Express Routes* (Glendale, Calif: Arthur H. Clark Co., 1949) is a classic on transportation into the Hills.

15. Estelline Bennett, *Old Deadwood Days* (New York: J. H. Sears and Co., 1928), has a whole chapter on the trails; Shorty's story is on pp. 95, 96.

16. Carl Leedy's *Golden Days in the Black Hills* (Rapid City: Holmgren's, 1961), p. 106, is one of several sources on the famous load of cats; Ellis T. Peirce wrote the version that appears in Brown and Willard's *Black Hills Trails*, pp. 432–34, and Bullock, "Account of Deadwood," p. 357, gives it very nearly firsthand. Badger Clark's poem "The Cat Pioneers" is in his *Sky Lines and Wood Smoke* (Custer: The Chronicle Shop, 1935).

17. Bennett, *Old Deadwood Days*, p. 248, quotes Keets; *Black Hills Daily Times*, 11 January 1883.

18. Bennett, *Old Deadwood Days*, chap. 3, lists the stage drivers and the guards.

19. Kellar, *Seth Bullock*, p. 160. Irma H. Klock, *All Roads Lead to Deadwood* (Aberdeen: North Plains Press, 1979), is a detailed account of the locations of all the old trails.

20. Bennett, *Old Deadwood Days*, p. 4, quoting a conversation she had with Buffalo Bill.

21. Mildred Fielder's writings on Black Hills railroads are useful: "Rail-

roads of the Black Hills," South Dakota State Historical Society, *Collections* 30 (1960): 35–316, and *Railroads of the Black Hills* (Seattle, Wash.: Superior Publ. Co., 1964).

CHAPTER FIVE: A BOOM IN CYANIDE

1. R. E. Driscoll, *Diary of a Country Banker* (New York: Vantage Press, 1960), pp. 24, 36; Deadwood Business Club, *Deadwood of Today* (1903); *Black Hills Residence and Business Directory* (Deadwood: Enterprise Printing Co., 1898), p. 8, provides the statistics of mining employment, as do successive directories and the biennial *Reports* of the South Dakota state inspector of mines.

2. David W. Ryder, *The Merrill Story* (n.p.: The Merrill Co., 1958), pp. 34–50.

3. Baldwin, *Black Hills Illustrated*, pp. 25, 31–33, 53. This book was issued at the height of the cyanide boom.

4. The Lexington Hill's money-raising project is mentioned in the *Pioneer-Times* on 7 November 1905.

5. Driscoll, *Diary of a Country Banker*, p. 25.

6. Grantz's story is told in Baldwin, *Black Hills Illustrated*, p. 21; the Black Hills Mining Men's endorsement of the Hidden Fortune's management is in the *Pioneer-Times*, 20, 21, 26 July 1905.

7. The Burlington Route's *Mines and Mining in the Black Hills* (ca. 1904), p. 9, lists many of the mills; Baldwin, *Black Hills Illustrated*, p. 93, lists some more; *Deadwood of Today* (1903) gives the most comprehensive list, and of course the *Reports* of the state mine inspector provide still further details.

8. The chart was compiled from the *Reports* of the state mine inspector.

9. Moses Manuel, "Forty-Eight Years in the West" is a firsthand manuscript account of the founding of the Homestake, copies of which are in several Black Hills libraries; Stokes *Deadwood Gold*, is brief but good; the Homestake Mining Company's booklet *Homestake Centennial* (1976), their annual *Reports*, and their illustrated employee magazine *Sharp Bits* (1950–1970) provide the basic information on this great mine. John Tait Milliken's "Report on Oro Hondo Mining Property, 26 May 1918," is in the Adams Museum in Deadwood. Mildred Fielder's *The Treasure of Homestake Gold* (Aberdeen: North Plains Press, 1970) is a history of the company.

10. Baron E. de Mandat-Grancey, *Cow-Boys and Colonels: A Narrative of a Journey across the Prairie and over the Black Hills of Dakota* (New York: E. P. Dutton and Co., 1887) was William Conn's translation of Mandat-Grancey's *Dans les Montagnes Rocheuses* (Paris: E. Plon, Nourrit et Cie, 1884) and is full of references to Deadwood and Lead; he reports the great cave-in which

took place during his visit. Other disasters are mentioned in the *Reports* of the state inspector of mines for 1893, 1907 and 1920.

11. Kellar, *Chambers Kellar*, chap. 5, deals extensively with Jenks's suit.

12. The reader will have to adjust today's wildly fluctuating gold prices for himself, to see what the Homestake's production would mean in terms of today's dollars. Production figures are mainly from Homestake annual *Reports*.

13. Hughes, *Pioneer Years*, p. 287, tells of Professor Underwood. I would surmise that the swindle was that involving the Safe Investment mine at Greenwood.

14. Professor Murphy is praised in the 20 May 1880 issue of the *Daily Times*.

15. *Cheyenne Daily Leader*, 17 August, 13, 24 November 1877; Brown and Willard, *Black Hills Trails*, pp. 359–61; Tallent, *Black Hills*, pp. 534–35; Bennett, *Old Deadwood Days*, pp. 51–53; Kellar, *Seth Bullock*, pp. 97–99, all tell of the Keets Mine battle. The question whether Bullock used asafetida or burning sulphur (which might be dangerous to the mine timbers) has never been settled that I know of.

16. Consultation with Black Hills mining engineers confirms the miner's inclination to augment his salary underground, and to justify his ill-gotten gains by a pretended mining claim.

17. Joseph H. Cash, *Working the Homestake* (Ames: Iowa State University Press, 1973), is the story of Homestake labor to 1942, using much original material and interviews with the participants in the great strike of 1909.

18. Otis E. Young, Jr., *Western Mining: An Informal Account of Precious-Metals Prospecting, Placering, Lode Mining, and Milling on the American Frontier from Spanish Times to 1893* (Norman: University of Oklahoma Press, 1970), is excellent on all phases of the subject. Ronald C. Brown's *Hard-Rock Miners* (College Station: Texas A & M University Press, 1979) and Mark Wyman's *Hardrock Epic: Miners and the Industrial Revolution, 1860–1910* (Berkeley: University of California Press, 1979), are both useful on labor in the western mines, but the reader should remember that to the average miner, simply going underground constituted so great a risk that he was not much interested in taking minor safety precautions which might be a nuisance without noticeably improving his chances for survival.

19. As a child, visiting neighboring mines, I was always cautioned *never* to speak to or intrude upon in any way, the attentive engineer: men's lives literally hung upon the wire rope that he commanded.

20. I am indebted to Albro Ayres of Deadwood for information about these two deaths from cyanide.

21. Young, *Western Mining*, is good on claim salting, and provides the quote from Harte; Tallent, Rosen, Stokes, and others already mentioned in these notes are also useful; *Frank Leslie's Illustrated Magazine*, 8 September 1877, mentions the use of the edge of a brass cartridge.

22. The guards are mentioned by Mandat-Grancey, *Cow-Boys and Colonels*, pp. 159–61. The packrat story comes from Frank Hebert, *Forty Years Prospecting and Mining in the Black Hills of South Dakota* (Rapid City: Rapid City Daily Journal, 1921), pp. 88–89. The dying miner is mentioned in Bennett's *Old Deadwood Days*, pp. 184–85. The joke must be an old one, for Coronado, I have heard, took as his cattle brand three Christian crosses, the implication being that he, too, had thieves on either side of him.

23. *Report* of the South Dakota state inspector of mines, 1927, deals with the blue ores. Lincoln et al., *Mining Industry of South Dakota* provides a useful account of mining activity including that of the 1930s boom, and mentions Grauman and Al Jolson.

24. *Black Hills Daily Times*, 8 October 1880, written presumably by a "stockholder in the Caledonia mine," although it may have been borrowed from some other mining area.

25. Ryder, *Merrill Story*, p. 40.

CHAPTER SIX: REFRACTORY ORE

1. Driscoll, *Seventy Years of Banking*, p. 13.

2. Leander P. Richardson, "A Trip to the Black Hills," *Scribner's* 13 (April 1877): 755; *New York Times*, 13 August 1877.

3. Robert Strahorn, *To the Rockies and Beyond* (Omaha: Omaha Republican, 1878), p. 20, deals with the honesty of the early miners; the quotation is from George Stokes, in the *Denver Tribune*, quoted by Spring, *Cheyenne and Black Hills Stage*, p. 167.

4. Tallent, *Black Hills*, pp. 252–53; *The Black Hills: America's Land of Minerals* (Omaha: Herald Job Printing Rooms, 1889), p. 6.

5. Diary of Irene Cushman (Mrs. A. D. Wilson), 1890–91, 7 April 1890, Deadwood Public Library.

6. Matilda H. White Starbuck, "My Trip to the Black Hills" (ca. 1924), South Dakota State Historical Society, mentions many of the characters met in 1876; Young's erratic and mendacious *Hard Knocks*, p. 198, lists many others of that era.

7. Old Frenchy, "the bottle fiend" lived in Deadwood about 1876–1880 and is frequently in the *Times* during that period; Morris, the second of that nickname, died in 1899, according to the *Pioneer-Times* of 23 March.

8. Bennett, *Old Deadwood Days*, p. 7.

9. Bennett, *Old Deadwood Days*, records many conflicts with the contumacious Madam Henrico.

10. *Black Hills Daily Times*, August 1880.

11. Phillip Durham and Everett L. Jones, "Negro Cowboys," *American West* 1 (Fall 1964), discusses Nat Love; McClintock, *Pioneer Days* lists the ensuing four "Deadwood Dicks"; Edward L. Senn's little booklet *Deadwood*

Dick and Calamity Jane (n.p., privately published, 1939), uses much the same material; Warren Morrell's "Through the Hills" column in the *Rapid City Journal*, 2 August 1955, adds the detail about Clark's funerary inclinations.

12. Kellar, *Seth Bullock*; and Bullock "Account of Deadwood," are basic to the study of this sterling western man; Elting E. Morison, et al., *The Letters of Theodore Roosevelt* (Cambridge, Mass.: Harvard University Press, 1952), 6:104, gives Bullock's letter, which has been widely quoted, on the election of 1908.

13. Prior's lines were "O day, the fairest one that ever rose / Period and end of anxious Emma's woes." Hughes's *Pioneer Years*, p. 104, tells firsthand of "Oh, Joe!"; and p. 68, of Smokey Jones and his wolf's howl.

14. Titles are laughed at in the *Black Hills Weekly Times*, 31 May 1879; Mandat-Grancey, *Cow-Boys and Colonels*, p. 21, was the man who found eight hundred colonels in Fort Pierre. Doane Robinson, *History of South Dakota* (n. p., B. F. Bowen and Co., 1904), vol. 2, is a splendid example of the "mug book" with its generous biographies and excellent steel engravings of Dakota worthies.

15. An otherwise undated newspaper clipping of 1877, "Facts about the Black Hills," in the Deadwood Public Library gives details regarding actual words and phrases used during the gold rush times.

16. Patricia Lavier Mechling, "Blanche Colman and the Pioneer Jewish Community of Deadwood," *Black Hills Nuggets* 12 (May 1979): 127–29, mentions many eminent Jews. George Frink of Mystic led me to the top of the peddler's trail, and pointed out the inlet of the Volin Tunnel, far beneath it.

17. L. J. O'Grady, "Old Aunt Lou in the Hills Rush," *Sioux City Sunday Journal*, 3 January 1926. The Spearfish Creek outing is mentioned in the *Black Hills Weekly Times*, 2 August 1879. "Colonel" Lawrence is in the *Times*, 16 April 1880. The "colored" and the "plain" man are in the *Times*, 17 May 1883, and Bo Williams's party on 13 April the same year. The "cutting affray" is in the *Pioneer-Times*, 23, 27 July 1905.

18. *Black Hills Daily Times*, 29 March 1883.

19. *Black Hills Daily Times*, 6 January [?] 1890; and Robert J. Casey, *The Black Hills and Their Incredible Characters* (Indianapolis: The Bobbs-Merrill Co., 1949), pp. 268–73, the latter by a native of the Hills, and chock-full of useful lore.

20. Clipping from an unidentified Deadwood newspaper, *about* February 1893, re Two Sticks's execution, Adams Museum.

21. Joe Sulentic, *Deadwood Gulch: The Last Chinatown* (Deadwood: Deadwood Gulch Art Gallery, 1975); Mildred Fielder, *The Chinese in the Black Hills* (Lead: Bonanza Trails Publishers, 1972); and Grant K. Anderson, "Deadwood's Chinatown," *South Dakota History* 4 (Summer 1975): 266–85, augment the frequent mentions of the Chinese which regularly appeared in the Deadwood newspapers. Mandat-Grancey's *Cow-Boys and Colonels*, p. 133, mentions the oriental appearance of lower Deadwood.

22. Bennett, *Old Deadwood Days*, pp. 175–76, mentions the Chinese school and its products. The *Times* reporter wrote of the opium den on 10 July 1878.

23. Bennett, *Old Deadwood Days*, p. 30; the hot bread is mentioned in the *Times* on 9 July 1880.

24. Driscoll, *Diary of a Country Banker*, pp. 122–23, mentions lawyer Frawley's odd plea; the *Pioneer-Times*, 23 May 1967, gives Hunter's story of his youthful abuse of the Chinese; the story of the hoodlums is in the *Times*, 7 March 1882; that of the unkillable Chinaman is on 28 March 1880.

25. *Black Hills Daily Times*, 19 May 1880, 12 April 1883.

26. *Pioneer-Times*, 10 March 1899.

27. *Pioneer*, 24 March 1877; *Times*, 28 June 1879, 4 July 1880, 22 March 1883.

28. *Times*, 21, 22 March 1883, 17 April 1883; *Pioneer-Times*, 6 June 1950.

29. City government is covered in more detail in Chapter 9; Seth Bullock, "Account of Deadwood," p. 322, discusses Deadwood's early sanitary arrangements.

30. Spring, *Cheyenne and Black Hills Stage*, p. 178, quotes the lousy bullwhacker; advertisements for the Deadwood bathhouse can be found in the *Pioneer*, 16 December 1876 and other times, but as early as 31 October 1876 the *Cheyenne Daily Leader* reported that this edifice has fallen into disuse and decay.

31. The tale of the demented wife was a current jest in the Hills.

32. Patton's hearse is mentioned on 16 January 1880.

33. F. S. Howe, M.D., *Deadwood Doctor* (n.p., n.d.) cheerfully illustrated by Diana Tollefson, provides the tales of Mount Moriah and of the curious tourists.

34. The Sozodont poetry appeared in the *Daily Times*, 11 May 1883; Dr. Spinney's ad on 6 January 1880 in the same paper, and dentist Buchanan's ad in the *Lead City Daily Tribune*, 26 February 1882.

35. This aged wheeze was a favorite of my father's, who obtained it locally in the Hills.

36. Bent and Deetkin's ads ran in the *Times*, 20 May 1880.

37. Tutt's Pills are advertised in the *Times*, 11 May 1883; Phosphoric Air, in July 1880; Hood's Sarsaparilla in the *Pioneer-Times*, 8 April 1899.

38. Dr. King's nostrum advertised in the *Pioneer-Times*, 23 March 1899; The Pink Pills for Pale People on 29 April the same year, and H. T. Helmbold's Buchu, 7 January 1880 in the *Times*.

39. Watson's "Beautiful Snow" can be found in *The Best Loved Poems of the American People*, ed. Hazel Felleman (Garden City: Garden City Books, 1936), p. 188. Langrishe's parody is quoted in Brown and Willard, *Black Hills Trails*, p. 547; and the *Cheyenne Daily Leader*, 22 November 1876, deplores the poetic excesses.

40. Brown and Willard, *Black Hills Trails*, pp. 436–38 discuss the blizzard of 1878; Roland R. Hamann, "The Remarkable Temperature Fluctuations in the Black Hills Region, January, 1943," *Black Hills Engineer* 29 (July 1949): 44–49.

41. *Black Hills Daily Times*, 19–24 May 1883, tells of the great flood of that year. The poem about the 'Frisco fire (for the inhabitants would never in this life admit that there had been an earthquake) was written, in a slightly different version, by Charles K. Field, quoted by Walter Lord in *The Good Years* (New York: Bantam Books, 1965), p. 135, but I was brought up on the version given here, and so prefer it.

42. *Andreas' Atlas*, p. 122; *Pioneer-Times*, 15 April 1899, deals with both the bad city water and the better Kidney Springs product, advertisements for which, disguised as news items, continue throughout the year.

43. The flood is discussed in the *Pioneer-Times*, 26 March 1899.

44. The 12 and 14 January 1883 *Black Hills Daily Times* contain the coroner's report. Mark Twain's *A Tramp Abroad* gives comparable death rates in U.S. and foreign cities, Dublin leading the list with forty-three deaths per thousand per year. The Lawrence County *Record of Deaths*, 1877–98, in the Deadwood Public Library, although incomplete, provides a feast for the statistically inclined.

CHAPTER SEVEN: A SOCIABLE PEOPLE

1. It probably isn't true: Young, in *Hard Knocks*, pp. 209–10, is notable for the inaccuracy of his recollections.

2. Preacher Smith's poem may be found in Brown and Willard, *Black Hills Trails*, pp. 400–402, and his notes for his last sermon in McClintock, *Pioneer Days*, pp. 124–27.

3. Rosen, *Pa-Ha-Sa-Pah*, pp. 381–82.

4. Hughes, *Pioneer Years*, pp. 235–36, tells of the Reverend Rumney's sermon in a bar, as do McClintock, *Pioneer Days*, pp. 146–47; and Brown and Willard, *Black Hills Trails*, pp. 422–23, each adding a few details.

5. The basic source for much Deadwood church history appears to be *Andreas' Atlas*; Bennett's *Old Deadwood Days* contains several useful stories, as does Tallent's *Black Hills*, here and there.

6. The *Times* mentioned the scarcity of small coins on 6, 20 January 1880.

7. This marriage service and others appear in Rosen, *Pa-Ha-Sa-Pah*, p. 384 and passim; Tallent, *Black Hills*, pp. 553–54, has another.

8. *Black Hills Daily Times*, 22 June 1878, although the date is not clear, entirely.

9. Deadwood Lodge No. 7, undated pamphlet *Organization and History*.

The doings of the Nobles of the Mystic Shrine are fully reported in the *Pioneer-Times*, 22, 23 June 1905.

10. The Deadwood Board of Trade's *The Black Hills of Dakota* lists eight fraternal societies; the city *Directories* for 1898, 1902, and 1908 add extensively to the list, as does Baldwin, *Black Hills Illustrated*, p. 93.

11. The hospital association is mentioned in the 8 August 1877 *Times*; the lecture association is spoken of in the WPA "Annals—Culture," 28 December 1879, typescript in the Rapid City Public Library; W. H. Bonham's scrapbook in the Adams Museum has a clipping about the 29 January 1883 meeting of the library association, and the *Pioneer-Times*, 8 November 1905, tells of the opening of the Deadwood Library. Mrs. R. Anna Morris Clark, president of the Thursday Club, wrote "Women's Literary and Social Clubs of the Black Hills" in Baldwin, *Black Hills Illustrated*, p. 66.

12. The fire-fighting companies are treated of in more detail in Chapter 9; their social nature is indicated by a notice for the Homestake Hose Company's grand ball, in the *Times*, 29 September 1880, which firmly announced that "no questionable person will be admitted to the hall." The secretary's record book of the Deadwood Pioneer Hook and Ladder Company No. 1, showing meetings up to 1936, is in the Adams Museum.

13. The Pleasant Hours Club is mentioned in the *Pioneer-Times* on 15 March 1899; the Athletic Club appears in the Deadwood Rotary Club's Deadwood chronology in the Deadwood Public Library; the Plug Hat Society in the *Times*, June 1883; the Mumm Club in the *Pioneer-Times*, 10 August 1905.

14. The "By-Laws, Articles of Incorporation and House Rules," with brief biographical sketches of the officers and members of the Deadwood Club, was printed in 1892; a copy is in the Adams Museum, as is their minute book for 1892–1906. The 1898 *Directory*, p. 12; "Deadwood," in Baldwin, *Black Hills Illustrated*, p. 93; and "Olympic Committees," in the *Pioneer-Times*, 23 April 1899 describe the Olympic Club in some detail.

15. The record book of the Society of Black Hills Pioneers, beginning in 1889, is in the Adams Museum; the society's pamphlet *Constitution and By-Laws* (1908) casts much light upon the organization. The two competing Pioneer societies are mentioned in the 1898 *Directory;* the poetry is in the Black Hills Pioneers' minute book for 11 January 1908. The Spearfish Local Pioneer's Club minute book covering meetings from 1893 to 1926 is also in the Adams Museum.

16. Nuttal and Brown's ad was in the *Black Hills Pioneer*, 2 December 1876.

17. Henriette Naeseth, "Drama in Early Deadwood, 1876–1879," *American Literature* 10 (November 1938): 297, quoting the *Daily Times* of 6 January 1876.

18. *Black Hills Pioneer*, 3 February, 14 April 1877.

19. Bourke, *On the Border with Crook*, p. 385.

20. William Littlebury Kuykendall, *Frontier Days: A True Narrative of Striking Events on the Western Frontier* (n.p.; J. M. and H. L. Kuykendall, 1917), pp. 194–95; *Pioneer*, 26 August 1876, as quoted in the *Cheyenne Daily Leader*, 12 September 1876.

21. Hughes, *Pioneer Years*, p. 113, quotes "The Days of Forty-Nine," apparently from memory, and on pp. 114, 117 tells of the death of Shaughnessy. The *Cheyenne Daily Leader*, 21 November 1876, is another contemporary source; and Miss Garrettson's letter is in the *Leader*, 16 December 1876. Lawrence Carl Stine's "A History of Theatre and Theatrical Activities in Deadwood, South Dakota, 1876–90" (Ph.D. diss., State University of Iowa, 1962) provides over five hundred pages of detailed and useful information on the Deadwood theater in general.

22. Tallent, *Black Hills*, pp. 277–79, has much on Langrishe; Bennett, *Old Deadwood Days*, p. 235, provided the quotation about Mrs. Langrishe; the *Cheyenne Daily Leader*, 10 February 1877, tells of Langrishe's short-lived change of pace.

23. There is a New Opera House playbill for the *Mikado* dated 20 December 1886 in the collection of such memorabilia at the Adams Museum; the Gem Theater program, dated 24 February 1887, provides the material on that presentation; the dismal amateur production was reported in the *Pioneer-Times* on 8 April 1899.

24. The depressing movie bill was advertised on the Days of '76 program for 4 August 1927.

25. Casad's Minstrels were condemned in the *Daily Times*, 21 February 1890; the Olympic Club's playbill for their minstrel presentation, 17 February 1899, reassures the public; Duncan's misnamed Lady Minstrels are criticized in the 20, 22, 23 April 1899 *Pioneer-Times*.

26. Tallent, *Black Hills*, pp. 258–59; and Hughes, *Pioneer Years*, pp. 138–39; both were present at the Fourth of July festivities of 1876.

27. *Daily Times*, 4 July 1880; Mandat-Grancey, *Cow-Boys and Colonels*, p. 174, deals with 1883, and the *Times*, 27 June 1883, printed the order of march for the parade for the benefit of both participants and spectators.

28. Stokes, *Deadwood Gold*, p. 76; Bennett, *Old Deadwood Days*, pp. 254–55; the concluding jest is of course not peculiar to Deadwood, but has enjoyed a long run elsewhere.

29. The *Pioneer* usually avoided frenchified affectations, but slipped up on 16 December 1876; the vesture of Miss Ulrick is mentioned on 2 December; the *Deadwood Western Enterprise* spoke of the grand masked ball and its participants on 1 March 1879; the *Pioneer-Times*, 17 December 1905, mentions exclusion of improper persons.

30. The young lady's tale is told in the *Times*, 6 January 1880; the young mother's in the *Pioneer-Times*, 3 October 1905.

31. The great wind is reported in the *Times*, 11 February 1880.

32. The diary of Irene Cushman (Mrs. A. D. Wilson), 1890–91, in the Deadwood Public Library, gives fascinating insights into Deadwood's social life.

33. Dr. Nelson Armstrong, V.S., *Nuggets of Experience* (San Bernardino, Calif.: Times-Mirror P. & B. House, 1906), p. 150; chaps. 11, 12, 13, concern Nelson's trip to Deadwood; the *Daily Times*, 14 July 1880, describes the race meeting from which Armstrong was excluded.

34. I was happy to interview Paul Martin, a college friend of my father's, in the 1970s, at which time his recollections of the trip were still green in his memory.

CHAPTER EIGHT: FÊTES WORSE THAN DEATH

1. Finerty, *War-Path and Bivouac*, pp. 313, 317, 322, describes the liquor generally available in Deadwood.

2. *Black Hills Daily Times*, 4 June 1877; *Pioneer-Times*, 4 June 1877, 19 September 1905.

3. Howe, *Deadwood Doctor*, pp. 26–27; Hebert, *Forty Years*, p. 45; *Times*, 13 February 1880; Zack T. Sutley, *The Last Frontier* (New York: Macmillan Co., 1930), pp. 128–31, tells of a cowboy's adventures visiting a Deadwood bar.

4. 1898 *Directory*, p. 105.

5. McClintock, *Pioneer Days*, pp. 53–67; the Bodega's gambling account books are on display in that famous saloon.

6. Kellar, *Seth Bullock*, p. 78.

7. Bennett, *Old Deadwood Days*, pp. 146–48.

8. Nuttall and Brown advertised in the *Pioneer;* Harry Young, who tended the bar, in *Hard Knocks* spells it "Nuttle"; *Frank Leslie's Illustrated Magazine*, 8 September 1877, describes the cancan and the jokes.

9. *Pioneer*, 23 September 1876; Tallent, *Black Hills*, p. 290.

10. Troy L. Parker was of course my father, and he delighted to tell of his innocence on his first trip to the Hills.

11. Ecker is mentioned in the *Times*, 4 May 1895; Sullivan's advertising is in the *Pioneer-Times*, 3, 24 September 1905, and Green Front advertisements passim; *Belt Cities Directory* (1908) has the slogan.

12. *Pioneer*, 7 April 1877; the new Gem, after the 1879 fire, opened about 1 January 1880, according to the *Times* of that date. McClintock, *Pioneer Days*, pp. 69–71, is highly critical of the Gem.

13. *New York Times*, 4 May 1879, tells of the departure of the sharpers; McClintock, *Pioneer Days*, pp. 66–69, tells of several con men; and Spring, *Cheyenne and Black Hills Stage*, pp. 284–85, quotes the *New York Tribune*, 3 January 1878, regarding Lurline Monte Verde, or Verdi as Collins's 1878 *Directory* lists her.

14. Young, *Hard Knocks*, p. 227 and elsewhere is full of tales of the antics of Deadwood's low characters mentioned in the paragraphs above.

15. Mrs. Erb deserves a biographer; the *Black Hills Central* (Rochford), 22 December 1878; the *Times*, 9 August 1879, 29 September 1880; and Armstrong, *Nuggets of Experience*, pp. 145–46, all mention her.

16. Poker Alice has been frequently written up. Nolie Mumey, *Poker Alice* (Denver, Colo.: Artcraft Press, 1951); and Courtney Riley Cooper, "Easy Come, Easy Go," *Saturday Evening Post*, 3 December 1927, p. 20, are useful. She was a Sturgis citizen, but often a visitor in Deadwood.

17. Joseph G. Rosa, *They Called Him Wild Bill: The Life and Adventures of James Butler Hickok* (Norman: University of Oklahoma Press, 1964, 2d ed. 1974) appears to me to be far and away the most judicious biography of Hickok, about whom the legends swarm.

18. Young, *Hard Knocks*, pp. 214–15, tells of the Montana men, and mentions Hickok's approaching blindness. The death of Wild Bill and the trial of his assassin was reported in the *Pioneer*, 5 August 1876. His epitaph, which varied as headboards and stones were replaced, is variously given.

19. The literature about Calamity Jane is extensive. Her own pamphlet autobiography, for what it's worth, spells her last name "Cannary"; J. Leonard Jennewein, *Calamity Jane of the Western Trails* (Huron: Dakota Books, 1953) is as even-handed an account of her as I know of. Kathryn Wright, "The *Real* Calamity Jane," *True West 5* (November-December 1957): 22 maintains that Jane was married to Wild Bill, but not many historians would agree. Her appearance and conduct in Custer in 1876 are mentioned in Brown and Willard, *Black Hills Trails*, p. 76; her similarity to a busted bale of hay is in Martha Ferguson McKeown's *Them Was the Days: An American Saga of the Seventies* (Lincoln: University of Nebraska Press, 1961), pp. 205–6. The nature of her "calamities" is entirely my own invention, the surmise of an old army medical NCO.

20. Mrs. Drowley's comments are written on the flyleaf of chapter 8 of my copy of Bennett's *Old Deadwood Days*. Warren Morrell's column "Through the Hills" in the 30 April 1956 *Rapid City Journal* comments on her appearance and conduct during the 1893 Columbian Exposition. "D Dee" (Dora Du Fran) is quoted by Senn in his *Calamity Jane* pamphlet in regard to her howling on the streets.

21. A good many of Calamity's biographers try to make out that she died on the anniversary of Wild Bill's death, but this does not seem to be correct. Her account in Jake Goldberg's store was incurred on 10 October 1895, says the *Rapid City Journal*, 11 February 1978.

22. *Times*, 20 January 1880; *Cheyenne Leader*, 11 August 1876; Bourke, *On the Border with Crook*, p. 386; and Finerty, *War-Path and Bivouac*, pp. 319–20, noticed the large number of highly evident harlots.

23. McClintock, *Pioneer Years*, p. 75.

24. Quiett, *Pay Dirt*, p. 252, tells of the jigging match, and p. 251, of

the dark eyes; the *Times*, 18 July 1896, speaks of Annie Carr; the "well known character" is mentioned in the *Times*, 10 January 1880, and the erring husband on 13 January the same year.

25. *Times*, 28 April 1883, quoted in Harold E. Briggs, *Frontiers of the Northwest* (New York: D. Appleton-Century Co., 1940), p. 86; and the *Times* itself, 18 May 1883.

26. *Times*, 13 August 1877; *Pioneer*, 10 February 1877; Bennett, *Old Deadwood Days*, pp. 177–78; *Times*, 1 January 1896, quoted in Lee, *Gold— Gals—Guns—Guts*, p. 171.

27. Bennett, *Old Deadwood Days*, pp. 6, 112; Howe, *Deadwood Doctor*, p. 11.

28. In the summer and fall of 1979 the local Black Hills newspapers had considerable news on a then current attempt to suppress Deadwood's most distinctive industry. By the summer of 1980 the houses were closed.

29. Linus P. Brockett, *Our Western Empire* (Philadelphia, Pa.: Bradley and Co., 1881), p. 772; Nathan Butler manuscript, in B986, Box 1, Minnesota Archives; *Manitowoc Pilot*, 23 August 1877; McKeown, *Them Was the Days*, p. 198; Baldwin, *Black Hills Illustrated*, p. 91; *Times*, 22 March 1883; *New York Times*, 21 June 1878; McClintock, *Pioneer Days*, p. 105.

30. *Black Hills Weekly Times*, 31 May 1879.

31. These miscellaneous crimes were noted by John A. Lammers in "Deadwood, Deadmen, Deadbeats," which covers the 1890s; a copy of this manuscript is in the Deadwood Public Library.

32. A quick riffle through the Deadwood newspapers during the gold-rush days will reveal references to stage robberies in almost every issue; Tallent, *Black Hills*, pp. 385–94, discusses them; the poem on Lame Johnnie's grave is from the *Times*, 27 February 1883.

33. The Cold, or Canyon, Springs holdup is mentioned in every history of the early Hills; my informant about Old Man Griffith phrased his departure: "And then he up and left his whole frightened family [I think "frightened" was the word] standing there and they never seen him again."

34. Lammers, "Deadwood, Deadmen, Deadbeats."

35. WPA, "Annals—Crime," 11 January 1879, p. 10, typescript in the Rapid City Public Library.

36. *Manitowoc Pilot*, 8 March 1877.

37. Bullock, "An Account of Deadwood," p. 347; and Kellar, *Seth Bullock*, are both full of early law and cases of its enforcement.

38. Stokes, *Deadwood Gold*, p. 64; *Times*, 3 February 1880; Kellar, *Seth Bullock*, p. 59; Ryder, *Merrill*, p. 39.

39. Brown and Willard, *Black Hills Trails*, is full of references to lynchings; Gilmore's 1882 execution was rehashed in the *Pioneer-Times*, 17 November 1905, which rejoiced that the rope used to hang him had been discovered in that year.

40. Young, *Hard Knocks*, does not mention Baum's murder, but he does

tell, pp. 232–34, of his association with Slippery Sam; Bennett, *Old Dead-wood Days*, p. 128; and Casey, *The Black Hills*, pp. 151–52, tells of poor Bummer Dan.

41. *Times*, 7 January, 1 February and passim, 1880; Howe, *Deadwood Doctor*, pp. 27–28.

42. Rev. C. B. Clark, "Churches of the Black Hills," in the *Black Hills Illustrated*, comp. Baldwin, p. 67; Samuel Butler, *Hudibras* 1:215; Kingsbury and Smith, *History of Dakota Territory*, vol. 3, chap. 19, deals with the state's tangled temperance movement; Stine, *History of Theatre*, pp. 482–83, deals with lectures given in unused theaters; Bennett, *Old Deadwood Days*, pp. 157–59, tells of Romeo Dwyer's troubles with Sol Star.

43. The *Pioneer-Times* during 1905 is full of the good effects of the abolition of gambling; see 18 July, 9 August for the quotations.

44. Leedy, *Golden Days*, p. 75; his informant regarding pleasure and potations seems to have been Dora du Fran; The Family Liquor Store is condemned in a broadside written by Freeman Knowles entitled "Work for the Grand Jury"; it seems to be from about 1898, and is pasted into a scrap book in the Adams Museum. It condemns the whole town, complaining that "every citizen of Deadwood is a partner in this industry," and it lists by name those many eminent citizens who had petitioned the city fathers to allow the place to stay in business.

CHAPTER NINE: THE VOICE OF THE PEOPLE

1. *Andreas' Atlas*, p. 122; *New York Times*, 23 December 1877.

2. *Pioneer*, 5 August 1876; *Andreas' Atlas*, p. 122; *Cheyenne Daily Leader*, 11 August 1876; Bullock, "An Account of Deadwood," pp. 322–23.

3. *Pioneer*, 28 October 1876.

4. Bullock, "An Account of Deadwood," deals thoroughly with early city government; Kellar, *Seth Bullock*, pp. 77, 109, and passim, has many interesting stories; even the crusty McClintock, in his *Pioneers Days*, p. 166, is generous in his judgment of Bullock.

5. *Cheyenne Daily Leader*, 8 May 1878; and *Times*, 15 June 1878.

6. Baldwin, *Black Hills Illustrated*, p. 11, tells of the idleness of the police and the merits of Mayor Mac.

7. The references to the proposed territory are voluminous: *Harper's Weekly* 20 (23 December 1876): 1031, and 21 (17 November 1877): 899; *New York Times*, 4 February, 22, 23 April, 21 May, 1 June, 13 October 1877, and regarding Absaroka, 13 October 1935; *Cheyenne Daily Leader*, 19 January, 22 April 1877, 4 April 1878; *Black Hills Daily Times*, 9 April, 22 April, 23 April, 21 May, 14 August 1877; U.S., Congress, Senate, *Congressional Record*, 1877–79; Rosen, *Pa-Ha-Sa-Pah*, pp. 422–25, gives a summary which most scholars have since relied upon. Professor C. M. Rowe of the South

Dakota School of Mines appears to have been a leader in the Absaroka movement, and showed me an automobile license plate which he had had struck off for the occasion.

8. Kellar, *Seth Bullock*, pp. 62–63.

9. *Times*, 22 May 1877; Kingsbury and Smith, *History of Dakota Territory*, 1:981–82.

10. *Andreas' Atlas*, p. 213; Bennett, *Old Deadwood Days*, p. 38 and passim; *New York Times*, 8 August 1878; *Black Hills Weekly Times*, during June 1878, lists many charges made against Bennett, and comes to his support against them.

11. *Times*, 14 July 1877; Kellar, *Seth Bullock*, pp. 80, 101.

12. *Pioneer*, 28 October 1876; *Times*, 12 January 1883.

13. *Pioneer-Times*, 5 November 1905.

14. *Pioneer*, 30 December 1876; The Deadwood Pioneer Hook and Ladder Company No. 1 Secretary's record book is in the Adams Museum. Articles in the *Times*, 20, 23, 26 June 1877, tell of its founding.

15. *Times*, 7 May 1880; incendiarism is mentioned on 9 December; the new hook and ladder house on 13 March; the various fire companies are listed in detail in the 1898 *Directory* on p. 11.

16. Every history of early Deadwood tells of the great fire of 1879. The late September newspapers of course give the details, and *Harper's Weekly* 23 (18 October 1879): 827, has a summary. Langrishe's remark is from Bennett, *Old Deadwood Days*, p. 121.

17. Pamphlet, *Twin City–Black Hills Railway* (1896), contains Selbie's letter.

18. Baldwin, *Black Hills Illustrated*, pp. 5–7.

19. *Pioneer*, 16 December 1877; *New York Times*, 21 May 1878; a diligent search has not brought to light any further news of the depressed diarist.

20. Rogers' ad is in the *Pioneer-Times*, 16 July 1905.

21. Deadwood's transformation is mentioned in the Deadwood Business Club's *Deadwood of Today* (1903); most of these promotional pamphlets can be found in either the Adams Museum or the archives of the South Dakota State Historical Society at Pierre.

22. *Times*, 14 January 1883.

23. Deadwood Board of Trade, *Deadwood, Metropolis of the Black Hills* (1892).

24. Ibid.; Baldwin, *Black Hills Illustrated*, pp. 15–17.

25. *Cheyenne Daily Leader*, 4 April 1876, speaks of Carpenter; 13 April mentions the valuable assay, and 10 December speaks of Smokey Jones's promotional activities in Chicago. Stokes's load of ore is mentioned in the *Leader*, 16 November, and in Stokes's own *Deadwood Gold*, pp. 94–99.

26. Bennett, *Old Deadwood Days*, pp. 290–91.

27. Lee, *Gold—Gals—Guns—Guts*, p. 4; *The Black Hills Engineer* (May 1926) contains an advertisement for Camp Jubilee.

28. Brochure, *Days of '76* (1927?); the program in the *Days of '76 Historical Pageant of Deadwood, South Dakota, August 5, 1927* (Fostoria, Ohio: John B. Rogers Producing Co., [1927]), gives the detailed description of this spectacle. A similar pageant, *Gold Discovery Days*, is still presented each summer in Custer, sixty miles to the south.

29. Coolidge was actually denominated something like "Chief Leading Eagle"; Potato Creek Johnny was in the news pretty regularly in the Hills newspapers; Mildred Fielder's pamphlet *John E. Perrett* (Lead: Bonanza Trail Publications, 1973) is a brief account of him.

30. Deadwood Business Club, *Deadwood of Today* (1903): the many Black Hills promotional pamphlets issued by both the Burlington and the North Western railroads would make an interesting study; Deadwood Business Club, *Souvenir Book of Deadwood* (Deadwood: Pioneer Times, 1915) urges summer travel; and the same organization's *Deadwood: What to See and How to See It* (n.d., [after 1919]) lists suitable trips around the town, and tells of the city's campground.

31. McKelvie's 1927 Christmas booklet, *By the Way—III*, is a fifty-four-page illustrated account of Coolidge's visit to his Squaw Creek cabin; only its foundations now remain. The *Days of '76* (promotional brochure of 1927) tells of Coolidge in the Hills; Howe, *Deadwood Doctor*, p. 61, tells of Coolidge's summary of the sermon, but I would judge that the tale is also attributed to other places.

32. No one ever stops to consider that when Deadwood really was the mining camp that local businesses are trying to recreate, its boards and buildings were not old and weathered but bright and new, but so deeply is the notion embedded in the public mind that a replica of something old must *look* old that I suppose this anachronism will never be rectified.

Selected Bibliography

BIBLIOGRAPHIES AND INDEXES

I have not tried, in this bibliography, to provide an exhaustive listing of all of the sources of Deadwood's plentiful history, or even to reiterate each of the sources mentioned in footnotes dealing with specific topics. Instead, this bibliography mentions those sources which seem most likely to be of use or interest to the reader, or which would fill in the gaps which a study of the standard sources on the Hills reveals. This abbreviation is both possible and desirable because the many writings on the history of Deadwood and the Black Hills have already been well recorded, and there is no need to list them here in profuse detail, for a glance at the various bibliographies available can direct the student wherever his interests lie. Cleophas Cisney O'Harra's *Bibliography of the Geology and Mining Interests of the Black Hills Region*, South Dakota School of Mines Bulletin no. 11 (Rapid City, May 1917) and Joseph Slouber's *Index for Bulletin 11* (Rapid City: South Dakota School of Mines, n.d.) provide a scientifically oriented guide to Black Hills books. Willard L. Roberts and George Rapp, Jr's. bibliography in their *Mineralogy of the Black Hills*, South Dakota School of Mines and Technology Bulletin no. 18 (Rapid City, 1965) provides an alphabetical updating of O'Harra's chronological *Bibliography*. *Master, Professional, and Senior Theses and Class Reports, 1904–1965* (Rapid City: South Dakota School of Mines and Technology, 1966) extends the two above works to include less formally published items. The bibliography of J. Leonard Jennewein and Jane Boorman's *Dakota Panorama* (Pierre: Dakota Territory Centennial Commission, 1961) is an extensive listing of Dakota materials, and Jennewein's own *Black Hills Booktrails* (Mitchell: Dakota Territory Centennial Commission and Dakota Wesleyan University, 1962) tells the history of the Black Hills through a chronological listing of books written about them, an effort which was extended to include both periodicals and books in Watson Parker's "Black Hills Bibliography," South Dakota State Historical Society, *Collections* 35 (1970):169–301. Charles Tank and Watson Parker's *Bits and Pieces: A Cross-Referenced Index of Volumes 1–11 for the Years 1966*

Through 1977 (Spearfish: Friends of the Leland D. Case Library for Western Historical Studies, Black Hills State College, 1979) provides easy access to the many Black Hills articles in that Newcastle, Wyoming, periodical. *The Checklist of South Dakota Newspapers in the South Dakota State Historical Society* (Pierre, 1976) is a helpful guide to available newspaper sources.

GENERAL BLACK HILLS HISTORIES

The classic account of the first twenty-five years of Black Hills history is Annie Donna Fraser Tallent's *The Black Hills; or, The Last Hunting Grounds of the Dakotahs* (Saint Louis, Mo.: Nixon-Jones Printing Company, 1899); republished (Sioux Falls: the Brevet Press, 1974) with the addition of a much-needed index. Mrs. Tallent was a member of the 1874 Gordon party which built its stockade near Custer, and she lived in the Hills thereafter, teaching and writing with quiet dignity. Her book leans somewhat upon the Reverend Peter Rosen's *Pa-Ha-Sa-Pah; or, The Black Hills of Dakota* (Saint Louis, Mo.: Nixon-Jones Printing Co., 1895), which contains much extraneous and legendary material, and which in its turn leans rather heavily upon the historical portions of A. T. Andreas's *Andreas' Historical Atlas of Dakota* (Chicago: A. T. Andreas, 1884), the latter being one of the major secondary sources of early Hills history. George W. Kingsbury and George Martin Smith's five-volume *History of Dakota Territory* (Chicago: S. J. Clarke Publishing Co., 1915) contains much primary quoted material of value for the study of the Hills and of the gold rush to Deadwood. Jesse Brown and A. M. Willard's *Black Hills Trails: A History of the Struggles of the Pioneers* (Rapid City: Rapid City Journal Co., 1924) is a compilation of recollections of both the authors and many others, and deals extensively with holdups, massacres, and lively doings, both of the compilers having been stagecoach guards in the early days. John S. McClintock's *Pioneer Days in the Black Hills: Accurate History and Facts, Related by One of the Early Day Pioneers*, edited by Edward L. Senn (New York: John S. McClintock, 1939) is sceptical about many of the marvels related by earlier Hills historians, and equally critical of the wayward ways of many of his fellow townsmen in the north, or lively, end of Deadwood. Robert J. Casey's *The Black Hills and Their Incredible Characters* (Indianapolis: Bobbs-Merrill Company,

1949) is a combination history and guidebook, told by a gifted writer who spent his early years in Rapid City around the turn of the century. The Federal Writers' Project, the Works Progress Administration's *South Dakota Guide* (Pierre: State Publishing Company, 1938) was reprinted in 1952 (New York: Hastings House) and is a fertile source of lore, fact, and legend, and provides much useful background for a visit not only to Deadwood but to the area around it. Herbert S. Schell's *History of South Dakota* (Lincoln: University of Nebraska Press, 1961) and subsequently issued in a new edition (1975), similarly provides not only Black Hills history but the state background needed to fully understand it. Leland D. Case's *Lee's Official Guide Book to the Black Hills and Badlands* (Sturgis: Black Hills and Badlands Association, 1949, 1952) is an invaluable tour guide to the whole Hills, relating the tales, histories, and legends which adorn each mile of their highways. Bob Lee, who edited *Gold—Gals—Guns—Guts* (Deadwood: Deadwood-Lead Centennial, 1976) and those who worked with him on this outstanding project have provided a delightful illustrated history of the major towns of the northern Hills, and one which future scholars will use extensively.

CHAPTER ONE: HOPE IN THE MOUNTAINS

The story of the Black Hills' exploration is well told, I have always believed, in Watson Parker's "The Exploration of the Dakota Black Hills" (M.A. thesis, University of Oklahoma, 1962). Cleophas Cisney O'Harra's "A History of the Early Exploration of the Black Hills," in the South Dakota School of Mines, *Bulletin*, no. 4 (ca. 1900) is even more reliable. C. C. Beckwith's "Early Settlements in the Black Hills, 1874–1884" (Ph.D. diss., University of Michigan, 1937) is a broadly conceived treatment of its topic, and is equally useful in its coverage of the gold rush and early hardrock mining days. Lt. Gouverneur Kemble Warren's *Explorations in the Dacota Country in the Year 1855* (Washington, D.C.: Government Printing Office, 1856) covers the Black Hills exploration of this famous mapmaker of the West. LeRoy R. and Ann W. Hafen's *Powder River Campaigns and Sawyers Expedition of 1865* (Glendale, Calif.: Arthur H. Clark Co., 1961) tells the story of Colonels Cole, Walker, and Sawyers, whose commands variously encircled the Black Hills and provided knowledge of the trails by which they could be reached to two or three thousand soldiers. The literature of Custer's 1874 expedition to the Black Hills is extensive. "The Black Hills Expedition," in *Harper's Weekly* (12 September 1874), p. 753, is one of many widely read contemporary accounts. Capt. William Ludlow's *Report of a Reconnaissance of the Black Hills of Dakota* (Washington, D.C.: Government Printing Office, 1875) is the official report; Herbert Krause and Gary D. Olson's *Prelude to Glory: A Newspaper Accounting of Custer's 1874 Expedition to the Black Hills* (Sioux Falls: Brevet Press, 1974) will be useful to the student and enthusiast alike. Pvt. Theodore Ewert's *Diary of the Black Hills Expedition of 1874*, ed. John M. Carroll and Lawrence A. Frost (Piscataway, N.J.: Consultant Resources Incorporated, 1976) and Lawrence A. Frost's *With Custer in '74: James Calhoun's Diary of the Black Hills Expedition* (Provo, Utah: Brigham Young University Press, 1979) are two recent additions to the primary literature of the Custer expedition. The 1875 expedition of Col. Richard Irving Dodge and Walter P. Jenney is described in Dodge's *The Black Hills* (New York: James Miller, 1876) and in Jenney's *The Mineral Wealth, Climate, Rainfall, and Natural Resources of the Black Hills of Dakota* (Washington, D.C.: Government Printing Office, 1876), the latter being expanded in 1880 into Henry Newton and Walter P. Jenney's *Report on the Geology and Resources of the Black Hills of Dakota, with Atlas* (Washington, D.C.: Government Printing Office).

The early days of the 1874–80 gold rush to the Hills have been repeatedly described by participants. David Aken's *Pioneers of the Black Hills; or, Gordon's Stockade Party of 1874* (Milwaukee, [1920?]) is a firsthand account, as is that of Annie Tallent, mentioned earlier. T. H. Russell's *The Russell-Collins 1874 Gold Expedition to the Black Hills* (facsimile reprint, Don Clowser: Deadwood, 1974) seems to be Russell's own recollections of the inception of the expedition, but repeats word for word Annie Tallent's description of the expedition in the Hills, and I have not been able to determine which of them copied from the other. Richard B. Hughes's *Pioneer Years in the Black Hills*, ed. Agnes Wright Spring (Glendale, Calif.: Arthur H. Clark Co., 1957) was written in his elderly but active years by a pioneer prospector and newspaperman and is highly readable, for Hughes had an eye for a good story and well knew how to tell one. George W. Stokes and Howard R. Driggs's *Deadwood Gold: A Story of the Black Hills* (Chicago: World Book Co., 1926) is the first-person account of Stokes's activities as a Deadwood prospector, merchant, and newspaper reporter. Jerry Bryan's *An Illinois Gold Hunter in the Black Hills*, introd. and notes by Clyde C. Walton (Springfield: Illinois State Historical Society, 1960) shows how much pith can be packed into a few words when they are written on the spot, and Martha Ferguson McKeown's *Them Was the Days: An American Saga of the Seventies* (Lincoln: University of Nebraska Press, 1961) is the story of her uncle, Mont Hawthorne, who as a youth joined the gold rush in 1876. James E. Smith's *A Famous Battery* (Washington, D.C.: W. H. Lowdermilk and Co., 1892) contains a little-known section, "Early Days in the Black Hills," which, if inaccurate, is at least interesting. Frank Hebert's *Forty Years Prospecting and Mining in the Black Hills of South Dakota* (Rapid City: Rapid City Daily Journal, 1921) is about as close as you can get to the genuine recollections of an unlettered but determined miner, and the papers of Nathan Butler, B986, Bx1, Minnesota State Archives at the Minnesota Historical Society in Minneapolis, tell of a trip to the gold rush in 1876 or '77. Zack Sutley's *The Last Frontier* (New York: Macmillan Co., 1930) tells of visits to the gold camps, and all of these accounts are but representative examples of the many others which are available.

Watson Parker's *Gold in the Black Hills* (Norman: University of Oklahoma Press, 1966) is a history of the rush from 1874 through 1879, when the great Deadwood fire burned the mining camp and let it rebuild as a city. Glenn Chesney Quiett's *Pay Dirt: A Panorama of American Gold Rushes* (New York: D. Appleton-Century Co., 1936) relied heavily on the pungent articles in the *Deadwood Daily Times* to enliven its already lively tales. Harold E. Briggs's "The Black Hills Gold Rush" in the *North Dakota Historical Quarterly* 5 (January 1931): 71–99, is a convenient brief account. William S. Greever's *The Bonanza West: The Story of Western Mining Rushes, 1848–1900* (Norman: University of Oklahoma Press, 1963) and Rodman Paul's *Mining Frontiers of the Far West, 1848–1880* (New York: Holt, Rinehart and Winston, 1963) both give useful summaries of the rush and boom in the Black Hills. Lawrence R. Olson's "The Mining Frontier of South Dakota, 1874–1877" (M.A. thesis, State University of Iowa, 1931) is valuable, as is Beckwith's dissertation which has already been mentioned. Linus P. Brockett's *Our Western Empire* (Philadelphia: Bradley and Co., 1881) has an extremely useful section on the Hills, and Russell Arthur Gibbs's "The Gold Boom in the Black Hills" (M.A. thesis, University of Nebraska, 1932) is well worth looking into.

The promotional material written and published during the years of the rush casts a bright, indeed a lurid, light upon the history of those gaudy times. *The Black Hills Bulletin* of the Wright expedition, published apparently in at least two volumes of more than one number each during 1875 and 1876, was certainly optimistic. Franklin Wixson's *The Black Hills Gold Mines: A Book for the Times* (Yankton: Taylor Brothers, 1875); J. E. Triggs's *History of Cheyenne and Northern Wyoming* (Omaha, Nebr.: Herald Steam Book and Job Printing House, 1876); H. N. Maguire's *The Black Hills and American Wonderland*, The Lakeside Library, 4th ser., no. 82 (Chicago: Donnelly, Loyd and Co., 1877); Maguire's *The Coming Empire* (Sioux City, Iowa: Watkins and Smead, 1878); Edwin A. Curley's *Guide to the Black Hills* (Chicago: privately published, 1877; facsimile reprint, ed. and introd. James D. McLaird and Lesta V. Turchen, Mitchell: Dakota Wesleyan University Press, 1973); and Robert E. Strahorn's *To the Rockies and Beyond* (Omaha, Nebr.: Omaha Republican, 1878) are all examples, more of which may be found in Jennewein's *Black Hills Booktrails*, of the promotional excesses which brought the prospectors to the Hills.

Newspapers of gold rush times which are particularly useful are the *Cheyenne Daily Leader*, the *Yankton Press and Dakotaian*, the *Black Hills Pioneer*, the *Deadwood Daily Times*, the *Rapid City Daily Journal*, and the well-indexed *New York Times*. Gold rush items, however, may be located, usually by accident, in any newspaper located in a town which sent miners to the Hills and received letters back from them; items in the *Oshkosh* (Wisconsin) *Northwestern* and the *Manitowoc* (Wisconsin) *Pilot* are merely examples which came to my attention.

CHAPTER TWO: UNGODLY MILLS

The student of Western mining would do well to begin with Otis E. Young, Jr.'s *Western Mining: An Informal Account of Precious-Metals Prospecting, Placering, Lode Mining, and Milling on the American Frontier from Spanish Times to 1893* (Norman: University of Oklahoma Press, 1970), a masterful and well-written compendium of mineralogical lore and information. The pages of the *Engineering and Mining Journal*, a publication which spans the entire period of Black Hills mining, are full of interesting promotions and condemnations of

Black Hills mineral prospects and efforts and have for the most part been ignored by Black Hills scholars. G. Thomas Ingham's *Digging Gold Among the Rockies* (Philadelphia: Cottage Library Publishing House, 1881) is one of those ponderously subtitled surveys so popular in Victorian times; its pages 167–218 deal extensively with the hardrock mining of the Black Hills. H. N. Maguire's *Black Hills Exposition Offering* (n.p., [1882?]), a four-page tabloid newspaper, is typical of the general hardrock promotional efforts of the area and provides an optimistic background for a study of the mines of its time. H. O. Hofman's "Notes on Gold Milling in the Black Hills," the South Dakota School of Mines, *Bulletin* (1888), pp. 80–105 gives useful technical details, and the closely packed "Dakota," in *Report of the Director of the Mint upon the Statistics of the Production of the Precious Metals* (Washington, D.C.: Government Printing Office, 1883) pp. 596–618, usefully surveys the early Black Hills mines. Two examples of the prospectuses of the early mines are the *Prospectus of the Black Hills Placer Mining Company* (Dakota, 1879), and the *Prospectus* of the Cheyenne Gold Mining Company (New York: Mining Record Press, 1879). Both appear to be unduly optimistic, as was the custom in those untrammeled times. Many of the sources listed under the cyanide books (Chapter 5) will also be of interest to the student of the earlier hardrock booms of the 1870s and '80s.

The literature of the Indians and the Black Hills is so extensive as to defy even abbreviation. For the years of the Black Hills gold rush the annual *Report of the Commissioner of Indian Affairs* (Washington: Government Printing Office) is of course invaluable, as is C. J. Kappler's *Indian Affairs: Laws and Treaties*, 2 vols. (Washington, D.C., 1904), for it is simply astonishing to see the number of historians who talk of "broken treaties" without ever having read the documents in question in their entirety. The *Reports* of the secretary of war are similarly valuable in presenting the little-known picture of ongoing warfare on the Plains. Mark H. Brown's controversial "A New Focus on the Sioux War" in *Montana* 11 (Autumn 1961): 76–85, lays the blame for the Sioux War of 1876 upon the Indians, and Watson Parker's "The Majors and the Miners: The Role of the U.S. Army in the Black Hills Gold Rush," in the *Journal of the West* 11 (January 1972): 99–111, endeavors to give a balanced account of both sides of the question. The books of three correspondents who accompanied Gen. George Crook on his 1876 military expedition which ended in the Black Hills provide not only a military account of the campaign but an informed and on the whole accurate description of the early days of the mining camps of the area: John G. Bourke's *On the Border With Crook* (New York: Charles Scribner's Sons, 1892); Capt. Charles King, *Campaigning with Crook* (Norman: University of Oklahoma Press, 1964); and John F. Finerty's *War-Path and Bivouac: The Big Horn and Yellowstone Expedition*, ed. and introd. Milo Milton Quaife (Lincoln: University of Nebraska Press, 1966; a reissue of the Lakeside Press 1955 edition). A recent account of the events leading up to the Battle of Wounded Knee in 1890 is Rex Alan Smith's *Moon of Popping Trees* (New York: Reader's Digest Press, 1975), and his bibliography provides a guide to many of the more significant books written about this tragedy. The last Indian battle in the Black Hills area, "The Lightning Creek Fight" of 1903, is given a modern interpretation by Barton R. Voight in "The Lightning Creek Fight," *Annals of Wyoming* 49, no. 1 (Spring 1977): 5–21, and a more traditional description is provided by Ernest M. Richardson in his pamphlet *The Battle of Lightning Creek* (Pacific Palisades, California: privately published, 1956).

CHAPTERS THREE AND FOUR:
DUST IN THE BALANCE and THE PROFESSIONAL MEN

The story of Deadwood's business and professions during the days when gold dust was the little city's circulating medium is much less thoroughly covered than are the mining excitements, and much of the business history of the town must be extracted piecemeal from the general histories already mentioned. A major source is banker Robert E. Driscoll's *Seventy Years of Banking in the Black Hills* (Rapid City: First National Bank of the Black Hills, 1948), his pamphlet *The Black Hills of South Dakota: Its Pioneer Banking History* (New York: The Newcomen Society in North America, 1951), and *Diary of a Country Banker*, (New York: Vantage Press, 1960). The writings of Baron E. de Mandat-Grancey *Brèche aux Buffles* [Buffalo Gap] (Paris: E. Plon, Nourrit et Cie, 1889) and *Dans les Montagnes Rocheuses* (Paris: E. Plon, Nourrit et Cie, 1884), translated by William Conn as *Cow-Boys and Colonels* (New York: E. P. Dutton & Co., 1887) include mention of vivid trips to the fleshpots of early Deadwood. Of much use in determining what Deadwood thought about itself are the Deadwood Board of Trade's frequent pamphlets, including *The*

Black Hills of Dakota (Deadwood: Daily Pioneer Book & Job Office, 1881) and *Deadwood, Metropolis of the Black Hills* (Deadwood: 1892), combined with other promotional materials like the anonymous *The Black Hills: America's Land of Minerals* (Omaha, Nebr.: Herald Job Printing Room, 1889) and government publications like A. F. McClure's "Dakota," House Executive Document no. 6, 51st Cong., 1st sess., vol. 23, 1889, part 2, ser. 2738, which appears to have been printed in aid of obtaining statehood for North and South Dakota and consequently is elaborate in its praise of both these areas. Douglas Crawford McMurtrie's *Early Printing in Wyoming and the Black Hills* (Hattiesburg, Miss.: the Book Farm, 1943) is an excellent history of newspapers, and the many publications of the Forest Service of the U.S. Department of Agriculture are typified by the pamphlet *Black Hills National Forest Fiftieth Anniversary* (n.p., September 1948). Bob Lee and Dick Williams' *Last Grass Frontier: The South Dakota Stock Grower Heritage* (Sturgis: Black Hills Publishers, 1964) is outstanding on the cattle industry, which provided at least some of the money ultimately spent in Deadwood's places of edification and entertainment.

The literature of Black Hills transportation is extensive. Hyman Palais's "A Study of the Trails to the Black Hills Gold Fields" in the South Dakota State Historical Society, *Collections* 25 (1951): 212–64, is thorough and scholarly. Agnes Wright Spring's *Cheyenne and Black Hills Stage and Express Routes* (Glendale, Calif.: Arthur H. Clark Co., 1949) contains innumerable useful anecdotes, and Irma H. Klock's *All Roads Lead to Deadwood* (Aberdeen: North Plain Press, 1979) is an extremely able survey of the entire stage trail and station picture. Richard C. Overton's *Burlington Route: A History of the Burlington Lines* (New York: Alfred A. Knopf, 1965) tells the story of one of the national railroads which was extensively involved with the Black Hills. Mildred Fielder's "Railroads of the Black Hills," South Dakota State Historical Society, *Collections* 30 (1960): 35–316, and her illustrated *Railroads of the Black Hills* (Seattle, Wash.: Superior Publishing Co., 1964) will be of great help to the railroad buff who is interested in following the old lines either on the page or in the timber. The *Annual Register of the United States* from about 1877 to 1911 lists by counties the post offices of the Black Hills areas of both Wyoming and Dakota; George H. Phillips's *The Post Offices of South Dakota, 1861–1930* (Crete, Nebr.: J-B Publishing Company, 1975) and Daniel Meschter and Ruth Dolezal's "The Post Offices of Wyoming" in *La Posta* 4, no. 5 (March 1973): 10–15, provide excellent insights into the often transient postal facilities of the Hills.

The various city directories of the Black Hills, but especially Charles Collins's *Collins' History and Directory of the Black Hills* (Central City, 1878) are invaluable in any study of Deadwood's business and population, and Collins's history of the opening of the Hills is a great aid to any student. The historical section of *Andreas' Atlas* gives many thumbnail sketches of Deadwood's businessmen of the early 1880s, and partially fills the gap between Collins's and subsequent directories, which include the *Black Hills Residence and Business Directory* (Deadwood: Enterprise Printing Co., 1898); Charles W. Sherman's *Black Hills Belt Cities Directory* (the mining towns of the northern Black Hills were assumed to lie pretty much along a single mineral belt) (Lead: Charles W. Sherman, 1902); and the *Belt Cities Directory* (Deadwood: Deadwood Daily Telegram, 1908). All of these directories include not only names and businesses, but societies, churches, and at least some local history. Kenneth C. Kellar's *Seth Bulloch: Frontier Marshal* (Aberdeen: North Plains Press, 1972) and *Chambers Kellar: Distinguished Gentleman, Great Lawyer, Fiery Rebel* (Lead: Seaton Publishing Co., 1975) deal with two of Deadwood's notable leaders. Frank G. Lydston's *Trusty Five-Fifteen* (Kansas City, Mo.: Burton Publishing Co., 1921) is an extraordinary novel, the last half of which tells of a Deadwood lawyer, though it appears to be more based upon the dime novels of an earlier age than upon much personal experience in the Black Hills, and I wish that I knew more about its origin.

CHAPTER FIVE: A BOOM IN CYANIDE

Charles Washington Merrill, described by David W. Ryder in *The Merrill Story* (n.p., The Merrill Co., 1958) was the founder of the cyanide process in the Black Hills. Charles H. Fulton, "The Cyanide Process," South Dakota School of Mines *Bulletin*, no. 5 (February 1902), pp. 15–87, is a contemporary description, and may be augmented with the *Papers Read Before the Monthly Meetings* of the Black Hills Mining Men's Association (1904). Essential to a study of Deadwood at the turn of the century is the Black Hills Mining Men's Association's, George P. Baldwin, comp., *The Black Hills Illustrated: A Terse Description of Conditions Past and Present of America's*

Greatest Mineral Belt (n.p., privately published by the Association, 1904). It has been excellently reprinted by Deadwood Graphics, 1978. Jesse Simmons's *Gold Mines in the Black Hills* (Deadwood: privately published, 1904) is an excellent example of the promotion of the cyanide prospects of the times. Francis Church Lincoln et al., *The Mining Industry of South Dakota*, South Dakota School of Mines Bulletin, no. 17 (February 1937) is valuable, but in part has been superseded by the Bureau of Mines, U.S. Department of the Interior's *Black Hills Mineral Atlas* part 1, Information Circular 7688, July 1954 (covering the northern Black Hills) and part 2, Information Circular 7707, May 1955 (covering the southern), both sections compiled by Professor Paul Gries of the South Dakota School of Mines and Technology, who assures me that one day his further researches will result in a new and expanded edition of this invaluable aid.

The more-or-less biennial *Report*s of the state inspector of mines for the state of South Dakota are available from 1893 if not earlier, and not only describe the mines and their production but deal extensively with accidents and working conditions. Joseph H. Cash's "History of Lead" in the South Dakota State Historical Society, *Collections* 34 (1968): 33–141, is extremely useful for the town and the Homestake Mine's influence upon it, as is his history of labor in that great mine, *Working the Homestake* (Ames: Iowa State University Press, 1973). Various histories of the Homestake itself are available, the earliest being that of Moses Manuel, one of its founders, as dictated to Mary Sheriff, "Forty-Eight Years in the West," typescript in the Homestake Library at Lead. Emma George Myron's "A History of the Homestake Mine" (M.A. thesis, University of South Dakota, 1928) is a formal study. Mildred Fielder's *The Treasure of Homestake Gold* (Aberdeen: North Plains Press, 1970) used many company sources, and the Homestake Mine's own employee magazine, *Sharp Bits*, comprises an illustrated history of the entire Black Hills area, published from 1950 through 1970.

C. L. Fuller's *Pocket Map and Descriptive Outline History Accompanied by a Compendium of Statistics of the Black Hills of Dakota and Wyoming* (Rapid City: Black Hills Bed Spring Co., 1887) is a useful summary of the hardrock mines, and the Burlington Route's *Mines and Mining in the Black Hills* (n.p., n.d., [ca. 1904]) deals with the mines which came into prominence during the cyanide boom. William Turrentine Jackson's "Dakota Tin: British Investors at Harney

Peak, 1880–1900" in *North Dakota History* 33 (Winter 1966): 22–63 deals with the abortive tin boom in the Hills. The ghost towns of the Deadwood area, many of which arose from mineral activities, are covered in Watson Parker and Hugh K. Lambert's *Black Hills Ghost Towns* (Chicago: Swallow Press, 1974; reprint, Athens: Ohio University Press, 1980) and in further detail in Irma H. Klock's more geographically restricted *Yesterday's Gold Camps and Mines in the Northern Black Hills* (Lead: Seaton Publishing Co., 1975).

CHAPTER SIX: REFRACTORY ORE

The social history of Deadwood, like much of its business history, must be gathered from the newspapers or inferred from the kind of sources which have already been mentioned. The diary of Irene Cushman (Mrs. A. D. Wilson), 1890–91, has been typed and made available at the Deadwood Public Library by Mrs. Cushman Clark and gives more insight into the society of its time than an historian has any right to expect. Raymond Auzias-Turenne's *Cow-Boy* (Paris: Calmann-Levey, 1896) mentions, as does Mandat-Grancey, visits to Deadwood in its early days. Various books of photographs are helpful in visualizing the life of the city and the area around it: the Reverend John I. Sanford's *Black Hills Souvenir* (Denver, Colo.: Williamson-Haffner Engraving Co., n.d. [1902?]); the *Souvenir of Lead: Black Hills Metropolis* (Lead: J. E. Meddaugh, 1892); *Black Hills Views* (Deadwood: Peterson and Carwile, n.d. [ca. 1907]) are early examples, and Cleophas Cisney O'Harra's *O'Harra's Handbook of the Black Hills* (Rapid City: Black Hills Handbook Co., 1913; rev. ed. 1927) shows the trends in the taste and appearance of the area. Alvin W. Josephy, Jr., *Black Hills, White Sky: Photographs from the Collection of the Arvada Center Foundation, Inc.* (New York: Times Books, 1978) contains splendid reproductions of photographs taken in the Black Hills from 1886 to 1915. Estelline Bennett's *Old Deadwood Days* (New York: J. H. Sears and Co., 1928) is a classic account of a childhood in Deadwood before the railroads reached the town. It is packed with both personal recollections and anecdotes of Deadwood's turbulent society, both high and low, and it has influenced Deadwood's image of itself perhaps more than any other book available. Carl Leedy's *Golden Days in the Black Hills* (Rapid City: Holmgren's, 1961), reissued as *Black Hills Pioneer Stories*, ed. Mildred Fielder

(Bonanza Trails Publications: Lead, 1973), is a splendid collection of legend, hearsay, and personal observation by an old-timer. Mel Williams's "Tales of the Black Hills" in the Chicago Westerners' *Brand Book* 23 (June 1966): 25, is another collection of Hills anecdotes collected by an expert, and Bob Lee's *Gold—Gals—Guns—Guts*, already mentioned as one of the basic books of northern Hills history, is similarly full of stories useful to the historian of society.

Patricia Lavier Mechling's "Blanche Colman and the Pioneer Jewish Community of Deadwood," in *Black Hills Nuggets* 12 (May 1979): 127–29 is one of the very few studies of this ethnic group in the Black Hills. Mildred Fielder's pamphlet *The Chinese in the Black Hills* (Lead: Bonanza Trails Publishers, 1972); Grant K. Anderson's "Deadwood's Chinatown" in *South Dakota History* 4 (Summer 1975): 266–85; and Joe Sulentic's *Deadwood Gulch: The Last Chinatown* (Deadwood: Deadwood Gulch Art Gallery, 1975), all deal briefly with Deadwood's Chinese population, and a quick riffle through the Deadwood newspapers will reveal additional stories in almost every issue. A demographic sampling of the 1880 U.S. census of Lawrence County, done at the College of Wooster, by Rebecca Ellen Parker, reveals a good deal about the mobility of their mining population, and reference to both Tallent and Rosen, previously mentioned, will show much about the social structure of the community.

CHAPTER SEVEN: A SOCIABLE PEOPLE

As previously mentioned, the city directories of Deadwood provide a useful guide to the various churches, societies, lodges, and social organizations of the city. Leland D. Case's pamphlet *Preacher Smith, Martyr* (n.p., Preacher Smith Memorial Association, 1929) and Edward L. Senn's booklet *Preacher Smith, Martyr of the Cross* (Deadwood: privately published, 1939) both describe the ministry and death of Deadwood's pioneer religious leader. *Steeples Above the Stopes: The Churches in the Gold Camps, 1876–1976* (n.p.: Deadwood-Lead '76 Centennial, 1976) provides brief sketches of churches in the northern Hills. The *Black Hills Illustrated* also has a section on churches, and the local newspapers habitually published news of them, and especially of their many social events and festivities. Irene Cushman's (Mrs. A. D. Wilson) diary, already mentioned, describes activities in these myriad organizations and their place in

everyday life during the early 1890s. Minute books of various organizations are in the Adams Museum in Deadwood, and the minutes
of the Society of Black Hills Pioneers are also available to show the
strong historical inclination of the community from its early days
onward. The *Constitution and By-Laws of the Society of Black Hills Pioneers, together with a Roll of Members* (Deadwood: Times Job Printing
House, 1891) describes not only the organization, but the dates of
birth and nationalities of the members, and is thus a resource for the
analysis of Deadwood's pre-1879 population. The place of the theater in Deadwood's social life is described in Henriette Naeseth's
"Drama in Early Deadwood, 1876–1879," *American Literature* 10
(November 1938): 289–312, and in excellent and scholarly detail in
Lawrence Carl Stine's "A History of Theatre and Theatrical Activi-
ties in Deadwood, South Dakota, 1876–90" (Ph.D. diss., State
University of Iowa, 1962).

CHAPTER EIGHT: FÊTES WORSE THAN DEATH

The literature of Deadwood's wild life is extensive and unreliable.
Bennett, McClintock, Brown and Willard, and Tallent, and others
already mentioned, deal with it to some extent, and with evident
distaste. "Judge" William Littlebury Kuykendall's *Frontier Days: A
True Narrative of Striking Events on the Western Frontier* (n.p.: J. M.
and H. L. Kuykendall, 1917) is the account of the man who presided over the trial of Jack McCall for the killing of Wild Bill
Hickok. George Ward Nichols [GWN] in an article, "Wild Bill," in
Harpers New Monthly Magazine 34 (February 1867): 273–85, did
much to get the Wild Bill legend off to a good start. Joseph G. Rosa's
*They Called Him Wild Bill: The Life and Adventures of James Butler
Hickok* (Norman: University of Oklahoma Press, 1964; 1974) has
always appeared to me to be the most trustworthy account of this
frontier fighting man. Mildred Fielder's *Wild Bill and Deadwood* (Se-
attle, Wash.: Superior Publishing Co., 1965) is profusely illustrated.
About the only easily available contemporary account of low life in
Deadwood's badlands is that of Harry "Sam" Young, whose *Hard
Knocks: A Life Story of the Vanishing West* (Chicago: Laird and Lee,
1915) which is both inaccurate in detail and unreliable in general.

The literature about Martha "Calamity Jane" Cannary Burke
would fill a small library without improving it in the least. Her

pamphlet *Life and Adventures of Calamity Jane by Herself* (n.p., n.d. [ca. 1896 or earlier]) is unreliable. Duncan Aikman's *Calamity Jane and the Lady Wildcats* (New York: Henry Holt and Co., 1927) appears to be reasonably accurate; Kathryn Wright's "The *Real* Calamity Jane" in *True West* 5 (November–December 1957): 25, is not widely accepted, especially its contention that Jane was married to Wild Bill. The most reasonable biography is J. Leonard Jennewein's *Calamity Jane of the Western Trails* (Huron: Dakota Books, 1953, 1958, 1965) which includes a seventy-seven-item bibliography of references to her. Deadwood Dick Clark and his predecessors in that title are discussed in Edward L. Senn's pamphlet *Deadwood Dick and Calamity Jane* (Deadwood: privately published, 1939) and in Mildred Fielder's booklet *Deadwood Dick* (Lead: Bonanza Trails Publishers, 1974). Poker Alice Tubbs, an occasional but notable visitor in Deadwood's gambling hells, is described in Nolie Mumey's *Poker Alice* (Denver, Colo.: Artcraft Press, 1951).

CHAPTER NINE: THE VOICE OF THE PEOPLE

The nature of Deadwood's government is best determined from an examination of pertinent portions of the general histories which have already been cited, Andreas, Rosen, Tallent, Hughes, Stokes, Kellar, and the newspapers being the most frequently useful. Seth Bullock's "An Account of Deadwood and the Northern Black Hills in 1876," ed. Harry H. Anderson, appeared in the South Dakota State Historical Society, *Collections* 31 (1962): 287–364, and is especially valuable in regard to early laws and law enforcement. The agitation for a Territory of Lincoln can be followed in the *Congressional Record*. The *Act to Incorporate the City of Deadwood* (Deadwood: Evening Free Press Publishing Co., 1881) shows what the Deadwoodians could do when left untrammeled to their own devices, and subsequent newspaper articles descant with enthusiasm upon the theme of local government.

The publicity with which Deadwood and the Black Hills endeavored, often successfully, to boost their share of the gross national product, consists mainly of ephemeral publications, a few of which may be found in each of the several archives around the state. They range from the guidebooks already mentioned in regard to the early gold rush to the yearly fliers and brochures issued to advertise the

events which the community puts on to attract the tourists, and a
sampling of them is all that can be profitably attempted.

H. N. Maguire's *New Map and Guide to Dakota and the Black Hills*
(Chicago: Rand, McNally & Co., 1877) is detailed but unrestrained.
Frank Bower's *Gold Mining and Prospects in the Black Hills* (n.p., n.d.
[ca. 1900]) is obvious puffery. The Burlington Route's *Little Journeys
in the Black Hills* (ca. 1904) aims deliberately at the tourist business
as does that railroad's 1932 guide *The Black Hills Detour*. The Deadwood Business Club's *Deadwood of Today* (1903) appeared during the
cyanide boom, to be followed by the Black Hills Trust and Savings
Bank's profusely illustrated pamphlet *Old Deadwood* which was published about 1905 and the Deadwood Business Club's *Souvenir Book
of Deadwood* (Deadwood: Pioneer Times, 1915) continued in about
the same format. The Chicago and North Western Railway's *Black
Hills* (1916) urged tourist travel to the area, and indeed both railroads printed advertising brochures for dude ranches in the Black
Hills in the hope of increasing train travel to the area. The North
Western brought out yet another pamphlet in the early 1920s, *The
Black Hills of South Dakota: An Ideal Summer Resort*, a trend of promotional activity which continued up to the Second World War.
From the 1920s onward a wide variety of Black Hills pamphlets,
some of them elaborately printed and colored, were published by
various promotional organizations: *The Black Hills* (1923?) consisted
of full-page photographs of local scenes, with maps and modest descriptive text. It was followed by similarly titled brochures in 1926
and 1929, and by *The Black Hills of South Dakota 1929*, which followed the horizontal format of the 1923 publication. In 1932 at least
two large and illustrated brochures appeared to advertise the Black
Hills, and of course all of this promotional excitement was spurred
on by the heady tourist prosperity generated by the welcome 1927
visit of President Calvin Coolidge, whose presence at the appropriate showings of Deadwood's Days of '76 did much to publicize the
Hills. The brochure, *Days of '76 Historical Pageant of Deadwood, South
Dakota, August 5, 1927* (Fostoria, Ohio: John B. Rogers Producing
Co., [1927]) gives the text of this magnificent festival, and annual
pamphlets and booklets have since described each year's offering of
the now somewhat truncated Days of '76 event as it occurs. The
creation of Mount Rushmore National Memorial near Keystone is
described in scholarly detail in Gilbert Fite's *Mount Rushmore* (Nor-

man: University of Oklahoma Press, 1952), and this great tourist attraction has of course brought ever-increasing hordes of tourists to the Hills, and within reach of Deadwood's promotional activities, which continue unabated to the present day.

Index